The Psychology of East-West Trade

Illusions and Opportunities

The Psychology of
East-West Trade
ILLUSIONS AND OPPORTUNITIES

Zygmunt Nagorski, Jr.

Foreword by

Jean-François Revel

 Mason & Lipscomb PUBLISHERS   NEW YORK

ISBN: 0–88405–088–2

Library of Congress Catalog Card Number: 74–13931

Printed in the United States of America

First Printing

Library of Congress Cataloging in Publication Data

Nagorski, Zygmunt, 1912-
   East-West trade.

   Bibliography: p.
   1. East-West trade (1945-   ) 2. International
economic relations. I. Title.
HF499.N33   382'.09171'301717   74-13931
ISBN 0-88405-088-2

To Krysia—
    a newcomer to the family
        a vivid link between the past and the present,
            between the country of birth and the country
                of adoption

Contents

Foreword

Technology transfer is one of the key issues which dominates our era. This issue will be crucial in rectifying the stupendous economic and even biological imbalances that fragment the modern world. It is surprising to discover that, with the unique exception of Japan, technology has local roots only where it was invented during a long historic process. These are the areas where scientific thought was conceived, from which modern technology emerged. By this, I mean technology as an applied science, the only one capable of increasing production on such a scale as to assure continuing development and mass consumption.

Elsewhere one often observes a superimposition of technology upon societies, the acquisition of a technological "veneer," made possible by the importation of foreign tools and instruments. But in terms of development, it is one thing to use self-invented tools and another to work with imported ones, without understanding how they function or without being able to produce them. In other words, it is possible to talk about a successful transfer of technology only when a society has begun to create it. It is only then that it acquires technological autonomy, or, at least, a place and an active role in a larger technological entity which has achieved technological independence.

Such a success assumes that other areas of development of the society in question (political, cultural, etc.) are abreast of the new technology. It assumes parallel developments in the fields of education, government institutions, administration, values, laws, relations between individuals, ethics, art, and social behavior. It is impossible

ix

to determine precisely the link between the practice of open discussion and public, theoretical debate originating in Greece in the 5th century B.C. and the invention of the transistor, but this link does exist.

By technology, we mean, of course, something more than pure technology. The know-how which shapes development, and therefore also has to be transferred, sometimes derives from methods of work and organization very distant from the current progress of basic research. It is harder sometimes to successfully manage a 1,000-room hotel or a grocery chain than to send rockets into space. This last technique requires, apart from vast sums of money, the formation of an elite, whereas making a hotel or a grocery chain work is based on the development of an "average man" who must participate in the original conception, realization, ultimate use, and consumption.

Between the underdeveloped and (more or less harmoniously) developed societies, there are also those which are overdeveloped in certain sectors and underdeveloped in others: underdeveloped—outside of the military sector—in the most important areas affecting the daily lives of most of the population.

The USSR appears to illustrate this definition best. But if her leaders want to stimulate consumer industry and improve daily life, can they do it simply by injecting capital and foreign know-how, or will they have to accept, at the same time, the seeds of social and moral metamorphoses? And will these, in turn, endanger the authoritarian and centrally controlled structure of Soviet bureaucracy?

As they launch themselves into a policy of exchanges with the West, Communist leaders, of course, assume that they will be able to secure access to an era of opulence for the USSR and to raise the standard of living, while limiting changes to a purely economic plane, without provoking any social, political, or cultural upheavals. Western experts, on the contrary, assume that commercial, scientific, technical, and business exchanges will have a cultural impact on the people of the East, to be followed by adjustments in their social values. These will loosen once and for all the totalitarian corset, thereby facilitating the rapprochement of the two world views at the level of the masses. This will create a community of interest and serve the cause of world peace. This is the thesis, as we know, which Samuel Pisar espoused in his well-known work, *The Arms of Peace*, and defended in many articles.

The value of Zygmunt Nagorski's book is not only in gathering together all the information dealing with this problem, but also in showing that this is a cyclical development, having parallels in the past. The czarist regime, on several occasions, and the Soviet regime at its early stages and then again during World War II, engaged in commercial and technological dealings with the West. Even then, they were already preoccupied with the same problems as today:

1. How to enter into commercial transactions without paying for the merchandise, or paying as little as possible—in any case, not in cash.
2. How to import technology without importing ideas, especially political ones, or social values of the exporting countries associated with the development of that technology.

This historical perspective, of course, should not prevent us from evaluating what is radically new in the present situation. It is here that Zygmunt Nagorski's analysis is one of the most precise and at the same time most subtle. He takes note of the additional fixity of purpose of both worlds that has been created by the nuclear confrontation, of the break, deeper and more self-imposed than ever, but also of certain new experiences which bring the two systems closer together—for instance, the Hungarian New Economic Mechanism.

We have learned to be cautious with futurology, and Zygmunt Nagorski always reminds himself that, in the words of Paul Valery, *"nous entrons dans l'histoire à reculons"* (we enter into history by going backward). One of the most savory, and least expected, examples which he gives us is the role of multinational corporations in the new East-West economic relationship: "The change, the détente, and Soviet needs have produced one of those topsy-turvy situations which delight sociologists and bring political scientists to the depths of despair. The Soviet Union, the first socialist country in the world, the arch-enemy of cartels, monopolies, and the like, began glancing in the direction of multinational companies. The courting began in a moment when the giant companies needed friends more than ever. Under considerable scrutiny within their own family environments in the capitalist world, the multinationals are delighted."

And besides, what this remarkable book demonstrates—and this is probably most important—are the limitations of political powers of the states. Political restraint on the development of economies and civilizations is the key phenomenon of our times. Political will rarely coincides with people's aspirations, and most often thwarts natural currents of exchanges and contacts between men and cultures. But the importance of this book lies in its pointing out the fact that possibly never before have the contradictions and tensions been as strong as they are now between the policies of nation-states and the dynamics of societies. Societies have needs which push them toward rapprochement, while states respond to national interests which push them toward separation. Societies engage in exchanges; states engage in mutual relations which are appropriately qualified by the adjective "foreign."

Are the states going to be able to continue channeling the forces that move societies closer to each other? Or will they, jointly with their own bureaucratic-military structures interested in self-preservation, be drowned in the marshes of unpredictable exchanges?

It is to these fundamental questions that Zygmunt Nagorski provides essential elements of an answer.

JEAN-FRANÇOIS REVEL

Acknowledgments

Acknowledgments have traditionally been heir to a margin of dullness for authors and readers alike. A long recitation of the men and women who have assisted, edited, typed, or simply lent emotional support often is merely a preface to a larger ceremony. All pious and humble, the writer pontificates at a high mass of self-effacement, confessing guilt for errors committed and refusing credit for any worthy ideas that might follow. As the ceremony draws to a close and the reader moves on to Chapter 1, the author smiles modestly to himself with the knowledge that what in fact follows is a reading of the gospel.

There are, of course, significant exceptions. In the preface to *Unity in Diversity*, a study of the Italian Communist party, Donald L. M. Blackmer tried to combine a description of the theme of his book with a listing of "my many blessings," including a reference to his family. He succeeded admirably, even managing to convey the feelings of one genuinely touched by the experience of writing a major book. His greatest debt, he concluded, was to his family: "This book owes much to them but nothing so irreplaceable as the compelling proof their presence and personalities provide that life is indeed full of richer things."

I could almost stop with that, except for putting my own thoughts into proper perspective. This is my first book of any significance. It is an attempt to enter into an area of great complexity by someone who is not really equipped with the proper economic tools. It is the by-product of a speech, followed by a series of smaller studies and steady writing on the subject. My only justification for adding to the literature is perhaps simply the fact that I feel strongly about the need to understand international economics as applied to East and West.

Historically, prerevolutionary Russia and the Soviet Union have shown a willingness for peaceful cooperation when their economic needs were acute. In less trying times, however, political constraints have tended to take precedence over economic expediency.

The eastern European countries have had their political flexibility drastically reduced over the last decade, leaving economic cooperation as their only open avenue to the West. In order to anticipate just how much and what kind of cooperation is feasible, then, the West must gain a precise understanding of not only the political limitations and economic needs of the East, but the psychological nuances as well.

This explains the title of the book. When I started to look for source material, I was overwhelmed by the sheer volume. Inquiries sent to the four corners of the earth produced an avalanche of replies. Studies produced in Japan, Iran, India, Hungary, Germany, Poland, France, Italy, and many other countries started piling up on my desk. When half-delighted, half-frustrated, I confessed to one of my colleagues that my early ambitions to be original and creative might have been overly optimistic, he smiled the smile of a well-seasoned and internationally acclaimed economist. You can be original, he said tartly, only if you are willing to be wrong.

It took me a long time to recover from that blow, but recover I did. People were ready to help, to read, to analyze, to correct, and to discuss. John P. Hardt of the Library of Congress, a friend, a specialist, an historian, and wonderful human being, whose understanding of the Soviet Union is deep and of long standing, provided the main push and the most stimulating critique.

Many others collaborated and guided. Most of them agreed with my friend's notion about originality, although as a reporter I could hardly refrain from projecting my own convictions. But this book has only been possible because so many before me have thought and written so much, and many have been generous in sharing their thoughts with me.

The last and final part of this note can only belong to my wife, Marie. Her involvement was total. It was up to her to research, to edit, to change, and to orchestrate. It was up to her to see that the accuracy was unchallengeable, that the facts were solidly rooted, and that the flow of thoughts met the rigid requirements of her precise mind. It was not an easy task. She had to test and to challenge me daily. She asked for clarity when obscurity abounded, and she had to bear the moodiness of the writer which accompanied the ebb and flow of ideas. It was not unusual for her to suffer to no end when in the early mornings she saw the typewriter itself ready to throw up its keys. It was not unusual for her to be forced to collect perfectly readable pages thrown in anger into the nearest wastepaper basket. It was not unusual to see her argue, explain, soothe, and guide— sometimes to no avail.

She has done this and much more. Sensing when fatigue blurred my vision, she would urge me into the fresh air or the clear waters of the ocean, to interrupt what often seemed a tiresome obligation, changing it after a walk, a swim, or just a plain drink into a labor of love.

Introduction

A book on East-West trade is usually approached with justifiable trepidation. Businessmen assume that in their professional activities they do not need the depth of a book. Political experts and activists are apt to leaf through a trade book with professional detachment and even disdain. Academicians usually seek a volume dealing with socioeconomics, preferably written in the familiar academic jargon used with great relish by social and political scientists.

Who, therefore, is this book written for? It is difficult to say. Trade relations do not exist in a vacuum. They usually rest on a solid foundation of mutual political interests. In the case of East-West trade, the political foundation—often shaky—is, nevertheless, indispensable. The mutual will to adjust and accommodate is another prerequisite. Finally, clear lines of communication must be established between two (or more) partners. And here enter the problems of values, concepts, and goals.

How different is the contemporary situation, compared to that between East and West in the past? Has there been a real change, or is this another variant of historical continuity, a continuity which has never augured well for the long-term improvement of a relationship? But if it is a real change, what makes it so?

The difference—and it will be argued that this is a meaningful difference—stems from the new world order. The Soviet-American condominium, an umbrella of power provided by the two superpowers, has added a new dimension to the international situation. The change has been forced upon all concerned—small, medium, and large—by new circumstances. It is a new and interesting evolution, creating within the overall rigidity of the two-superpower world considerable unexpected flexibility.

The rigidity can be explained simply. It is within the limits of national survival (the survival of both) that the two powers are forced to operate. The newly emerging flexibility is possible because of that first inflexible premise. The difference between political, economic, and cultural systems is important but no longer crucial. In order to survive, the superpowers must accommodate themselves to internal changes. Some of them may be considered an irritant while others are almost sacrilegious; but no matter—they must be faced and tolerated.

If this assumption is correct, then the traditional Western notion of Eastern dogmatism must be revised. If ideological principles have been relegated to the lower echelon of Soviet priorities, then the Marxist-Leninist system must have acquired a new dimension. That is what makes the change meaningful, interesting, and politically significant.

A look at various economic reforms undertaken in the East confirms that there is a new, more permanent, change. The East is evolving; it is adapting itself to new circumstances, to a new age. Hungary and Poland have translated their desire to change into practical reforms. Both countries, profiting from their lack of larger international responsibilities, have introduced measures which permit new, more efficient, scientific and technological innovations into the mainstreams of the nations. Other, smaller, east European nations have followed a similar pattern. Even in the Soviet Union, there is some progress. The reform of economic institutions, the introduction of monetary incentives, even attempts to satisfy consumers' needs, have been observed.

Is this enough to make a system flexible and different? Probably not fully, yet the introduction of reforms in Hungary, for instance, has produced sociopolitical changes which the regime neither wanted to stop nor could stop. Consumer-oriented industries have sprung up. Much freer movement of people and goods has been introduced in Hungary—new ideas and a new awareness. Aside from the issues of defense and foreign policy, the Hungarians have been able to develop a large degree of internal flexibility without forgetting the limits of the new world order.

The permanence of the change, at least in Hungary, thus becomes visible.

The evolving Eastern scene, however small, parochial, or internationally insignificant, imposes on the West the requirement of a *conceptual* approach. Does the West have any role to play? Should it play a role or let things develop under their own momentum? A significant number of businessmen and bankers in the West hope the West will play a role. The question that remains unanswered is, What kind of role? There is a gradual converging of commercial and developmental interests between East and West. Is it enough to assure the permanence of this new set of relationships? Or is it just a temporary, expedient approach, not very different from what the world witnessed in the 1920s, 1930s, and 1940s?

The very nature of the contemporary change requires more than merely a convergence of commercial and developmental interests. It calls for a better understanding of the interrelationship and interdependence of the two principal sources of power. The umbrella of parity of strength creates for the West a challenge as well as an opportunity. The challenge can be translated into a call to revise old stereotypes about the Eastern system. There is now the opportunity, in the form of involvement in economic reforms, reforms which will not change the political philosophy but which may (as in Hungary) loosen institutions and permit people to lead better lives.

This interdependency, of course, can be translated into more pedestrian, prosaic, commercial terms. The 1973 Middle East war is a case in point. The oil embargo is viewed by the East as a satisfactory move. It slowed down Western development, development the East has been unable to catch up with. At the same time, Western countries eagerly looking for alternative sources of energy are ready to take a second look at the Siberian oil deposits. Eastern bargaining power has risen; the West has taken notice.

The intricate link between politics and trade in East-West relations remains strong. Formal and informal discussions on both sides emphasize the political rewards of trade. There is a strong prejudice —again, on both sides—against compromise, that is, against compromise of national or transnational ideologies, which implies that economic negotiations cannot be insulated from their political consequences.

The Soviet Union, as a rule, balks at introducing elements of a market economy into her system, to permit more competition and create a more attractive market for the West. The United States refuses to lift total embargoes, fearing a potential strengthening of an enemy. While in some cases (a number of large Soviet-American deals can be cited as examples), there is real bargaining and give and take, when the issues concern the transfer of highly sophisticated technology, with military implications, Western governments come into the picture, where their interests are political and strategic, not commercial.

This is a crucial point. Current Western policy may be less fragile than have been the earlier cycles of similar change, because political and strategic considerations will probably remain constant, due to the parity of strength. There is little likelihood of a major new approach or a major evolution in Soviet-American relations—short of an economic or political upheaval in one or the other. Historically Russia, and later, the Soviet Union, have looked to the West for needed technology, modern equipment, and modern technology. Peter the Great introduced Western imports into Russia; Catherine the Great used and exploited these imports. Nikita Khrushchev performed the same role as Peter—he opened the Soviet gates to Western imports. And today it can be said that Brezhnev, like Catherine, is exploiting the new opening.

But something has changed. Peter the Great, Catherine, and Nikita Khrushchev made their moves in order to strengthen their country militarily. Today the two superpowers are about equally balanced militarily; both have highly sophisticated military weapons. America's smaller allies, such as Israel and South Korea, feel that the Soviet Union provides her allies with better technology and better equipment than the United States does her allies. The fact that the Soviet domestic economy suffers as a result does not change this situation.

The two systems—U.S. and U.S.S.R.—continue to be sharply different. They continue to be diametrically opposed in their philosophies on the relation of men to society, men to government, and government to national economy. The leaders of both systems remain suspicious of each other—for good, solid political reasons. As long as this situation exists, trade will suffer. Hungary and Poland were able to enter into the delicate fields of liberalized commercial interaction partly because of their different power positions; they do not have the security responsibilities the big powers do.

Differences in basic philosophy have also created great gaps in the process of communications. When the United States entered the underdeveloped world with a massive economic and technical assistance program, it transplanted into foreign cultures, innocent, well-meaning, technically competent individuals who proceeded to apply their methods (the only methods they knew) to cultures with wholly different chemistries. The results were costly, in human and material terms. If the assumption of permanence of today's change in East-West relations is correct, one of the modest objectives of a book like this one is to assist in avoiding similar instances of individual and national agony.

Therefore, this book's target is a broad range of individuals. Those who will be looking for a know-how approach may wish to look elsewhere. But many others—businessmen, bankers, students of the east European scene, political scientists, and plain, interested laymen —may find some insight into the environment of change in which the United States and the Soviet Union have been living for approximately the past generation. These readers may discover trends for relations to come. They may also start looking at the entire issue of East-West trade, not only through the narrow window of mutual economic advantage—limited or not, universal or not, profitable or less so—but as an opening toward the gradual establishment of a common denominator of global concern.

This book proposes that economic cooperation between the two ideological adversaries has, in a way, been forced on them by chains of events they could neither control nor predict. The mutual accommodation to change, superimposed by parity of military power, has been boring into the glacial walls created by seemingly inflexible dogma. In the case of the Soviet Union, the relative stability of its maturing system and the need for a modern economy have urged a better life, one in which there is less ideological zeal. In the case of the United States, it has been the restlessness of her society and the dynamics of her economic system that have permitted, and forced, various administrations to adopt more flexible, realistic policies.

Both changes require new and additional outlets. Trade is one of them.

Each system is intrigued with the other. Both, at the time of a closer approach, tend to attribute their flexibility, openness, and readiness to talk and change to the benefits of their respective national philosophies. In the process of the interaction, self-perceptions are being altered in the light of an increased knowledge of each other.

In some cases, individuals acquire a different self-perception as a result of change in objective outside conditions. Ota Sik, a Czechoslovak reformer who was deputy premier during the brief period of his country's liberal regime, is one example. A long-time Communist, a man of strong convictions, Sik was a Stalinist and close collaborator of President Novotny, the very symbol of Soviet influence and subservience. Yet he has changed; he has changed not because he was a career-oriented person, but because conditions permitting his country's survival as well as his own, have changed in his own eyes. There is some similarity between Sik's change and that of the superpowers: the conditions necessary for survival have changed. This change has grave implications for the world at large; it indicates more local wars and more compromises to avoid large wars, compromises likely to be achieved at the expense of the smaller powers. But the nature of the change and its permanence may be one of the most significant in the history of East-West relations.

It was Sik, now living in the West, who testified one day at a hearing conducted by the Subcommittee on Foreign Economic Policy of the Joint Economic Committee of the 91st Congress. He vividly described the issue of East-West trade: "Economic relations," Sik said, "involve, above all, contacts between men; they lead to the overcoming of distrust, they assist technical comparisons and self-critical evaluations and promote new needs and economic incentives. From time immemorial, active economic contacts have led to progressive changes in, and approximations between, systems, while autocratic aspirations have only served the purposes of nationalistic warmongers."

Ota Sik's perception of change had changed. It was now in trade and commerce that he saw openings and hope.

There is always a valid argument on the Western side, that with all the goodwill, political evolution, and liberalization of trade, the volume of East-West trade will remain fairly insignificant. But more than auditing statistics, this book will try to examine the political, psychological, and ideological underpinnings and the way in which they have influenced changing East-West relations. We will look at past and present euphoria, past and present frustrations, and examine the differences in their roots and perspectives. One of the objectives of this book is to show that with the current process of mutual understanding, new military parity means a new political reality; to trace the trade relationship and link it with changing political attitudes; to indicate how a mutual approach has softened political tension; to suggest that trade and politics are intermingled, each influencing the other; that political tension occasionally dissipates after two sides take note of each other's wares.

The other objective will be to link the changing relationship between the east European countries and the Soviet Union, on one side, and between the Soviet Union and the United States, on the other, to a conscious political decision related to trade and economics. This presupposes a Soviet-American umbrella, a mutuality of interests, as well as similar inner problems and outer conflicts. Two vital factors are deliberately left out of the discussion: China, because it is not germane to the broader aspects of the power relationship under discussion and therefore is not central to the thesis of this book; and Yugoslavia, where foreign investments are heavy, but the political climate is different and very special.

Eastern Europe is and will most likely remain within the Soviet sphere of influence. This is a conclusion which both the Americans (who at one time propagated the liberation of eastern Europe) and the east Europeans have arrived at separately. The east Europeans have tried on numerous occasions to recover some of their past glories and past positions; Hungarians, Poles, East Germans, and Czechs have bloodied themselves in the process. They have also discovered—to their great and deeply anguished disappointment— that those in the West willing to fight for Vietnam were not ready to do the same on their behalf. Americans, after periods of reappraisals and national debates, have settled into the pragmatic conclusion of the limitations on their power and political will to face a major Soviet adversary across east European boundaries.

Once this sank into the political consciousness of all concerned, east Europeans settled down to the business of better living. Trade with the West grew. For the Westerners, in general, and Americans in particular, opening new east European markets had a double attraction: it could be profitable and commercially interesting for some companies. The governments looked upon it (and continue to do so) as the best available substitute for their earlier, defunct policy. Modernization and a higher living standard—or so the saying goes—

may lead to pluralistic reforms and may also whet people's appetite for all kinds of interesting reforms.

Should the West, in general, and the United States, in particular, be a party to such a scheme? The answer is an emphatic yes. The scheme itself, however, is not a scheme at all. It has not been calculated, prearranged, planned, or blueprinted. It just arrived. It came by itself, caught in a web of interdependency and change. The theory of transition, rationalized at one point by Bukharin and later adopted by Lenin—has come home to roost. The transitional nature of Soviet society has brought with it a softening of dogma and permitted a subtle change, leading to what may appear on the surface to be more of a convergence than change itself. It is more of a transition from one form of domestic relationship to another, influenced by a similar trend in the broader field of international relations. Short on major political concepts, the United States ought to plug itself into this stage of transitional change. An active commercial and economic policy—conducted with wide-open eyes and solid roots in historical frustrations—is the course that should be followed.

This book, therefore, will try to till the subsoil of motivations, history, psychology, and political evolution behind trade. It will deal with such obvious issues as the transfer of technology and its past and present impact. It will touch upon availability of credits, solidity of potential sources of raw materials, and similar areas. But principally, it is to be a story of evolution, a story of changing policies, looking at those which appear to be stable, as well as those that are perishable. It will point to mutual interests rather than mutual conflicts. It will examine the web of interinvolvement, the relationship between accommodation and change, retreats and transitions, the reversibility of decisions, and the events that have overtaken decision-makers. But above all, this book is an outline of two major currents in the present international order: one flowing horizontally at high levels of the superpowers' interdependence, and the other flowing vertically, as tributaries of the major sources of that power toward smaller units, peoples, and institutions.

This book does not intend to be an optimistic prediction that trade is the way between the East and the West, that it is going to grow and flourish, leading to the happy ending of diluting Soviet-Western tensions. The limited ability of the two sides to trade is well known; these limitations are often more mechanical than substantial.

What are sometimes overlooked are the different kind of obstacles: varied motivations on the part of the negotiators; different approaches to the issues of profit and cost effectiveness; fear—translated in different notions—that one or the other side will, through trade, encroach upon the territory of the other; fear of ideological contamination; frustration and bafflement when different values face each other without either an effort or a willingness to understand the difference.

The reader, when he gets to the end of this book, may not be much wiser in terms of learning the technique of the trade, but he should have a better understanding. And since trade and commerce rest firmly on the subsurface of human psychology—which, in turn, is rooted in history and politics—the entire issue of East-West trade is being approached from that rather particular angle.

There are no better negotiators in the field of trade than men who, transplanted into a different cultural setting, are able to find their way around, who within a different political environment can detect the motivations, the desires, as well as restraints, of their counterparts. There are no better or more successful businessmen than those who can look at a potential contract or potential agreement from the point of view of their partner sitting on the other side of the table. Within the setting of international negotiations, with basic commercial complexities compounded by conceptual differences in the economic and political systems, a Westerner needs all of the unorthodox tools he can get.

This book is meant to be just such an unorthodox tool. Its approach is not that of a textbook, but rather a thought process entering a hidden part of a human brain as an intuitive reflection, permitting an intuitive and a fairly intelligent, as well as coolly calculated, action.

The Psychology of
East-West Trade

Illusions and Opportunities

CHAPTER 1

Men at Work

There is a stretch of road in southern New England where a sign saying MEN AT WORK has become almost a permanent fixture. It calls for a detour. A road under repair is not unusual and does not usually call for irritation or impatience, but this one has been in its present state of disrepair for years. As soon as one segment is fixed, another calls for more repair. Travelers who use the road frequently have accepted the situation as something one must live with, even smile and joke about. But when on rare occasions, the sign disappears briefly and the road looks new and finished, a condition of near euphoria descends on motorists. But no one dares say out loud that the sign will be back before long.

The road of political and economic relations between the East and the West, the Soviet Union and its east European allies, and the United States and western Europe, parallels that road in New England; it is constantly under repair. Men have been at work on the politico-economic road ever since the modern Soviet state came into existence. In earlier times, it was traveled by merchants and American investors, by Russian nobility and their European counterparts. But since the October Revolution transformed Russia into a complex society with a new ideology, economy, and politics, the West has been confused and bewildered. It knows it has to make another detour but doesn't know where it will lead.

There is, however, an encouraging factor. Cycles of history have a tendency to repeat themselves. The pre-World War I period was punctuated by political and economic distrust between the West and Russia, as happened again after the Revolution. Politically, Russia turned out to be a doubtful ally; economically a good customer, an excellent potential developer of virgin lands and explorer of raw materials, but still, a difficult partner. When the Revolution came, the fledgling Soviet Union made it clear that foreign capital was unwelcome, that foreign business interests were unwelcome, that the past must be erased from the history books. A wave of seizure and nationalization followed, leaving a shambles of past trade relations.

Then came a moment of reflection, a small moment in time for the new Soviet leaders. Through Lenin's policies, another cycle was begun. His New Economic Policy (NEP) lasted eight years, from 1920 to 1928 and was followed by the first Five-Year Plan, which for the first time since the Revolution created a need to import technology.

This time it looked as if the road was finally repaired and that the MEN AT WORK sign would disappear. Under the NEP, concessions were granted to foreign industrialists, and Western partners—almost as euphoric as their counterparts on the road in New England—were ready to drive in at full speed. Lenin viewed the change, the new historical cycle, as a logical, pragmatic one. In the West it was interpreted as a victory, as a departure from the communist bible. But each side misread the other. Both sides took risks. Lenin consciously defied some of his earlier principles, while Westerners consciously (and naively) risked their capital and industrial plants. The earlier cycle was forgotten, and the new promises were viewed with enthusiasm.

When the day came for another change, travelers looked incredulously at the reappearance of the road sign. Again? they asked themselves. Was this highway ever going to be finished? Was there any chance for an East-West road one day to dispense with this endless uncertainty?

This time the sign marked another wave of seizures and confiscations. When World War II descended on humanity, the relationship between the Soviet Union and the rest of the Western world was strained, to say the least. It took a dire threat from the enemy to make them allies and friends. The road sign was hastily taken down, and in its place, a broad seaway opened, a seaway along which thousands of tons of supplies were sent from the West to the Soviet Union. A new cycle, different yet similar, dramatic and meaningful, began. The Soviet Union, battered by the enemy, was given a daily transfusion of materiel and technological know-how by the West. Its purpose: to win the war.

The honeymoon did not last long enough, however, for either side to forget that the road sign still signaled trouble. The Soviet-Allied victory brought new discord. Eastern Europe, the remnants of lend-lease, economic differences, and political ambitions were all part of a mosaic of mutual discontent. The United States launched the Marshall Plan, and the Soviet Union reacted angrily, telling its two new allies, Poland and Czechoslovakia, that the American offer extended to them was unacceptable to a truly socialist country. And so, the cold war began. The new detour on our now-familiar road froze, this time, apparently for good.

It lasted a long time, indeed. Another cycle of history, almost another chapter of human behavior, had to be written before the road sign was removed again.

East and West went through a period which brought humanity close to another calamity. There were wars in Korea and Vietnam. A balance of mutual terror was somehow attained. There was a short-lived triumph of the socialist bloc when Sputnik I orbited the earth, and a subsequent, more stable, but less spectacular, development of Western technology.

During that period, another change occurred, this one subtle, psychological, and never fully articulated by either the United States or the Soviet Union. At some point, the two superpowers realized that there was a limit to their respective power, so the next, logical step emerged by itself: the U.S. and U.S.S.R. reluctantly agreed that they needed each other. Security and the instinct for self-preservation was one reason; a mutual desire to grow and prosper was another.

When the sign on our metaphorical road again faded from sight, its disappearance seemed more permanent. Mutual doses of humility were added—a sign of hope.

Count Witte and the Russian Peasants

The beginning of these cycles, the start of the modern period of East-West relations, goes back many years. Their roots are not in either the beginning of the United States or the movement to consolidate Russia as a power and end the fragmentation of what is today western Europe. The roots lie in the birth of mutual, ordinary interests. Nineteenth-century Russia was already bent on industrializing.

Russian rulers, especially Peter the Great and Catherine, sensed the Achilles' heel of their country: it was a primitive society; it lacked industry, it had a stagnating population.

One Russian leader who knew this all too well was Count Witte (1849–1915), an urbane, highly respected court counselor. Witte was a strong proponent of using the West as the main source of future Russian industrial strength. He was well aware of the growing indebtedness of the country, an indebtedness which had begun with Russia's discovery in the mid-18th century that she could borrow from Dutch banking houses. The debt itself did not trouble Count Witte; his worry was that the West would not be willing to help Russia.

Witte firmly believed that Russia and the West were adversaries, not potential allies, and he was willing, even eager, to use the capital, advanced knowledge, and technological know-how of the West. But would the West respond? To his great surprise, it would. In a memorandum written to the tsar, the count succinctly made his point: "Why create with their own hands an even more terrible rival? For me it is evident that, in giving us capital, foreign countries commit a political error, and my only desire is that their blindness should continue for as long as possible."[1]

Lenin could have written the same memorandum a quarter of a century later. Count Witte viewed 19th-century Russia. His main motivation was power rather than ideology or social structure. His Russia traded with the West, importing Western products and capital. Mining and related industries provided the bulk of Russia's exports. As they were to later, agricultural commodities led all others —cereals, eggs, butter, sugar, seeds, hides, and skins. Cotton textiles accounted for about half of the manufactured goods exported, and there was a considerable amount of petroleum. These products reflected the social structure of Count Witte's Russia: it was the peasantry who counted, who provided most of the salable products.

When the Communists took over and Lenin realized the potential power of the Russian peasantry, he turned in the direction of making them into an urban proletariat. Witte had been preoccupied with industrializing Russia, using its peasants as a natural resource; Lenin wanted to change the entire social landscape. The two men, who, in a way, succeeded each other in the field of Russian development, could hardly have been in more contrasting situations. Both inherited a people with strong traditions and a history of hard, painful struggle for survival. The peasants formed the class from which today's trade and political negotiators are descended. As early as the 13th and 14th centuries, Russian farmers faced a power vacuum in their society caused by the inability and unwillingness of a weak central government to control regional development. So the farmers formed agricultural-social units strong enough to govern, protect, and feed their members. Prince and landowner played an active part, as did the church. Naturally this was done within the overall, existing social structure, with all its stratifications and values.

Was the Russian peasant living in a feudal, or only a semifeudal, society? Did he have a taste of free choice, and if so, to what extent did that taste carry over into this turbulent century, the century that brought the October Revolution?

The medieval Russian land structure, unlike that of western Europe, did not connote strong ties or automatic allegiance to a prince on whose property landowners and boyars lived and tilled the soil. The first social layer—prince and landowner—was formed voluntarily. Landowners and boyars freely chose which prince would be offered their services (usually soldiering). A similar free choice was transferred to the lower social level, whose members also had a free choice in selecting their masters.

As tenants, the peasants remained free. When they joined their masters, they offered their services in return for shelter. This was a strong incentive. While it was required that a peasant on an estate commit himself and his family to a specified period of work, after the expiration of that period, he was free to leave. Another factor was of considerable value to the peasants: neither offices nor tax privileges were hereditary in medieval Russia, and they were granted only for a limited time. Peasants whose landowner suffered a loss were not bound to share the landowner's loss; they could go elsewhere.

It is this point—lack of inherited rights and privileges—that has caused several authorities, including some Marxist historians, to dispute the existence of feudal institutions in early Russian development.

The situation changed later, however. Freedom of choice disappeared when serfdom was officially introduced, and even when it was legally abolished in 1861, Russian peasants did not fare very well. Russia's arable land was roughly halved, with the landowners getting half and their former serfs half. The result was that peasants owned less land than they had farmed before, and the average size of their plots diminished by about a third.

Thus the peasants moved from a relatively free Middle Ages to a more feudal, restrictive, repressive 19th century. Along the way, they had acquired a taste for freedom, a taste which Count Witte dismissed with a shrug of his shoulders, but which Lenin was ready to build his theory of Russian socialism on. Why would peasants submit to those conditions, Lenin asked. Why wouldn't they move, revolt, change? The peasantry, the backbone of Russia, was ripe for transformation into a Marxist society, Lenin believed.

Were they ready? There was certainly little in 19th-century Russia for them. They were tied to the land by contracts with the landowners, who could dismiss them for practically any offense, alleged or real, major or minor. Escaped farm laborers were hunted down by the police. The taxes of the farmers were heavy, and their indebtedness was virtually unending. But still, were they angry enough to take up arms against the state, which was responsible for their fate, or just against individual landlords? An additional complication which Lenin perceived was the birth of a new class of well-to-do peasants; it was toward them, as much as if not more than the landlords, that Lenin's attention was directed.

The institution of *mir*, a type of village commune of the mid-19th century, looked as if it would gradually give way to more commercially-oriented farms. Land distribution was changed more in the farmers' favor.

The total arable land of prerevolutionary Russia was 367.2 million hectares (1 hectare equals 2.2 acres).[2] The landlords, royal family, and church, among them, owned 152.5 million; the rest, 214.7 million hectares, were the peasants'. Within these statistics were others more indicative of the direction of Russian agriculture. Well-to-do, prerevolutionary farmers accounted for only 12 percent of the population, yet they held about 31 percent of the arable land. Peasants and others of limited means amounted to 81 per cent of the population; their share of the land was 35 percent. Somewhere in between were the medium-size landowners, with farms averaging 35 to 50 hectares. They were 7 percent of the rural population and held 7 percent of the land.

Lenin saw the trend. He was concerned that the peasants were drifting into a farm capitalism. Count Witte had felt that this trend was beneficial, but Lenin, long after Witte, drew his own conclusion: a Marxist type of revolution *could* be sustained in Russia, where the basic social class—the peasants—were in danger of becoming capitalists.

Industrialization and Politics

Count Witte—observant, tolerant, ready to deal and talk with anyone useful to Russia—saw in industrialization issues larger than merely the economy. In order to make Western countries more receptive, he thought, Russia should make some kind of political accommodation with the West. In addition, the count looked for ways and means to lighten Russia's financial burden.

Military defense was the largest item in the budget. Witte saw a way to please the West, reduce armament expenditures, and continue the flow of foreign capital, all in one stroke. He persuaded Nicholas II to take the initiative in calling a major world disarmament conference. The idea was to organize an international conference to deal with the problem and elicit pledges from the other powers to reduce, or at least limit, their armies. The purpose was to create a climate that would permit Russia to reduce her own armies, which, it was hoped, would have the effect of diminishing the treasury burden. The conference, held at The Hague in 1899, accomplished much of what Count Witte had hoped it would.

The timing was appropriate for imperial Russia. Its economy was in trouble; its internal structure was showing signs of considerable strain. Although Count Witte was not outwardly troubled by Russia's foreign debts, he could not disregard their steady growth. At the turn of the century, they amounted to 30 percent of Russia's national debt. By 1905—when the first violent outburst in the streets of Russian cities signaled the beginning of another revolutionary movement—foreign debts comprised 46 percent of the national indebtedness, and they were growing. (Great Britain and France were the principal creditors.)

Russia just before World War I did much better in securing a steady inflow of foreign private capital. The flow was linked to foreign debts because foreign banks, as they are today, are much more

willing to finance outside investors than to lend a hand directly to
Russian capital.

The input was encouraged by Witte and other Russian leaders.
In a move not unlike one later made by Lenin, Witte concluded that
no price was too high to pay for rapid Russian industrialization. In
pre-World War I days, Russian peasants had footed the bill. There
was little outside of agricultural products, furs, and timber that the
West wanted to buy. The Russian export drive meant exploiting the
farm population, something that did not escape Lenin's and his as-
sociates' notice later.

In the meantime, foreign capital flowed into Moscow in a steady,
solid, dependable stream.[3] In the first 13 years of this century, the
flow of outside money increased 85 percent, while native capital
investments increased only 60 percent. A number of Russia's industrial sectors were of interest to foreign investors—the metal goods
industry, 42 percent of which by 1913 was owned by foreigners;
chemicals, where the share was exactly half; and the woodworking
and textile industries, 37 and 28 percent, respectively. But the bulk
of the foreign capital went into oil, where the future seemed the
brightest.

The list of Western companies involved reads like a who's who
of the industrial world—the Rothschilds, Henri Deterding of the
Royal Dutch Company, Marcus Samuel of Shell, and others. In 1907
the Royal Dutch group was formed by a merger between Deterding
and Samuel. As a result of this heavy foreign involvement, Russia
became one of the world's top oil-producing countries. The Baku oil
fields, about six square miles of desert, yielded nearly half of the
world's needs at the time.[4]

Oil became a booming industry which earned valuable foreign
exchange; it entered foreign markets showing signs of helping stabil-
ize the market. It was, after all, a time when the auto industry was
beginning, an industry that was still far from being a prime factor in
oil consumption but one with enormous potential. Russian oil exports
grew steadily. By the time Count Witte's conference on world arms
limitation had been held, Russian exports of oil had reached 1.4 million tons a year (a decade earlier, exports were half that).[5] Oil exports
kept rising steadily until 1904 when they reached a peak of 1.8 million
tons. In 1913, the last year of peace, they were down to 945,000 tons
and thereafter dwindled to almost nothing.

It wasn't until the early 1970s that new possibilities for Russian oil emerged, in the vast, unexplored fields of Siberia. But by this time the necessary capital was virtually unattainable by one outside investor. Private and public capital had to be found, which cut across the national interests of at least two major powers, Japan and the United States.

During Count Witte's lifetime the capital was there; explorations were made, and there were export earnings. The only major price to pay was the fate of the Russian peasants who were forced to sell their products, products they would rather have consumed. By reducing consumption, it was argued, the peasants could increase their share in the national output available for industrialization.

Count Witte's mixture of political savvy and concern for the economic growth of Russia was subsequently adopted by others with responsibilities even greater than Witte's. Within the New Economic Policy, Lenin found a new place for Western capital, capital to enhance his own goals for development. At the Rapallo Conference, held when the NEP was getting underway, Lenin managed to calm many Western doubts about the Soviet government's sincerity and reliability. But parallel to the Rapallo negotiations, secret talks were being held between the Russians and the Germans, and it was the Russians' intention to assist Germany's rearmament plans.

Much later, when the Soviet Union's needs in the areas of advanced technology and industrial input were urgent, another team of Soviet leaders, with Kosygin at their head, applied similar tactics. An all-European security conference was held, which was instrumental in allaying Western fears and giving the Soviet Union a new economic lease on life. This conference, combined with the Strategic Arms Limitation Treaty and other security negotiations, played the same role as the conference held at The Hague 70 years earlier.

Another Look at the Peasants: Marx and Lenin

The most solid pillar of Russian society throughout its history has been the ever-present, ever-working, ever-suffering peasantry. The peasants have moved from serfdom to collectivization; they have prospered, and thus made it possible for the Communist party to use them as props and scapegoats. They are and have been the core of

Soviet society, a society which requires, and keeps requiring, Western technology. The needs of the farmers (technically Russian *peasants* do not exist; the *proletariat* does) are growing along with the personal and collective well-being of the farmers.

When Lenin arrived on the Russian political scene, he was torn between the Marxist credo and the realities of his country. Marx's interest had centered on the urban proletariat. His attitude toward the village dwellers was summed up in his famous reference to a chance to escape the "idiocy of the rural life." But Lenin knew that in Russia there was no escape. Marx looked forward to changing the lot of the west European peasant. His thoughts on the Russian peasant were at first unvoiced, then unclear. Finally, when pressed by Russian revolutionaries to speak out, what he said wasn't helpful—to Lenin. Marx viewed the peasants' communal life, which revolved around the *mir*, as not being conducive to socialism. He suggested a step in between: private ownership first and socialism second.

This concept was not acceptable to Marx's Russian-revolutionary contemporaries. For them, the peasants were the primary problem, whereas for Marx, they were a marginal one, something that did not matter much in advancing the revolution. Marx lived, worked, and wrote in industrialized England and Germany. His target was Germany as the first country to experiment with a proletarian revolution. He envisioned a situation in which capital, monopolists, and the masses faced each other across a sociopolitical barrier.

Lenin perceived the problem early in his political life. In one of his first books, *The Development of Capitalism in Russia*, two themes emerged. One was that, while Marxism should be applied to Russia, conditions comparable to those in western Europe did not exist in the Russian countryside. Therefore it was necessary to develop an interpretation of Marxism that would suit Russia. The second theme was Lenin's conviction that commercial capitalism was already established among the Russian peasants. Thus there was no need to follow Marx's prescription to try private ownership first; it was already there. Rich peasants formed a substantial proportion of the landowners. The situation was ripe for socialism. Collectivization was the proper approach. Elimination of the *kulaks*, or rich peasants, plus a more equitable distribution of land among the large collectives, would transform Russian rural capitalism into the beginnings of socialism.

Lenin attempted to accomplish a linking of nonsocialist elements with the socialist movement, to find a common ground between the peasants and the urban proletariat. He managed to do just this—build a union between the workers' revolution and the peasants' war of liberation—and he did so in the name of Marxism.

Lenin's accomplishment was significant. He was dealing with a traditional, basically conservative element of society, a group willing to change only out of desperation, a group who were suppressed but who had a deeprooted tradition of free choice and strong attachment to the soil. The October Revolution fired the peasants' imaginations with its boldness and the prospect of immediate change for the better. Poor peasants opened the gates of the large estates, thinking that the land was theirs. The new state was to be theirs too. The revolution, bent on the eventual elimination of private ownership, inadvertently played on the peasants' hope of ownership by themselves. The image of owning the means of production and the physical proof of being able to take over what had before belonged to the rich was enough for the moment.

Russian peasants were thus quite able to share the revolutionary zeal of their urban comrades. A much more distant and difficult goal was that of sustaining that zeal and forging out of it a new political system. In Lenin's view, it was to be a system based on the direct relationship of peasant and worker. Such a relationship required mutual interest, goals, and understanding. It also called for a series of grave, mutual sacrifices, the extent of which no one was able to foresee at that time.

Peasants and Foreign Trade

At first the Soviet Union was unwilling to impose hardship, to request that farmers continue to make the kind of sacrifices required of them before the Revolution. One area directly affected by the new policy was Soviet foreign trade. Soviet exports, which consisted mostly of agricultural products, ceased.

The benevolent attitude of the new government toward the peasants is not the whole story, however. It was true that rural consumption was no longer hampered by stringent, official, export requirements. It was also true that Lenin was more anxious than ever to underline the revolutionary regime's debt to the peasants, to show that he knew it was the peasants' army that had played a crucial role in the Revolution. "We had to show the peasantry," he told the Congress of the Communist Internationale in July 1921,

> that we could and would quickly change our policy in order to alleviate their want. . . . We are the state power. To a certain extent we are able to distribute the burden of privation, impose it upon various classes, and in this way alleviate the conditions of certain strata of the population. . . . We are assisting peasantry because it is absolutely necessary to do so in order that we retain political power.

With such strong beliefs, the problems of exports, balance of trade, and reliance on imports were relegated to second or even third priority. Besides, at the time of his speech, Lenin still subscribed to the earlier belief in economic self-reliance. It was a little later that the idea of the New Economic Policy was born, which represented a different approach to foreign trade.

Lenin's speech was in response to a sudden worsening of the peasants' condition. The euphoria of the revolution was a thing of the past; postrevolutionary chaos now had to be coped with daily.

First of all, there was a dramatic decrease in the land under cultivation. Second, distribution of food had practically ceased by 1918, the end of the first revolutionary year. The urban proletariat, who had acquired political power, found themselves short of food. A remedy had to be found in order for the new government to function, for Lenin realized that agriculture was absolutely essential to the survival of that government.

The Soviet government had to find a way to get the peasants to produce the needed food. A distribution system had to be reinstated. Lenin concentrated on the peasants at the middle-income and middle-production levels; they had to be organized and helped. At the same time, he saw the need to slow down collectivization. To help agriculture as much as possible, Lenin ordered industry to start mass production of tractors and other agricultural machinery, in addition to planning for the possibility of importing farm machinery.

A link between the welfare of the Russian peasants, the political stability of the Soviet regime, and East-West economic relations began to emerge. It is possible that the NEP was conceived at this time; it is also possible that the policy of using available resources from the capitalist world to strengthen the young communist state was formed by Lenin's efforts to revive the Soviet economy and agriculture.

Imports from the West were part of the Soviet Union's foreign trade—and they were in a miserable state. During World War I and immediately following, Germany, one of Russia's traditional partners, had dropped out of the Russian export market. Great Britain and Finland tried to fill the gap. Russian exports dropped about 33 percent during the war, while imports increased 40 percent. The Soviet Union's balance of payments was precarious, which made its bargaining position weak. The key problem, therefore, was how to obtain enough capital to revive the country's agriculture and industry.

Like Count Witte, Lenin looked westward for this capital, and like Witte, he knew enough about the relationship between the old and the new Russia and between Russia and the outside world not to have any illusions. He understood the economic motivation of the capitalistic world, which often transcended politics—and on occasion, common sense. In a controversial move, Lenin invited Western capital and technology into the Soviet Union, using an NEP provision which permitted foreign concessions to be established in the country. These concessions were to be based legally on a mixed formula which allowed foreign, private interests to be combined with Soviet state shares.

"Communism," Lenin is reported to have said, "equals Soviet power plus the electrification of the whole country." Soviet power was already established; now only outside help was needed to meet the second requirement.

Foreign Concessions

The General Electric Company vigorously took advantage of the new concessions. The Dnieper Dam got its hydroelectric units. Designed by an American engineer, the dam was built under Soviet-American auspices, some of it with Soviet materials. The five original generators were later joined by four more, of 77,500-kilowatt capacity each.

The dam was just one of the many electrification projects undertaken by GE in the Soviet Union. The company, which initiated an unbroken chain of long-range technological cooperation with the Soviet Union, proudly proclaimed the feasibility of working arrangements between the free-enterprise American economy and the state-controlled and -planned system. Its work did much to encourage other American and Western companies to enter Soviet markets.

Other GE projects included the first complete American outdoor substation, built for the Leningrad electric power supply system, as well as complete electrical equipment for a testing laboratory at the Electrical Institute in Leningrad. In subsequent years, GE either built or supplied the first power system in the Urals, the Stalingrad regional power station and substation for the tractor works and other factories, and the Nigres power station in the Gorki region. Later in the development of the trans-Ural system, GE was asked to supply a large number of steam turbine generators. Among the items it delivered were portable steam turbine electric power stations mounted on railroad cars and designed to operate as self-contained units. Diesel-driven generators, along with special switchgear equipment similarly mounted, were furnished in large quantities, equipment that was of considerable value when Germany invaded Russia in World War II.

GE's involvement is a good example of the wisdom of Lenin's New Economic Policy, but when the decision was made, there was little except his own intuition to rely on. He viewed the period as one of learning, in which the young socialist state should acquire knowledge and experience from every possible source. "The idea that we can build communism with the hands of pure communists, without the assistance of bourgeois experts, is childish," he wrote in an article in *Pravda* on October 31, 1921. Revolutionary enthusiasm was not enough. Socialism must be achieved in this "small peasant country by way of state capitalism." To allay fears and emphasize his faith in the strength of the Soviet system, Lenin added: "The bourgeois experts [who will come] must be so encompassed by organized, creative and harmonious work, that they will be compelled to fall in line with the proletariat, no matter how much they resist and fight at every step."

Accusations of selling out to the capitalists mounted among Russian as well as some Western Marxists. But Lenin was firm, confident that the way to proceed was to assist the Soviet economy through the infusion of outside muscle and capital. This conviction was based on cold analysis of the available domestic resources, of the inner system that linked the countryside with the cities, and of the inability of Soviet industry to pick itself up from the ravages of the war and the revolution that had followed. Lenin well remembered the years preceding World War I when foreign capital and trade had played such an important part.

Westerners were only too eager to reenter Russian markets. Russian agents shopping around for assorted goods were treated the way a rich customer is treated in a fashionable department store. Only a few, very astute merchants realized how much of a seller's market they were in.

A variety of foreign concessions were granted to outsiders. In June 1925 W.A. Harriman & Company received permission to prospect for, mine, and export manganese. Their concession was connected to the Georgian Manganese Company, which apparently had been able to do little alone. Another foreign concession was granted for mining gold along the Semartak River in Siberia. The American Asbestos Company and Russian-American Compressed Gas Corporation were authorized to work in their respective fields. Just about this time (in 1925) Armand Hammer began his own business-love affair with the Soviet Union by obtaining a concession to manufacture pencils, pens, and related products. The factory Hammer built is still in operation in the Soviet Union.

Western experts flocked into the country. Not much is known of their views and convictions, nor whether any "fell in line with the proletariat," according to Lenin's prediction, but their contribution to the revival of the Soviet economy is widely recognized.

It was an American, Harold Ware, who introduced the modern tractor to the Soviet Union, while his compatriot, Ethel Ely Pattison, successfully transplanted the first grapefruit trees to Russian soil. An agricultural researcher named H.J. Muller went to the Soviet Union in the early days of the NEP and helped found Soviet agricultural research.[6]

Soviet agriculture was enriched by the involvement of large companies. Du Pont provided technical assistance in building a series of fertilizer factories. The Nitrogen Engineering Company participated in constructing and providing operating assistance for a $10 million ammonia fertilizer plant. Because tractors were so important, Soviet planners wanted a tractor factory. One capable of turning out 40,000 tractors a year was built in Stalingrad in the late 1920s, with Albert Khan, Inc., designing the buildings.

A number of American companies and individuals were involved in nonagricultural areas during the NEP and post-NEP periods. An American expert, Leon S. Moisseiff, in the Soviet Commissariat of Transportation, specialized in bridge-building. John Calder came from Detroit to assist in the development of automobile plants, while a specialist in aluminum production, Frank E. Dickie, helped establish a domestic aluminum industry.

The Freyn Engineering Company was in steel production. It sent its consulting engineers to cooperate with the Soviet State Metal Works Planning Institute, where they helped design a large number of metallurgical plants. In housing, the Longacre Engineering and Construction Company contributed to a major building expansion program in Moscow, which consisted of apartment houses and public buildings.

The Ford Motor Company was involved in the Nizhni automobile plant; Roberts & Schaefer loaned mining experts to help develop a modern coal-mining operation in the Donets region, which yielded up to 3.5 million tons of coal a year. The Foster-Wheeler Corporation provided technical assistance to the Soviet oil-refining industry. And Arthur P. Davis studied and advised local authorities in the Asian part of Russia on irrigation.

All of this activity was controlled by the Soviet Union and took place unilaterally, for it was years before the United States established diplomatic relations with the Soviet Union. It was a time when legal and psychological restrictions made it difficult for American companies to trade freely and for American banks to extend large amounts of credit to Soviet enterprises. In spite of such restrictions, during the NEP period there were a surprising number of Soviet-American technical and business contacts. There were fewer contacts after 1933, the year of diplomatic recognition, but this was merely a coincidence, mostly the result of world economic conditions. In 1929, the year the depression began, there were an estimated 1,500 American experts and consultants on their way to or from the Soviet Union.

The Psychology of the Early Contacts

The motivations that prompted Lenin to initiate the NEP and include foreign capital in his planning were clear. He spelled them out on several occasions—never overly eager to placate his Western business partners, but most of the time candid enough to state his political and economic goals. Western reactions, particularly the American, were mixed. Officially, the lack of recognition was an excuse for discouraging American business interests from dealing with the Soviet Union. The belief that conditions there were far from stable, that the communist regime was a passing phenomenon, was widely held. But the U.S. business community was not convinced of this. Its experience was different, its memories longer. The reaction of businessmen was that of an investor viewing a promising deal. The business community had been influenced by its earlier dealings with the new Soviet state, dealings characterized by scrupulous Soviet adherence to the letter and spirit of business contracts. They remembered World War I and their discussions then about Russia as a potential market.

When, after the war, Russia was looking for new trading partners, with a defeated Germany now removed from competition, the United States was a natural choice, having emerged from the war as a creditor power. So the United States and Soviet Union began to eye each other in spite of, and in some cases because of, the U.S. government's line of ignoring the new communist regime.

As early as the middle of World War I, the American business community was interested in the postwar Russian economic potential. The Russian-American Chamber of Commerce and Russian Association of Commerce and Industry were organized about 1915 primarily to solicit American capital and trade. That year there was a dramatic rise in American exports to Russia, which nearly tripled the next year. Russia had emerged from the war with a population equal to that of Great Britain, France, Germany, and the Austro-Hungarian empire combined. Plans to enter this promising market occupied the best minds in American banking and corporate circles.

There was little reason, other than purely political pressure, not to take the opportunity at hand. In fact, it appeared downright foolish not to do so, with some business leaders asking: If, in spite of the Revolution and the communist takeover, Western capital and technology are needed, isn't that the best proof of the virility of the free enterprise system?

This was sufficient reason for the business community to move in and defy national policy. There was some degree of pride in doing so, in the feeling on the part of businessmen that they could discern the future better than Washington could. In retrospect, this feeling seems justified, but at the time, it brought about a bi-level approach. One was pragmatic, centering on the business opportunity represented by the situation. The other, political, approach was rooted in the idealism of America and its disdain for the system the Soviet Union had introduced. This dual approach served the Soviet leaders in two ways: it was economically vital to trade with the United States, and it bore out the Communists' contention that there were inconsistencies in the capitalist world's economy, inconsistencies, Marx and Lenin had said, that would make the capitalists their own gravediggers.

The situation wasn't simple. American businessmen had to deal with the Soviet government, which had taken over all Soviet production, as well as all public and private institutions. There was simply no one else except the Soviet state to deal with. The situation was simple in Washington's view, however. Washington did not consider the Soviet government viable, and Americans contemplating going to the Soviet Union were warned that a future regime might not honor the present one's obligations and notes. The stubborn Soviet refusal to honor prewar Russian debts or to pay for bonds and other promissory notes added weight to the Department of State's argument.

The argument was verbal only, but it wasn't the only pressure applied. The State Department was strongly opposed to the extension of credit to the Soviet Union by American banking and other lending institutions. In 1920 an official embargo was imposed on the importation of Russian gold. The moral argument for the embargo was the alleged use of slave labor in Soviet gold mines. Politically, it was another tactic to isolate Russia from the rest of the world. The embargo lasted for several years and wasn't lifted even in 1923, when, partly as a result of the massive American business response to the Soviet concessions, Washington relaxed slightly its trade restrictions with Russia.

The gold embargo was ignored when it suited U.S. purposes. In

1922 the Soviet government offered to pay, partly in gold, for the famine relief supplies sent by the United States. The Treasury Department, after some consideration, did not oppose the payment, and soon $12 million in Soviet gold was in American vaults.

In the Soviet Union, a different attitude was emerging. Once the idea of foreign involvement was accepted, once engineers, consultants, specialists, and experts from the U.S. began arriving, the Soviet government became impatient for results. And when results were slow in coming, the government found a convenient scapegoat—the foreigners. The Soviet system was beyond reproach; the Soviet economy needed only an additional input to make it work. A suspicion that the capitalists who had been invited to help had, in fact, come to sabotage Soviet national efforts, began to take hold. The American business community in Russia, which had taken such pains to remain nonideological and apolitical, was stunned.

But by this time, Lenin was dead and Joseph Stalin, a nationalist and a Georgian peasant deeply rooted in xenophobic Russian traditions, was at the helm. Another cycle was about to begin.

The Impact of Foreign Concessions

Did the foreign concessions have any impact? Had the Soviet leaders been right in criticizing foreign experts and companies, or were they merely looking for a scapegoat? Were foreign concessions worth the experiment, from the Soviet point of view? Had Lenin been justified in stepping outside the communist doctrine and allowing a temporary marriage of socialism and capitalism for the benefit of socialism?

When, in 1935, a number of earlier concessions were terminated, with some American assets confiscated and others on the verge of it, a prominent Soviet official faced an attentive audience in Chicago. Ivan V. Boyeff was at that time chairman of the board of directors of the Amtorg Trade Corporation, the only official Soviet trade agency operating abroad.[7] He came to deliver an important message and to explain the new set of Soviet trade barriers and customs regulations. The reason the Soviet Union had escaped the largest impact of the worldwide depression, Boyeff said, was its wise, perceptive, and socialist-oriented foreign economic policy. The Soviet people knew that the only way for the Soviet Union to continue to prosper was through its economic independence from the rest of the world. Then he added: "The foreign trade of the Soviet Union is also charged with a second task, namely that of assisting in the economic development and socialist construction of the country." Clear, blunt, and direct.

Had foreign concessions really done that much? Of course they hadn't. They weren't numerous enough, dynamic enough, or capital-intensive enough to play such a major part in alleviating the Soviet Union's economic ills. But they did make an important contribution to the reconstruction of Russia's basic industrial sectors.

The concessionists were working under various handicaps. In the West, they were accused of contributing to Soviet domestic and foreign practices, of encouraging the Soviet timber industry, which was operated by slave labor, including political and criminal prisoners. They were accused of assisting Soviet agriculture, which had dumped its butter on world markets. In the Soviet Union, the foreigners were viewed as a mixed blessing, and their freedom of movement, as well as their economic initiatives, had been curtailed.

Yet the concept, implementation, and follow-up, even after the NEP ended, were all useful. Interpretations of this usefulness differ, however. What Amtorg official Boyeff said did not jibe with what the Western business community said. Historians' versions are equally in disagreement. Soviet statistics for 1928, for instance, include a modest 68 foreign concessions, which accounted for a bare 0.6 percent of Soviet industrial output. It is likely that these figures did not take into account all types of concessions, but instead, concentrated on a "pure" type—the acquiring by the Western partner of all the rights, short of ownership, of property, with the simultaneous introduction of capital and technology. The other two types—joint companies, and straight purchasing of technology against permission granted to a Western company to exploit Russian natural resource—might have been left out of the statistics.

American sources later put the number of concessions at 156 in 1927, but agreed with the Soviets that their impact was small. Neither the Soviets nor the Americans ever spelled out their expectations. Lenin's objective was a limited input, an input, it can be said, that was reached, and more.

The Western energy sector felt it. Russian oil, a major source of energy supply for the West, was almost nonexistent at the time of the

Revolution, yet the oil fields had not been destroyed. Recognizing its limited capacity in oil technology the Soviet Union turned to the Western companies. The first concession was granted to an American company, International Barnsdall, with others following, including the Lucey Manufacturing Company and Metropolitan Vickers, both British. A genuine technological revolution occurred in Soviet methods of processing, producing, and distributing oil. New pipes were laid and new refineries built, with the result that the production of crude oil almost tripled during the five-year NEP period 1923–28. Soviet oil exports, while not reaching their 1904 peak, were increasing.

This is just one example of the impact of the concessions. It was a limited impact, but a significant one, as was the impact on some other key industries, among them, anthracite coal and metallurgy. Among the Western companies granted concessions were such large corporations as Union Minière Group (France), Thyssen, A.G. (Germany), and Stuart, James & Cooke Corporation (United States). The American outfit was chosen especially to reorganize and reactivate the Donbas coal basin. Selected by a Russian commission appointed to make a comparative study of methods of mining coal, Stuart, James & Cooke was asked to replace an earlier concessionaire, a German company.

A precise description of the impact of Western capital, expertise, and technology does not answer the extent of the impact. To do so, it would be necessary to compare what would have happened had Lenin not made his decision to allow concessions in Russia with what actually did happen. The sheer variety of the Western activity tells part of the story. It was felt in such diverse sectors as commercial farming, where the Americans, Germans, and British were granted concessions, and the quarries developed by Krupp, International Micca Corporation (U.S.), Lena Goldfields of England. Textile mills, apparel-manufacturing, wood products, electrical equipment, railroads, and communications were also affected.

One conclusion emerges from a study of the period: whatever was brought to the Soviet Union proved useful; whatever was introduced as a new technology whatever was constructed as an addition to existing facilities, remained. The Soviet Union lost nothing through the foreign concessions, and it gained much. The impact of the concessions was significant. In spite of the political and psychological problems created by the concessionaires, they left behind a residue of Western knowledge otherwise inaccessible to the Soviet Union.

The process, which began partly because of the Russian farmers' inability to produce enough, ended in the 1920s and '30s as one of the major channels for the transfer of capital and technology from West to East. Even if, as some suggest, the process was economically marginal for the Soviet Union, it was the first and most important one undertaken by the new Communist regime. Its impact was not confined to Russia, but was felt, in various ways, in western Europe and the United States.

Reactions in the West

A strange reaction took place in western Europe and North America. There was pleasure—that Russia was once again a commercial partner—and fear—how competitive was the Soviet Union going to be? How easy might it be for the Russians, using their newly acquired knowledge, to combine it with cheap labor and reenter world markets too aggressively? In the United States, where political opposition fed on concern over "unfair" competition, steps were taken to slow down trade with the Soviet Union. Soviet lumber, pulpwood, and matches were placed under embargo; the importation of Soviet asbestos and manganese was investigated (both were industries developed partially by concessions granted to American companies).

One of the reasons for Western fears was the figures released by official Soviet sources. The figures were not necessarily definitive, for they were not compiled on the same basis as Western statistics. Nevertheless, they showed dynamic export growth for the period when depression hit the industrialized world. West European exports declined, while in the Soviet Union in the early 1930s, exports jumped 35.7 percent. When, in 1932, Western exports sank to one-third of their 1929 level, the Soviet trend was only slightly downward.

Behind the Soviet drive were all the resources of the Soviet state. Foreign trade—a state monopoly—mobilized all possible channels to achieve a spectacular export volume. In statistics, *constant* prices were used. With the world commodity prices dropping rapidly, true

Soviet exports grew only in 1929–30. But later figures did not reflect the realities of world market conditions. The results were soon visible: during 1933–35 the Soviet Union suffered a greater drop in its exports than did the rest of Europe.

The early statistics, which were intended to prove Soviet economic viability, contributed to Western fears. Other fears stemmed from what was then viewed as a successful experiment with granting concessions to the West. Both East and West lacked basic, mutual understanding. Both had started from political adversary positions. Soviet economists despised and rejected the market economy of the West and were freely predicting the early collapse of capitalism. The West's understanding of the economic planning of the Soviet Union was elementary at this time. Parliaments busily went over their trade legislation, trying to erect barriers against a dangerous influx of Soviet goods. In Russia an amendment to the constitution legalized Soviet government jurisdiction over "the rights of Russians and foreigners alike."[8] This legislation eventually led to the arrest and trial of some members of the Western business community who lived in or near Moscow. In addition to representatives of large corporations and the experts who were officially invited, there were many independent merchants—fur traders, tobacco buyers, pig-bristle manufacturers, buyers of cotton waste, and many others—who were neutral, apolitical, and profit-motivated. They were the most vulnerable to official Soviet displeasure.

But this situation was minor compared to the fear of competition. How real the fear was can best be illustrated by the case of Canada. Canada felt threatened. These fears were hardly justified, and often based on ignorance. The Canadians failed to include any reference to the first Soviet Five-Year Plan in official documentation prepared for the imperial conferences.[9]

Two imperial conferences were held—in 1930 and 1932—with agendas full of items for the discussion of Soviet exports. A wheat quota system was considered in spite of the fact that the Soviet Union was exporting less wheat, rye, and barley than had Tsarist Russia in 1909–13. Further, collectivization of agriculture had reduced Soviet farm output. To a careful observer, it was clear that a shift was occurring in the composition of Soviet exports. The amount of finished commodities exported had been gradually expanding, while that of unfinished material was declining.

It appears that Ottawa, as well as other participants at the first Conference, made little effort to inquire about such details. It was the fateful year 1930, filled with economic disaster and gloomy predictions. The conferees apparently arrived in Ottawa with preconceived ideas, and papers prepared for them by the General Economic Committee of Canada only reinforced their views and concerns. Great Britain was concerned about Soviet coal, Australia about wheat,[10] and Canada, in addition to wheat, about the entire scope of the Soviet export drive.

In an irony of history, which often occurs when there is massive misunderstanding, the results of the conferences *helped* the Soviet economy, which was running in a direction counter to that of Russian goals. Some of the embargoes imposed on Soviet exports helped channel needed resources back into the domestic sector—which was exactly what the Soviets, without realizing it, needed.

Soviet exports had to be laboriously extracted from the domestic economy. The Soviet economy could easily have absorbed the timber, coal, and wheat that Russia produced. Now, with world prices for commodities hitting a new low, the Russians were squeezed between the large ambitions of the planners and the grim domestic reality of the low export returns. The Soviets' goal was to earn foreign exchange with which to pay for imports. For them, the best possible situation would have been an upswing in world commodity prices, which would permit them to earn foreign exchange and at the same time lower their volume of exports. The Soviet Union sensed the need to make better domestic use of its resources, but the exigencies of its rigid economic plan did not permit it to make the switch.

Canada competed with the Soviet Union for British timber markets, while Great Britain competed with the Soviet Union for Canadian anthracite markets. Australia's competition centered on wheat. British delegates to the first Imperial Conference in 1930 were pressed by their other colleagues to initiate an embargo. But Britain—always cool-headed, always willing to first listen to reason and to protect its business interests—was far from ready. She was much more interested in seeing the Soviet Union earn enough foreign exchange to pay for British-made machinery and equipment than to declare an embargo. Besides, there were quite a few British concessionaires operating in the Soviet Union, and an embargo would almost certainly have hurt them.

Canada was less inhibited. In February 1931 she declared an embargo prohibiting imports of Soviet coal, pulpwood, timber, lumber, asbestos, and furs. One of the arguments was the difficulty of fair competition between a free and a state-controlled economic system. The Canadian Forest System had publicly complained about its inability to compete with the Russians in the British timber market. The pricing structure, the Canadians said, was market-regulated in Canada and Britain and state-regulated in the Soviet Union.

In principle, this was a valid point, but the Canadians had failed to do their homework. Soviet timber was sold in Great Britain under an agreement which included a requirement that the price of the timber be regulated by the world market, not Moscow. This clause made Soviet timber a competitive, freely bought and sold commodity. The Canadian point was no longer valid.

Great Britain continued to be under pressure. When the second Imperial Conference was held, in 1932, it finally gave in and, in typically British fashion, agreed on a principle: if Soviet sales undermined the imperial preference scheme, London would take action. Satisfied, the conferees went home, only to learn less than a year later that a British consortium had contracted with the Soviet White Sea Timber Trust for a sizable purchase. Canada immediately lodged a protest, but Great Britain was too far along toward its first full-fledged trade pact with the Soviet Union to worry about the Canadian protest. Discord developed within the British empire; a pacifying step had to be taken, and was. The Board of Trade requested that the consortium—Timber Distributors, Inc.—reduce the size of the Soviet order, which was complied with. The problem of breach of contract and the ensuing Russian displeasure, however, remained. Therefore, the Board of Trade gave the group permission to keep the agreed-on price at the original level.

White Sea Timber Trust delivered less timber for more money, and there was little question who the ultimate winner was.

America Comes Around

The 15 years that separated the birth of the Soviet Union from official recognition by the United States were eventful ones which saw both the rise and fall of the new Soviet foreign economic policy.

During these years, the American business community raced to secure Soviet markets. Also during this time, the Soviet Union was transformed from a weak, defeated power after World War I into a major European political power. The year of American diplomatic recognition was also the visible beginning of the rise of new forces in Europe.

Russia and America, in diplomatic contact with each other for the first time in over 15 years, still had far to go. Their understanding, and thus opinion, of each other was shallow. The Soviet Union was convinced that it could use American capital and technology to turn its ailing economy around and make a truly socialist society, while the American business community, working hard to be accepted and to prove its usefulness to the Soviets, was equally convinced that the free-enterprise system would prevail through the sheer force of its logic. By the time business contacts and a gradual development of mutual political interests led to the recognition, some of this optimism was gone.

The Russians began to see American capital and credits as a political wedge with which to make Russia once again an area for easy exploitation. American interests in the Soviet Union began to feel the pressure of cumbersome Soviet state apparatus and police surveillance. While many companies continued to do business with the Russians—Douglas Aircraft, Packard, and General Electric, to mention a few—they were kept at arm's length. Jointly, along with the other foreign concessionaires, they were blamed for the Soviet economy's lack of progress. From a faulty, or mistaken, position on their respective economic systems, the two countries moved toward mutual recrimination. Both houses were built on moving sands. In the Soviet Union, the sands were politics and ideology, while in the United States, they were business and economic motivations.

The two countries seldom met in a spirit of understanding. Not that they did not try; they were simply unable to decipher each other's state of mind. They were, however, reaching a point in history in which they would be forced to try harder to forget their past differences. World War II caused everything else to fade into insignificance. Both powers tried to stay out of the war, but both were forced into it anyhow within six months of each other. America and Russia suddenly found themselves on the same side.

Once again, a dilemma had to be resolved by the two capitals.

How could they cooperate with each other without compromising their own political systems, their basic philosophies and economic goals? Moscow's answer was that it was fighting for its very survival, that American assistance was vital. There wasn't the slightest doubt that its system was superior, that it would eventually triumph. To the Russians, their risk was small and their gain potentially huge.

The natural tendency in Washington, London, and other Western capitals was to forget their differences and go ahead with the job of winning the war. This called for a careful explanation to people for whom communism equaled subversion and lack of freedom, but it was the only thing the Allies could do under the circumstances.

This policy led to the lend-lease program, a massive transfer of materiel from the West to the Soviet Union as well as to the other Allies. A trickle of American supplies early in the program changed almost overnight into a flood. The allies intended to rebuild the Soviets' ability to wage war against the Germans. They did—and more. The lend-lease program turned out to be one of the most significant transfers of economic strength in history. World War II was won by the Allies, including the Soviet Union.

After the war, the Soviet Union and United States once again found themselves in conflict. The forgotten sign, MEN AT WORK, reappeared. Restoration of the East-West road was badly needed.

CHAPTER 2

Profile and Psychology of the Lend-Lease Program

It was October 1972, 27 years since World War II had ended. The place was Washington, where the principal actors were the United States Secretary of State and the Minister of Foreign Trade of the Soviet Union. The occasion was the signing of an agreement to settle the lend-lease debts. Lend-lease, a supreme effort to win World War II, which had somehow become a source of discord, was now part of history. Historians were to be the only judge of how effective, selfish, or magnanimous lend-lease had been.

The ceremony was held, signatures were attached, smiling photographs taken. It looked as if the last hurdle to the opening of trade between the two superpowers had been overcome.

But the last hurdle hadn't been reached. Lend-lease wasn't yet entirely part of history. Although the problem of lend-lease debts had blocked so many other approaches to trade and was now being put aside, both parties to the agreement were uneasy. In the Soviet Union, lend-lease had left a bad taste; the United States, the power that had suffered the least during the war, was insisting on being paid for its wartime assistance. The U.S. had similarly developed a bad taste over the Soviet Union's reluctance to meet its obligation. Both countries were uneasy about the future reliability of each other.

The core of the conflict remained, probably for the same reasons that the act of granting concessions to foreign firms by the Soviet Union proved to be a mixed blessing. These concessions were permitted because of the Soviets' acute need for industry, capital, and technology. They were accepted on a pragmatic basis and rejected ideologically. All this time, cooperation was being belittled by political interpretations. It was argued that the concessions were needed temporarily in order to assist a system which would eventually prove how the other system was wrong—how those who had come to Russia with their wares had erred by being successful, how the socialist society was correct in borrowing the best in order to surpass and eventually destroy its capitalist creditor.

The Lend-Lease Act fell in the same category of interpretation. Its formal acceptance was first justified by wartime needs, by American self-interest, and later embraced with a powerful bear hug of official silence: it did not exist; its usefulness was no longer acknowledged. The flow of supplies was accepted and absorbed into the war machinery, but the origin of the supplies was carefully ignored. The socialist system was winning the war alone, it was claimed.

Some U.S. assistance was reluctantly acknowledged. Much later, when long-drawn-out negotiations to settle accounts had begun, the Soviet Union's official interpretation depicted the United States as a greedy, capitalist power which, even in war, had been commercially minded.

The idea of lend-lease was conceived early in World War II. Long before the Soviet Union's involvement and long before Pearl Harbor, when Great Britain was under heavy pressure from German air attacks, the President of the United States took action. Using a press conference, Roosevelt floated the idea of nonbelligerent assistance to Great Britain. He was careful to suggest only constitutionally acceptable ways to assist a traditional ally without violating the declared neutrality of the United States. If your neighbor's house is on fire, he argued, isn't it logical to loan him your garden hose?

The analogy caught people's fancy and took root. Lend-lease was accepted, but not before considerable arm-twisting. The groundwork for a solid, effective program had been laid. This was a radical step in an America deeply committed to staying out of Europe's affairs. Americans remembered World War I vividly. There seemed to be no good reason for getting involved once more in a war which many Americans considered entirely of Europe's making. The notion of an immediate danger to the United States was absurd. In its place emerged a plan for assisting America's fighting friends with her industrial capacity—to make them strong so they could fend off Germany and Italy without involving United States troops.

Roosevelt sensed this mood and acted accordingly: lend-lease was to decrease the chances of American military involvement. He wanted to make Britain self-sufficient in the war, strong enough to make American intervention unnecessary. The lend-lease bill went even further than this. It strengthened the President's hand by authorizing him to allocate certain production to meet the demand. In addition, it left the decision-making to the President, without the customary congressional authority, as well as the authority to determine the compensation a recipient would be asked to pay.

A crucial point in the proposed legislation was the possibility of extending the authorized assistance to other countries and not just to Great Britain. The drafters of the bill looked at the Soviet Union with the seriousness of futurologists. Western Europe was gone. France had been conquered, as had been the Benelux countries. Scandinavia, except for neutral Sweden, was occupied. It seemed inevitable that sooner or later, the Soviet Union would be on Germany's list. Few American planners thought a direct attack likely before an attempted invasion of Britain, but they did feel that the German war machine was contemplating a turn eastward eventually. Because of this, they wanted to make it possible for the President to act when the time came.

A powerful opposition group in the U.S. Congress feared the possibility of a move to assist the Soviet Union and counterattacked. At the time, the Soviet Union was an ally of Germany, linked to the Third Reich through the Ribbentrop-Molotov pact signed in August 1939. The Soviet Union was also a country governed by a regime inimical to the U.S. system, one which, for the second time within a generation, had hurt American and other Western business interests by, one, refusing to compensate the prewar investors and creditors, and two, by mistreating foreign concessionaires invited by the Soviet government itself. To assist such a government, even during a crisis, would, it was argued, be contrary to the national interest.

The opposition was vociferous, but such was Roosevelt's charisma that his proposals went through, with a loophole which permitted extending assistance to other countries. The new law gave the President authority to order the manufacture of war materiel which might be useful to any nation whose defense was considered vital to the defense of the United States. A two-year limitation clause was included, as well as a $1.3 billion limit on spending. Congress was granted the power to withdraw its delegated authority by a concurrent resolution.

The speed with which the bill went through was unprecedented in peacetime America. It was drafted in early January 1941, in little more than a week had received White House clearance, and on January 10 was introduced in both houses of Congress. The opposition managed to delay passage for two months by arguing that the bill was merely the first step toward bringing the United States into the war against Germany. The argument had considerable force, but by now the country was ready to take the risk.

The bill, which went through almost unchanged, was a triumph for the Administration. In the House, it passed 260 to 165, and in the Senate, 60 to 31. The President signed it into law on March 11, 1941, and Congress closed ranks behind it.

The Soviet Union Enters the War

On June 22, 1941, Germany invaded the Soviet Union. The Lend-Lease Act was about to be put to the supreme test. Should the Soviet Union—the latest victim of German aggression and now a potential ally of the United States in the war—automatically be given aid? Was her defense vital to the defense of the United States? The legal interpretation was clear; the Soviet Union *was* eligible. But politically, the issue was more complicated. Even the President wasn't ready to risk such an overt move, to include the Soviet Union in the lend-lease program.

Publicly, the Administration wasn't entirely consistent. Acting Secretary of State Sumner Welles icily commented at a press conference: ". . . to the people of the United States, the principles and doctrines of Communist dictatorship are as intolerable . . . as are the principles of Nazi dictatorship."[1] However, at a press conference two days after the German invasion of Russia, President Roosevelt struck a different note. The Soviet Union, he declared, would receive all the assistance the United States could possibly spare. He qualified this by stressing top priority for Britain's needs and refused to be drawn out on the applicability of lend-lease to Russia. He was also vague and purposely imprecise when asked whether the American national security was or was not vitally affected.

While America continued sharply divided, entering a period of deep internal examination of its priorities and motives, events in the Soviet Union moved rapidly. The German army swiftly struck at the

heart of the Soviet Union. Great Britain anxiously watched, urging
her allies to welcome a new combatant and give Russia a helping
hand. Under the circumstances, Washington decided to make it possible to give any help without forcing the issue of lend-lease. The
parallel tracks of official thinking and official action converged behind the President's lead, for Roosevelt was acting as a man who was
sure that the vital interests of the United States were being affected
by war in Europe and specifically by the German invasion of the
Soviet Union.

The Soviets well understood the Americans' dilemma. One week
after the German attack began, the Soviet ambassador to the United
States delivered his country's first list of procurement needs. It was
impressive. The list included fighter planes, cracking plants for aviation gasoline (which became postwar refineries), machinery for
manufacturing tires, light-alloy rolling mills, and other, less crucial
items. The ambassador presented the requirements without ever
mentioning the lend-lease program. These were simply the needs of
his country; he was ready to discuss the availability of his requests and
the method of procurement. To tie the request to lend-lease would
have been politically embarrassing to the President, which was the
last thing the ambassador—and Russia—wanted.

The American people were wavering, and the President needed
all the help he could get. The issue was political and psychological,
rather than purely military. The interventionists and the isolationists
were not debating the American role in the war; they were judging
the viability of their new partner in a war against Germany. Was the
Soviet Union worth assisting? A potential friend and cofighter? Was
the Soviet system as bad as Sumner Welles said, or was the type of
political system irrelevant, so long as the government that adhered
to it was willing to fight the Germans?

These were agonizing questions, questions that threatened to
polarize the country. One group was ready to overlook the Soviet
Union's political system, to subscribe to the President's view of helping anyone who was willing to fight alongside the United States in the
war. This group saw in the Soviet Union an ally that could make the
difference between defeat and victory. The other group, the isolationists and noninterventionists, had a different problem. Should
America help a Communist country? Should it help strengthen a
system so alien to all America stood for? Their instinct told them not

to, yet strengthening the Soviet Union as a war ally could be another deterrent to American entry into the war; a strong coalition between Great Britain and the Soviet Union might be adequate. Which way, then, to turn?

The American national mood fluctuated according to the latest news: the German attack on Russia, the President's appeals, his popularity and credibility. But the national trauma continued—what should they do when caught between the two evils of communism and nazism, between alternatives which were not alternatives at all?

It was during this time of searching that the basis for wartime cooperation between the allies, including the Soviet Union, was born. The crisis had brought America and Russia closer.

Stunned at first, the American public replied to the invasion of Russia in a variety of voices. The *Chicago Tribune,* reflecting the widespread isolationist view, professed hope for the mutual destruction of both belligerents, Germany and the Soviet Union. The national commander of the American Legion, hardly one susceptible to pro-Soviet attitudes, canvassed the membership. The results indicated a considerable degree of soberness and political sophistication. "The gist of the advice that I received . . . may be summed up in one sentence," wrote Milo J. Warner: "In no way changing our attitude toward Communism, the invasion of Russia by Germany forms an occasion for the United States to increase and speed up her aid to Great Britain."[2] Still others argued otherwise, in suggesting that neither a Russian nor a German victory would bring freedom or democracy to the world.

Shortly after the invasion on June 22, a public opinion poll conducted nationwide revealed an overwhelming majority in favor of helping Russia against Germany. The question, however, was poorly phrased: "In the present war between Russia and Germany, which side would you like to see win?" Of those who answered, 72 percent favored Russia and 4 percent Germany. The most revealing part was the 20 percent who felt that there was not much choice, nor that the outcome would make much difference.

The poll was taken only two days after the German attack. On the same day, the President made the first two major decisions affecting Soviet-American relations. By executive order, he released $40 million worth of Soviet assets frozen up to then and revoked the provisions of the Neutrality Act as they affected the Soviet Union.

Now Russian ports were open to American shipping, the most important of which was Vladivostok on the Sea of Japan. Roosevelt was entering a delicate web of Asian politics. He was now ready to test the Japanese intentions.

The move was bold and swift. It was also unprecedented, in view of the nonbelligerent status of Japan and the U.S. A presidential note was dispatched to Tokyo, expressing the hope that rumors about an imminent opening of Japanese hostilities against the Soviet Union were totally unfounded. Caught by surprise, Japan took some time to answer. Fears about too close a rapprochement between the Soviet Union and the United States softened her answer, which was couched in mildly reassuring terms but which did not fail to express the Japanese hope that rumors reaching Japan about the imminent intervention of the United States in the European war were also unfounded.

In the meantime, after the shock of the invasion had begun to wear off and the Russians appeared to display little stamina against the Germans, public opinion polls taken in July 1941 indicated a swing toward nonassistance. The Congress of the United States reflected this swing. Yet both sides of the argument held that American entry into the war would be less likely if Britain and Russia were better equipped to fight on by themselves. The difference centered on which European countries could best use American materiel and technical assistance.

On August 12, 1941, two tangentially related events occurred which illustrated the duality of political thinking and the dilemma of American politicians. While Franklin Roosevelt was signing the Atlantic Charter at sea, in the company of Winston Churchill, the British Prime Minister, the House of Representatives voted by a majority of one to extend the Selective Service Act.

The Soviet Union Endures the War

Anxiously and somewhat impatiently, the Soviet Union watched the American drama unfold. For most of the Russians, it was almost impossible to comprehend the interplay of American political forces. There were fluctuations of public opinion, congressional moods reflecting their constituencies, and voices of eastern European minorities irate over the Soviet treatment of Poland and the Baltic Republics of Estonia, Latvia, and Lithuania. Yet the President was determined to act and to act swiftly.

It was Roosevelt alone who was instrumental in mobilizing American resources behind the European (including the Russian) war efforts. The flow of materiel began. Roosevelt wanted military equipment shipped, spare parts provided, production facilities expanded, ships made available. In early August, the first legal opening was provided by the State Department when it made the Lend-Lease Act applicable to the Soviet Union. In a notification sent to the Soviet embassy, regarding a forthcoming shipment, a sentence was included which made the Russians cheer: "It is a conviction of the Government of the United States that . . . strengthening of the Soviet Union's armed resistance against an aggressor who is threatening the security and independence not only of the Soviet Union, but also of all other nations, is in the interest of the national defense of the United States."[3] The Soviet reply, unusual in its warmth and expression of genuine gratitude, carefully noted the forging of a semiformal alliance, an alliance the Soviet Union needed badly.

The war was beginning to take a heavy toll on the Soviet Union. The Soviet economic structure had begun to crumble. Production of key industrial commodities declined sharply. Pig iron dropped to one-third of its prewar level. Steel declined from 18.3 million tons a year to 8.1 million. Output of electric power decreased by half. The trend was not yet fully discernible during the early postinvasion months, but economic wartime indicators were not difficult to read. While Great Britain, due partly to her geographic location, was building a powerful military machine, the Soviet Union was fighting just to stay alive. The consequences for the flow of American assistance did not go unnoticed long.

The railroads, vital in the vastness of the Soviet Union, were crippled. Meager to begin with, they had been virtually paralyzed by air attacks. Water transportation was in a similar fix. For one thing, military operations had made the Volga River nearly useless as a transportation route. All kinds of ways had to be found to get oil from the Baku fields to its destination. First, it had to be shipped by rail to the central provinces of Russia, through Kazakhstan and Siberia, because the north Caucasus pipeline had been cut. Somehow, following the German invasion, the Russians had saved the bulk of their railroad rolling stock by evacuating it almost immediately (this permitted a rapid postwar recovery of the railroads).

The production of oil, an essential ingredient in mechanized war, had suffered. By the beginning of the second calendar year of the war—1942—production of Soviet crude oil had dropped from the prewar level of 240 million barrels to 150 million, a trend that continued.

Thus it was not surprising that the Soviet Union increasingly looked to the United States for "cooperation." (It was seldom seen as *help* or *assistance;* the term used was the *common war effort,* and any variation of the phrase was risky.) The Soviet Union looked upon the initial cooperation and subsequent lend-lease arrangements as an integral part of a natural American involvement, one in the United States' interests. The U.S. viewed things differently, however. Lend-lease was an American *economic* extension into the war zone; it was a gesture intended to supply a fighting ally with the means of fighting. The U.S. was entering into the agreement *politically* and *commercially*—an approach that had to be taken in order to make aid to the Soviet Union palatable domestically. The Russians were never able to understand this viewpoint or to agree with it. They quickly agreed to payment for wartime assistance but resented doing so when the day of reckoning arrived.

The Soviet-American wartime marriage was rich with complications. It was destined to end in divorce, and it is probable that at least one of the partners sensed this from the beginning.

The Lend-Lease Pipelines Open

The Japanese attack on Pearl Harbor changed everything. The United States, now officially at war, turned into an "arsenal of democracy"; she was willing to stretch the definition of *democratic,* the Soviet Union included. One of the first decisions taken by a full meeting of the cabinet in Washington was that American entry into the war would not be allowed to handicap lend-lease. On the contrary, it was to be accelerated, with Great Britain and the Soviet Union the principal beneficiaries.

The consequences exceeded most Soviet expectations. Between October 1941 and May 1945 a total of 16.5 million tons of supplies were shipped to the Soviet Union. About 2,660 ships were used; some were lost at sea and some were diverted en route to Great Britain due to emergencies there. The bulk of the shipments consisted of war materiel, much of it of both wartime and peacetime usefulness. Since the Soviet Union remained high on the American list of priorities throughout the war, all kinds of materiel were shipped. Wartime conditions blurred the difference between war needs and postwar uses. Food, clothing, factory units, machinery, ammunition, guns, and so on were included.

The supply routes, which were far from safe, went through the Soviet Arctic, Black Sea, Soviet Far East, and the Persian Gulf. Almost 800,000 tons was shipped via the Black Sea route, which was opened up late in the war. The safest but longest route went through the Persian Gulf and accounted for 4.5 million tons. The most frequently used route extended from the American west coast to the Soviet ports in eastern Siberia; it accounted for nearly 10 million tons.[4]

Soviet requests came thick and fast. They were indicative of the low level of Russia's state of war preparations as well as her high level of expectations. Shortly after the Second Washington Protocol was signed, assuring the continuation of the flow of supplies (about 7 million tons, worth some $3 billion), a series of requests were received, which included everything from munitions and industrial machinery to food. The fact was, not all of the Soviet requests were met.[5] This is illustrated by a sample list of requests and deliveries. The Russians asked for 4,200 aircraft of all types. Fine, Washington said, we'll start with approximately 212 planes a month. What about tanks? The Russians requested 5,250 and were promised 7,500. When it came to hot-rolled steel and duraluminum, they did not fare as well. These items were of high strategic importance to U.S. war production, so the Soviets got 107,000 tons of steel, against a request of 168,000 tons, and 16,000 tons of duraluminum, against 19,000 requested.

But the U.S. could comply with the Soviets' need for food—wheat and flour. The request for 2.4 million tons was fully met. The lend-lease pipeline to the Soviet Union went into high gear, but what was also needed on both sides was the soothing balm of mutual understanding and recognition—of mutual interests, mutual efforts, and mutual goals. This was not easy to achieve, as events were to demonstrate.

In the meantime, the Soviet economy was receiving a series of important injections of wartime strength and peacetime immunity against inherent Soviet economic weaknesses. Lend-lease was laying a solid foundation, which in time was to create a springboard for rebuilding and recovery. The Soviets had not made these requests with the express purpose of peacetime development in mind. But just as many foreign concessions of the 1920s and '30s had combined technology, capital, and industrial know-how, so had lend-lease, under different conditions and different needs. Both turned out to be important to the Soviet Union.

Transportation equipment and rolling stock is a good case in point. Lend-lease deliveries of about 2,400 locomotives during the war provided the Russians with a better combined rolling stock (her own and that provided by the Americans), as well as a better rail system, than she had in 1941. In addition to the locomotives, diesel and steam, lend-lease supplied Russia with nearly 10,000 flatcars, dump platforms, tankers, and heavy machine cars. Railroad tracks with Soviet gauge specifications were manufactured in the United States and shipped over.

Here was a link with prewar American involvement. In the thirties a team of railroad engineers had been sent to the Soviet Union to overhaul and modernize the Soviet railroad system. Their recommendations led to a major change, which, in turn, led to modernization. The process included double-tracking key routes and installing automatic block signals and similar devices. Union Switch, an American corporation, provided $10.9 million worth of railroad equipment, including signal-operating units installed along an additional stretch of about 2,000 miles. The new equipment left permanently in the Soviet Union was later used by the Soviets as prototypes for copying and expansion of existing facilities.[6]

After the war the Russians further modernized their rail system. For example, the Russian gauge had always been a problem, and the postwar relationship with east European countries required a greater volume of railroad freight. Unloading and reloading trains from one type of gauge to another was cumbersome and time-consuming. So a new system was introduced, which consisted of refitting the train wheels. Today traffic with the Soviet bloc is carried across Soviet frontiers with little trouble; trains are hoisted, new wheels are fitted, and the trains proceed with a minimum of delay.

Another sector of equal importance to the war effort was the generation of power. Power stations and power-generating equipment were a significant part of lend-lease shipments. The total capacity supplied is estimated to have been 1.5 million kilowatts, which included stationary steam and diesel plants, railroad power steam trains, diesel trains, and hydroelectric stations.[7] But not all of it was delivered under the original lend-lease agreement; an estimated 20 percent was the result of a postwar contract signed as late as October 1945. Supplies "in the pipeline" when the war ended constituted a significant input, which was of great importance to a war-ravaged country such as the Soviet Union.

The total delivered capacity of power-generating equipment, which was supplemented by shipments from Canada and Great Britain, was about 2 million kilowatts, enough to virtually replace what Russia had lost in the war with Germany. Toward the end of the war, the Soviet economic ministry specially requested a series of deliveries for the construction of hydroelectric power stations. In 1944 General Electric, which had installed the Dnieper Dam's original set of generators in the 1930s and which was still in the good graces of the Soviets, received a contract to furnish nine additional hydroelectric turbogenerators for the dam. GE was active in another sector where the war had handicapped production—the Soviet petroleum industry. Under the lend-lease program, GE furnished complete electrical equipment, including steam turbine generators, to a number of oil refineries.

The oil story was complex. One of the key contributors of hard currencies early in this century, the oil production declined between the world wars. Exploration for oil was limited by the lack of modern drilling equipment. When Germany attacked, the Caucasus fields (Baku and Grozny) were the principal producers, accounting for about 87 percent of Soviet oil production. Production rose to 230 million barrels annually.[8]

Understandably, lend-lease shipments were unable to replace all of these losses. The fact that for years the Russian (and later the Soviet) petroleum industry was closely linked to the United States helped to some extent. Actual shipments from American to Soviet ports—lend-lease and existing prewar pipelines—totaled almost 15 million barrels of oil and lubricants. About 700,000 barrels of motor fuel was added to production soon after the war.

In some areas, help was sorely needed, help the United States was unable to provide. In the latter half of the war, a shortage of aviation gasoline developed. With her air force moving from the defensive to the offensive, the Soviet Union risked a serious curtailment of air sorties. A U.S. offer to send a group of highly trained specialists to study Soviet refineries was turned down. This decision was later reversed, but the Americans, whose task it was to look into the possibility of speeding up the construction of refineries, were coolly received. They were refused access to sites, restricted in their movements, and were not permitted to look at any basic data. The mission was a failure, and the shortage of gasoline continued, but Soviet state secrets were preserved.

The most important part of the oil story concerned its infrastructure. While it might have been difficult to satisfy even temporarily the immediate needs of the Soviet Union, as in the case of aviation gasoline, long-term sufficiency had to be provided. Lend-lease was aimed at the wartime emergency, but the Russians were eager, especially later in the war, to look beyond the end of the war. The fact that oil exports accounted for 13 percent of Soviet foreign trade was not overlooked. Also not overlooked was the fact that the recipients of the oil and its byproducts were highly developed countries of western Europe. So while the Russians were indulging in the luxury of being choosy and difficult about their aviation needs, they were open, willing, even eager for juicier possibilities. Oil refineries—cracking plants, as well as lubricating oil—were built according to blueprints provided by the United States. In addition, through the lend-lease program, four complete refineries were shipped to the Soviet Union, which required the shipment of an estimated 100,000 tons of highly sophisticated equipment. The production capacity of the four units reached 7,000 barrels a day. When the war ended, the Russians requested additional refinery equipment, but the U.S. was not the only source of such equipment. Several British-built refineries, in addition to American-built ones, were installed in the Romanian oil field at Ploesti. As soon as the Red army was firmly established in Romania and a new Romanian government had been placed in power in Bucharest, the Ploesti fields were surveyed for whatever spare parts (even entire units) were needed in Russia. Then they were dismantled and shipped out.

The lend-lease contribution to rebuilding and maintaining the Soviet petroleum industry was considerable, but a layman reading the Soviet statistical material today would find scant evidence of it.[9] Lend-lease pipelines remained open for many other key products. Synthetic rubber-manufacturing plants found their way across the oceans, as did the latest American rubber technology. Machine tool plants were shipped to Russia and set up, thus permitting production of tools of varying complexity. For example, the Ford Motor Company shipped an entire rubber tire plant.

In the military sector there were large shipments of such things as shipyards (especially yards for building submarines), engine production facilities, as well as designs and parts for producing fighters and fighter bombers. After the war they were used as prototypes for producing civilian aircraft.

Finally, the interaction between skilled Soviet and American personnel throughout the war, particularly the engineers, added a special dimension to the usefulness and effectiveness of the lend-lease program. It was unfortunate, but inevitable, that a political interpretation was to emerge. Lend-lease worked well at the practical, but not at the political, level.

Areas of Conflict

Conflict between the Soviet Union and the rest of the Allies developed sooner than expected. Three issues were involved: the opening of a second front, the volume and frequency of shipments of supplies, and that of priorities. It was Stalin's firm belief that the Soviet Union had borne the brunt of the fighting and therefore should have priority in receiving American assistance. Whatever was shipped elsewhere, such as to Great Britain, Stalin considered "stolen."

In hindsight, such conflict was inevitable. The war clouded everyone's vision. Wartime rhetoric undercut the Allies' unity and helped generate intolerance of each other's viewpoint. The intolerance was greater in the West than in the Soviet Union, for readily apparent reasons. Two opposing forces were at work. The West feared criticism of the Soviet Union. Russia was a highly sensitive ally It was vital to keep her satisfied and unsuspicious, as if this were attainable. The mood of the West, especially the United States, was anti-Communist. A switch was needed, one that would separate the

Communists and what they represented from the wartime emergency. Thus Western spokesmen took great pains to underline unity and downplay differences.

The other force was at work in the Soviet Union, where the influence of the political system had begun to erode soon after the war began. The Soviet military was beginning to disintegrate, and Russia's economy was buckling under the pressure of the German invasion. But as soon as the tide began to turn, the Soviet government found it necessary to tell the Russian people that the turning was due to Soviet efforts. Whatever help came from outside was incidental. The thrust of ultimate victory was that of the people of Russia, motivated and led by the political system under which they were governed.

In the process, the lend-lease program became a victim of considerable distortion. The motivation of the United States, originally praised by the Soviet Union, was now cast in a different light. On the American side, this development was viewed with amazement and openly resented. In private, Soviet leaders were full of praise, while in public, they were full of criticism, a tactic which puzzled and angered the Americans.

In 1944, the last full year of the war, Eric Johnson, president of the U.S. Chamber of Commerce, went to Moscow and was received by all of the top Soviet leaders, including Stalin. In a lengthy interview, also attended by Averell Harriman, Stalin paid tribute to the wartime assistance of the United States. He felt that lend-lease had contributed greatly to the economy of Russia and made the observation that about two-thirds of the most important, large industrial enterprises in the Soviet Union had been built and made productive with the help of the U.S. Harriman reported this conversation in a dispatch to the State Department.

A year later, Johnson wrote a foreword to an important little book. Under the title, *We Can Do Business with Russia*, the author, Hans Heymann, a German refugee and a business consultant used by a number of Soviet officials, propounded the concept of future trade and commercial potential between Russia and America and appealed to the American business community for support. In his foreword to the book, Johnson drew heavily on his experience in the Soviet Union, underlining the fact of official Soviet recognition of the American wartime contribution:

Russia wants to rebuild her towns and industries, and to continue building up her consumer goods industry. . . . In addition, she has learned the technique of developing her own natural resources, and American mining machinery, American road-building equipment, American rolling stock are all on the list of "musts" for the Soviet Union. . . . Russia has looked to the United States in the past as a model of industrial production. She has relied heavily on American technological skill and . . . machinery.[10]

Heymann's book was for American consumption only, but it would have been more convincing if it had been available to the Soviets as well.

The Russians saw a different version. In 1947 a comprehensive study of Soviet economic development, written by Nikolai A. Voznesensky, deputy premier of the U.S.S.R. and chief of the State Planning Commission, was published in the Soviet Union.[11] It was aimed at "clarifying" a major point, that the Soviet system, based on centralized planning and inspired by Stalin's leadership, had won the war alone. The Soviet economy had survived and become highly productive because of the strength of Soviet communism.

The study contained a brief comparison of Soviet and American economic and political motivations. While the Soviet Union had survived and "assured the independence of its war economy during the most difficult periods of trial," in the United States, war meant extra money. "The driving power of the war economy are the capitalist monopolies, for whom war is an exceptionally profitable venture and a means of conquering world markets. The profits of capitalist monopolists in the United States increased from $6.4 billion in 1939 to $24.5 billion in 1943, and during the four years of the war, they amounted to $87 billion."[12]

There was a limited number of conclusions a Russian reader could draw from such a statement. He could dismiss it out of hand or he could assume that it was correct. In the latter case, his resistance to paying the United States for lend-lease supplies would be much greater. It would be more than that: it would be a matter of national pride to refuse payment.

Other parts of the study vacillated between political illusion and economic reality. Deliveries made by the Allies figured in the text as part of Soviet foreign trade. A sevenfold increase in Soviet imports and a sharp drop in exports were mentioned. The fact that Allied deliveries (lend-lease shipments) were made on a noncommercial basis was omitted. While Soviet imports grew rapidly, their industrial and economic significance was limited, it was claimed in the study, which estimated that outside help during the war had accounted for only about 4 percent of domestic production.

Descriptions of various other sectors of the Soviet economy, such as coal, iron, steel, metallurgical plants, transportation, and agriculture, were constructed so as to prevent the reader of the study from guessing that the outside help had made any difference.

When, on occasion, the issue of priorities caused the Russians to complain, the Allies were usually ready to make an extra effort. One of the most striking examples of this concerned the delivery of diesel engines for small naval patrol craft being built in the Soviet Union. Early in 1944 the Soviets urgently requested the engines. But the timing was awkward. Landing craft of all types were being built and readied for the Normandy invasion scheduled for that spring. Should or shouldn't the Russians' request be granted? The decision was to ship the engines. The Allies knew that patrol boats were already under construction in Soviet shipyards; not to send the engines would be a severe blow to construction. Not to do so would also be politically difficult. A total of 126 engines were taken from those earmarked for the invasion fleet and shipped to the Soviet Union. Replacements for the invasion fleet had to be manufactured hastily and at a higher cost, but a conflict with the Soviets had been avoided, and it looked for a while that this time, the cooperation had paid off.

But within a few months, there was another request. Would an American specialist in installing the engines come over? Russian shipbuilders needed instruction and training. A naval officer and an engineer were sent, and their report precipitated another strain in Soviet-American relations.

When they arrived, they found that only three of the American engines had been installed, with hulls ready for installation of another 45. These 45 engines were rusting in open storage.

The officer estimated that the engines already on hand would require a year for installation. Shortly after he returned home, a request for 50 more engines was received, which, this time, was quickly and decisively turned down.[13]

The issue of priorities, as well as allegedly slow deliveries, came up a number of times. The Russians used the visit of Wendell Willkie to air their complaints. Washington, they said, not only had dragged its feet when supplies were desperately needed in the Soviet Union, but they had shipped some of them to Great Britain instead. Between the two war fronts—the British, which was inactive aside from the air war, and the Russian, which was overactive—wouldn't it make more sense to choose the Russian? Or was there a political motivation behind this policy?

A similar argument was advanced by the Russians when an open clash occurred between Admiral William Standley and Premier Stalin. Acting partly on instructions from Washington and partly in his capacity as the American ambassador, Standley attempted to get data on the use of lend-lease supplies from the Russians. At this time, there was a running feud between Congress and the Lend-Lease Administration. Congress wanted more data and was more skeptical of Soviet needs than were the lend-lease administrators. Both Congress and the Lend-Lease Administration wanted evidence from the Russians which would substantiate their respective side of the dispute.

Ambassador Standley asked and asked and asked. Economic data wasn't adequate for his purposes. He also needed military facts.

The Soviets wouldn't be budged. Standley, irate and disgruntled, decided to go home for consultation and to explain the situation to Washington. To his Soviet contacts he repeated that a flow of reliable information would help, rather than hinder, the Soviet war effort. On the eve of his departure, Henry Cassidy, an Associated Press correspondent in Moscow, received an invitation for an interview with Stalin. Pleased and fascinated with the interview, Cassidy filed his story, in which he quoted Stalin as saying that the lend-lease supplies reaching Russia were slow in coming and hinting that Standley had been slow in responding to Soviet requests. The story reached Washington just about the time Standley was reporting to President Roosevelt.[14]

Standley's mission was certainly not helped by the story. He left the President without a clear idea of what Roosevelt really thought. But this was not the end of his troubles. On his return to Moscow, a period of even greater tension began, this time centering on Soviet impatience with the Allies' reluctance to open a second front. Lend-lease supplies continued to arrive, but Standley found it more and more difficult to get from the Soviets any public *or* private acknowledgment of the shipments.

Standley decided to take the initiative and called a press conference, in which he gave his version of the flow of supplies. He openly criticized the Russians for concealing the fact of the shipments from the Russian people and accused them of spreading propaganda that the war was being won by the Soviet Union alone. The press conference was well covered outside the Soviet Union. It stirred up a storm in Washington as well as the Kremlin.

But the situation did not improve. The Russian accusations continued, and American apprehension grew. The two powers, between whom the lend-lease program was intended to be a bridge, drifted further apart. In the meantime, the war ended.

Lend-Lease—A Memory and a Burden

Final victory was more of a triumph for the Soviet Union than for any other country. She had come back from the depths of military defeat and fantastic destruction of her people, land, and cities. Russia had lost more men than any other major belligerent. She had been all but given up by friend and foe alike, yet she had recovered to drive the Germans out and plant the Russian flag on the ashes of Berlin.

The Soviet victory was overwhelming and her political strength at its peak. She was to turn back and start living again, but in order to do so, bread, machines, tools, and the means of production in general were needed. There was no modern technology, no raw materials, no machines the Russians could produce themselves. Yet in a moment of national euphoria over her victory, Russia was sure she could produce these very things. Why worry? Why look to foreigners? Why compromise with those who had failed to stand by the Soviet Union when she was in distress? Why negotiate with those who still subscribed to the faulty system of capitalist economy and who h'd a class-oriented society? To the Soviets, somewhere in all this specious postwar reasoning, there was the inadequate and politically subversive concept of lend-lease.

Politically it was important for the Soviet Union to assume the posture of the sole winner. Acknowledging that lend-lease had helped (especially to the extent that it had) would have endangered this posture. Admission of a mutual war effort, admission of having needed and used Western help effectively would have been to admit the weakness of the Soviet government to the Soviet people. Lend-lease—indeed, the entire wartime cooperation with the West—was relegated to the history books. There was cooperation, yes; Western ships brought supplies; but this was only incidental to winning the war. And, of course, Western help had very little to do with the postwar reconstruction. Lend-lease, as a vivid, acknowledged fact, would have been a burden.

In the United States, the memory of lend-lease became a moral burden. The dream of a better, fuller, happier world emerging from the second worldwide conflict in a generation was shattered. Willingness to work and live with everyone else in peace—an ideal widely held in the U.S.—was there, but the realities of conflicting world interests eroded the ideal. Why had America helped Europe and Russia? What went wrong?

The seeds of the failure of wartime cooperation might have been planted at the very beginning of lend-lease, which was as much a political act as it was a military one. It was accepted as such. The difference lay in the different ways the political aspect was interpreted in the United States and in the Soviet Union. The U.S. viewed lend-lease as a political move to hold the Allies together in a death struggle with fascism. The Soviet Union knew this to be so, but to admit to the Russian people that Soviet communism had been inadequate to defeat the Germans would have been to invite domestic disaster. This, and its ramifications, was lost on Russia's Western partners.

Other gaps in a mutual understanding further complicated the matter. An embattled Soviet Union had demanded preferential treatment, forgetting the problems the Americans faced in helping her. After Pearl Harbor, the United States was willing to help anyone who would help the U.S., but she had to look after her own interests first. In the new alliance with the Soviet Union, Americans were hoping for something else: a change of political orientation, a little less rigidity, a little more democratic thinking on the part of the Russians. How could anyone who saw the strength of America do otherwise? The question was asked in all seriousness.

Due partly to lend-lease, the Soviet Union emerged from World War II stronger, more influential, more expansionist, than she had ever been. The United States also emerged stronger than ever, but she was ready to settle down and look inward, to rebuild, yet fearing (partly because of the lend-lease experience) the new mood of the Soviets. When they moved into eastern Europe and began acting aggressively toward Greece, Turkey, and Iran, this fear became something approaching reality.

The Soviet Union distrusted the capitalist nations, especially the United States, a distrust based on experience as well as the Marxist doctrine of the inevitability of conflict between East and West and of a socialist victory. The U.S. distrusted the Soviet Union because it was a Communist power. Memories of lend-lease, compounded by purely political difficulties encountered by the two powers in attempting to divide the fruits of victory, increased their mutual distrust. The road to the cold war stood open.

The Cold War

Before the day arrived when the United States and the Soviet Union met at the negotiating table to sign the final lend-lease settlement, the long road of the cold war had to be traveled.

The Marshall Plan, announced in 1948, was the first signal of America's new determination. The dynamics of a free-market economy were put into action with the express political purpose of stopping Communist inroads into western Europe. Earlier, the President's decision to sign the Turkish and Greek assistance program was aimed equally at Soviet-inspired and -supported forces. Both moves strengthened the West, but they also helped harden the Soviet position. To the Russians, this was additional proof that the Western wartime alliance had been a facade hiding sinister motives. To them, the Communist movements in the West were liberating, not subversive, forces. Once again, the question of political definitions made it impossible for the two sides to agree and work together.

The Berlin blockade was an act of hostility, viewed with alarm by the U.S., just as the American hard-line reaction surprised and alarmed the Russians.

The American policy of liberation, followed by events in East

Germany in 1953, the Hungarian uprising in 1956, the Polish uprising in 1959, and the Cuban missile crisis in 1962—all contributed to the creation of the Cold War. Any possibility of reviving the wartime debts, of meaningfully negotiating the lend-lease obligation—either payments or the return of unused materiel to the U.S.—was out of the question. By the same token, the possibility of lifting some of the embargoes on Soviet and American goods, respectively, was considered unrealistic. The two sides were frozen in their respective positions.

Only occasionally were there signs of a thaw, but the signs were not politically significant. Instead, they indicated an area in which political sensitivity could give way to common sense about mutual commercial interests.

In the early 1950s a small, unknown company in New York was looking for chrome ore. The company was headed by a seasoned, well-informed Armenian-American who knew that the Soviet Union had large reserves of the metal in the Kazakhstan area. He also knew that the United States needed chrome, a commodity on which there was no U.S. import duty because of its scarcity. The Russians were known to be interested in selling the ore. The question was, how could the political obstacles be overcome?

Preliminary inquiries were discouraging. The U.S. Department of Commerce felt that applying for an import license would be futile. American officials were convinced that the Russians would never agree to sell such a strategically important material to the United States. Unofficially, businessmen were equally sure that the major American buyer of chrome, Union Carbide, would not touch Soviet chrome with a 10-foot pole; it was too dangerous politically. When inquiries took the prospective trader to Moscow, the Russians declared their willingness to sell but were certain that Washington would never grant the necessary import license.

This was the beginning of the first commercial transaction of any magnitude between a private American company and the Soviet Union. Mutual misconceptions were wrong: the Russians agreed to sell and the Commerce Department, after long, careful deliberation, granted the import license. Tramp steamships were chartered, and thus a small New York corporation became the first American company in the postwar years to do business with the Soviet Union. Fifty thousand tons of chrome ore arrived in Ohio via Montreal. Union

Carbide paid for the shipment with a letter of credit. Payment was made in accordance with the general international practice—90 percent on acquisition of the bill of lading and the balance after unloading the cargo.

The entire transaction went smoothly. No duties were paid, and no punitive duties were levied. Contrary to earlier predictions, the deal didn't cause political repercussions. The news of it was carried by the American press as an interesting and rather unusual item.

In the meantime, the Soviet economy had begun to grow, to climb out of its postwar depression. Oil production, power-generating capacity, and coal and mineral explorations moved rapidly ahead. There was no way to judge the Western contribution to that progress. Years of foreign concessions and the lend-lease program made a difference, but their extent will probably never be known.

There was the residue of Western technology from the thirties and the war years, but its usefulness was diminished by the new, hostile atmosphere. Settlement of the lend-lease debts, one of the factors contributing to this atmosphere, was an important, but not decisive, step in the improvement. Other steps must come first.

As president, Dwight Eisenhower decided to decontrol some 700 items in 57 categories of commodities, to permit their export to Soviet-bloc countries. The Kennedy Administration introduced much more liberal legislation, governing medium-term credits linked to U.S. export transactions. Trade unions relaxed their official positions. An agreement concluded with the longshoremen allowed 50 percent of export cargoes to travel in non-American ships. This agreement paved the way for the first major ($110 million) sale of wheat to Russia. On Capitol Hill, hearings were held, during which the American business community advocated an expansion of trade and liberalization of laws governing trade with Communist countries.

In the Soviet Union, the groundwork for change was also being prepared. Participants in the 23rd Congress of the Communist Party of the Soviet Union received all kinds of directions before the meeting. These directions included suggestions that the delegates consider the importance of what was called the international division of labor. For instance, buying Western industrial licenses would eliminate the necessity of spending man-hours and money on scientific research which merely duplicated Western work and results. The participants (the Congress was held in 1965) duly noted these points. They appeared to make sense, without suggesting a compromise in terms of the principles that governed Soviet and socialist foreign trade philosophy.[15]

Still later—and in this case, the time segment has to be jumped—the 1971–75 Five-Year Plan officially included Soviet use of Western technology. The go-ahead was given to joint ventures, bank financing, and even bank mergers, to achieve Soviet economic goals. "Consideration is being given to mutually beneficial cooperation with foreign firms and banks, in working out a number of very important economic questions associated with the use of the Soviet Union's natural resources, construction of industrial enterprises, and exploration for new technical solutions."[16]

Lenin's ghost was back in town. A new version of the NEP was being announced, one which included a different type of cooperation with the West than Lenin had devised, but one which would lead to the same goals.

The Soviet Union and the United States had come full circle in their economic relations. The implementation of Article 7 of the Lend-Lease Act was finally about to be permitted. The article read:

> In the final determination of the benefits to be provided to the United States of America by the Government of the Union of Soviet Socialist Republics, in return for aid furnished under the Act of Congress of March 11, 1941, the terms and conditions thereof shall be such as not to burden commerce between the two countries, but to promote mutually advantageous relations between them, and the betterment of world economic relations . . . To that end . . . they should include provisions . . . regarding elimination of all forms of discriminatory treatment in international commerce, and to the reduction of tariffs and other trade barriers.

When an agreement was reached and the papers signed, the world was very different from what it had been in 1941 when the Lend-Lease Act was passed, the main difference now being the emergence of a divided Europe.

The agreement closed a wartime alliance that had helped the two powers reach several solutions, but it also created new problems.

Eastern Europe had come out of the war vastly different politically. It was weak economically and dependent on the Soviet Union. Economic growth, linked to foreign trade, was the only field that was relatively open, and in that direction the east European countries began to move. There they felt more competent and successful.

This postwar geopolitical occurrence created a new psychological climate for future commercial relations with the West. The term *East-West trade* was no longer sufficient. It had to be divided, treated differently, approached differently. Trade and commercial relations with the Soviet Union were one part of the story; trade with the east European countries was another. The premises differed; the approach had to be more subtle.

The results could have been much more satisfactory. The east Europeans were less powerful politically, less important. Their lack of prominence permitted more leeway in economic experimentation —economic reforms and slow, shy, but persistent attempts to merge the socialist and capitalist systems in various economic areas.

By the time the lend-lease program was being terminated at the end of the war, a new eastern Europe had been formed. One phase had ended, another was beginning.

CHAPTER 3

The Emergence of a Divided Europe

Both major wars of this century have brought destruction and reconstruction. Both were fueled by physical, spiritual, intellectual, even messianic, forces. Destruction came about for particular reasons; the justification for it was to make possible a better, fuller, more peaceful world. Reconstruction was a challenge, a way to create new institutions and new systems.

Nowhere was the process more visible than in Europe. Nowhere was it more painful—or significant. The old continent had been cut in half in the name of Allied unity. Europe was regarded by the two outsiders, the Americans and the Russians, as a potential source of another calamity. But the views of the two powers differed, as much as their national characteristics and outlook on life differed.

The United States viewed Europe as a natural ally in need of assistance. Europe was an unhappy continent whose unhappiness was being prolonged in spite of the war having ended. The Americans never lost faith in their European allies, and they never doubted the faithfulness of Europeans, in turn.

The Soviet Union viewed Europe as a continent filled with remnants of capitalism, hostile and unfriendly toward Russia. It was weak, ripe for exploitation, a beachhead for Soviet political incursion. It must be converted to socialism.

The two superpowers pulled out their knives and performed surgery. Eastern Europe and the city of Berlin were separated from the main body of Europe. National entities in eastern Europe remained but lost their sovereignty. Officially it was simply a change of systems, the rebirth of a number of countries within a new international framework. In fact, it turned out to be an extension of Soviet influence and power, both military and political.

The change meant different things to different people. To the Poles, it meant the resurrection of Russian preponderance, which had ended a generation earlier with the Treaty of Versailles. To the Hungarians, it meant new restraint in political choice, restraint that went beyond what Hungary had experienced under the Hapsburgs or the Ottomans. To the Czechs, it was the end of a brief period of independence. For Romanians, it was the end of a slightly longer period which had begun in 1877 with the coronation of King Carol I. Bulgarians started a similar process in 1878 when their national independence was proclaimed. Yugoslavs and Albanians joined these nations with new social and political systems. The Baltic states were now part of the Soviet Union.

The transition was traumatic. Bitterness ran deep. The new spheres of influence meant that the war had been fought for no gain. It took east Europeans years to learn that there was no way to stop the knife of history in the middle of an operation. It took them even longer to restructure their thinking and economy. Thinking was psychological, but the economy required a practical approach. Europe survived it well, however. Its western half soon regained its health. The eastern half took more time.

A Change of Direction

Social, political, and economic reorientation followed. Principally Western-oriented, east Europeans had to refocus their attention and change their priorities. In the past, most of the cultural flow had been to and from the west. Most of the trade, investments, and credit were westward. Their social philosophy, legal systems, and institutions had Western roots. The task of change would be enormous.

Reorientation toward foreign trade was also necessary. The new communist system considered, and still considers, foreign trade as basically a political tool, an integral, and active, part of foreign economic policy which goes considerably beyond actual trade. When the east Europeans emerged from the war in the new attire of People's Republics, the official Soviet policy was political independence combined with economic self-sufficiency. In practical terms, this meant a high level of inner-bloc trade and rejection of Western offers of cooperation (including the Marshall Plan for Poland and Czechoslovakia).

The reorientation of eastern Europe had to be drastic. Before the war, east European trade with western Europe was flourishing. Western exports included heavy industrial products, machinery, iron, steel, chemicals, motor vehicles of all descriptions, nonferrous metals, ships, and textiles. The composition of Western imports was different: foodstuffs, raw materials, and the products of light industry. Pulp, paper, coal and coke, wood, and cereals dominated the flow to Western countries. The total trade turnover was heavily Western-oriented. The figures for 1938 are a striking example of this trend: the total volume of eastern Europe's foreign trade was $1.081 billion. The neighboring countries of eastern Europe accounted for $147 million, the Soviet Union for $14 million, and the rest—$747 million—was the turnover with western Europe.[1]

This trend had to be reversed, and it was.

Poland and Czechoslovakia, one year after the war, are outstanding examples of successful change. Poland's prewar imports from the Soviet Union amounted to 1.8 percent of her total imports. In 1946 the percentage was 78 percent. Her exports to the Soviet Union rose to over 50 percent, against a negligible 1.1 percent before the war. The Czech case was less drastic, reflecting slightly different political circumstances in Prague right after the war. Forty percent of Czechoslovakia's trade was now with the Soviet Union.

Similar developments in Poland involved special lines of credit. Rather tough requests were made by the Russians. On one hand, they were willing to extend substantial credit to the Poles —$450 million—for Soviet industrial equipment, while on the other, stiff demands were made for Polish coal. Immediately after the war, the figure was 13 million tons. In 1947 the Poles were able to negotiate the volume and cut the request in half. The reason given by the Soviets for their demand for coal was the destruction of the coal mines in the Donets Basin and the resulting acute Soviet need for coal. The fact that the Poles, as weakened by the war as were the Russians, were obliged to make large deliveries was highly typical of the changed situation.

The trend continued. The internal orientation of the Soviet-bloc countries helped create a trade pattern that was heavily slanted toward each other. After some hesitation, the hope of more trade with the East dwindled among the Western countries. Eight years after the end of the war the amount of American trade with the Soviet-bloc countries was not significant. American imports, slightly higher than the other Western countries, were about one-half of 1 percent of all American imports. The Soviet Union and eastern Europe were being gradually phased out of the calculations, plans, and economic considerations of the West.

The change was calculated by the Soviet Union to link the newly acquired members of the socialist community with her. But there is another explanation, which is more in line with the official Marxist interpretation of events.

The Theory of Economic Independence

Marxist theoreticians saw many of their dreams come true after the war. Outside of the phenomenal expansion of the system, even before China had established her own Communist government, the classical Marxist-Leninist theory of economic evolution was about to be proved. Stalin, the postwar reincarnation of the founders of the Soviet Union, spelled it out in his writings.

The war weakened the capitalist world, and this weakness, added to prewar problems, was considered enough to bring about the early collapse of the non-Communist world. The creation of the socialist bloc of states was a blow to the market-oriented economy of the capitalist states, an area containing about 35 percent of the world's population. The West, deprived of such a large chunk of its traditional markets, would be faced with economic crisis and severe unemployment. This would lead to social unrest.

According to the Marxists, the response of the capitalist states would be highly predictable. Shrinking world markets would create competition. Each capitalist state would attempt to secure as many of the remaining markets as possible. Internal conflict would lead to local wars between the developed countries. Western Europe would be the first to attempt to isolate itself from the United States. The two defeated powers, Japan and Germany, would join the struggle for economic survival, and chaos would result.

The states that emerged from the war outside the capitalist system had to stay out of the system. For their own survival, they should abstain from any dealings with a world doomed to end its present form of existence. Association with the West would be temporarily beneficial, but fatal in the long run. While a tiny stream of trade could be maintained, nothing large should be permitted.

The theory of the early collapse of the capitalist states paralleled another theory, one which claimed economic self-sufficiency for the socialist bloc. It had all that was required to secure healthy growth and to avoid the calamity toward which the West was gradually moving. Raw materials were available in abundance. Labor, skilled and unskilled, was ready to resume its normal, peacetime activities. There existed financial and administrative institutions, as well as the basic institutional framework for creating technological and educational units. The theory of economic independence and self-sufficiency was thus fully documented.

Stalin's reasoning, aside from his basic assumptions, was faulty, with respect to the non-Soviet part of the bloc. In theory, the Soviet Union could pursue an autarchic foreign economic policy.[2] Small east European countries were in no position to even state a similar proposition. Their dependence on foreign trade was traditionally much greater. One of the results of the political changes that occurred in 1945 was a severe shortage of raw materials usually imported from the West.

Institutionally it also took eastern Europe some time to adjust. State ownership of the means of production and state monopolies introduced into east European countries were based on the Soviet model. Market mechanisms which existed before the war had to be eradicated and replaced by a new institutional framework. State planning·commissions, ministries of foreign trade, and other highly centralized units were created. The change was not easily digestible especially under postwar conditions. Economic retrenchment was inevitable. New priorities decreed by the Soviet Union led to several uneconomic investments, as well as the duplication of investments in a number of countries. Steel and various types of engineering were the two most frequent examples.

Agriculture, which was the basic economy of the area, had suffered greatly during the war and was now suffering from postwar neglect. Collectivization, bitterly resisted in most of the new socialist entities, was not an answer. A period of deep economic stress followed. But in spite of this stress, the Communist parties and their leaders were convinced that their theory of economic independence was correct. Outward signs in western Europe corroborated the theory. France and Italy had strong postwar Communist parties. Germany did not count. The United States had just launched the Marshall Plan to save the crumbling European capitalistic system, but it was too desperate a measure to be successful.

Just in case, though, the Soviet Union thought of a way to counter the Marshall Plan. A strong pitch for the economic integration of eastern Europe was made, and an institution was created in 1949 to carry it out: the Council for Economic Mutual Assistance (COMECON).

The Early Role of COMECON.

The economic integration of the socialist countries was the immediate goal. Integration meant independence; it meant the acquisition of enough strength to permit a firm rejection of such "dangerous" offers as the Marshall Plan. The Soviet Union wanted to prove to her allies (and probably also to herself) that the two systems were dynamic enough to be compatible. Of course, the theory went further and predicted the ultimate victory of socialism.

The COMECON charter (original members: Romania, Poland, Soviet Union, Czechoslovakia, Hungary, and Bulgaria) provided the blueprint for a major economic revolution. It pledged the creation of the proper institutional machinery for a steady exchange of technical assistance and technical information between its members. A system of mutual aid through the efficient distribution of raw materials, foodstuffs, and industrial machinery was envisaged.

The new institution, however, had much more ambitious goals. COMECON was to be a central agency through which overall economic planning would be funneled. It was also to be a body that would decide the production pattern of its members. Diversification of production would mean assignments of lines of products to individual countries. The system would avoid duplication of effort; it would assure needed production of basic agricultural and industrial commodities; and it would make the socialist countries truly independent of the West. COMECON's other role would be to synchronize foreign trade, to provide centralized access to modern technology, and later to deal on a multilateral basis with whatever type of integration western Europe accomplished.

The Soviet Union claimed, indirectly, that COMECON was an answer to the Marshall Plan. In an editorial in *Pravda* on January 25, 1949, COMECON was described as the result of political necessity created by the West. "The industrialized nations of the West," *Pravda* asserted, "were boycotting trade relations with the People's Democracies and the USSR in retaliation for their unwillingness to submit themselves to the dictates of the Marshall Plan."

In the West, there were different assumptions. COMECON was viewed as a real threat, as a well-organized, economically self-sufficient, group with high political motivation. It was also disturbing because of the widespread belief immediately after the war that foreign trade was to remain one of the important elements of inter-European relations. The trend of Western thinking ran along predictable economic lines, while the thinking in the East was politically motivated. The two ways of thinking never met.

The creation of COMECON delivered another blow to Western economic planners. Prewar production and foreign trade figures were used in drafting the Marshall Plan. Based on these figures, an assumption was made, that the prewar scale of commerce between eastern and western Europe could reasonably be assured.[3] Economically, the premise was sound, but a closer look at the growing dependency of eastern Europe on the Soviet Union should have sobered some of the planners. For a while, it did not.

There were sound economic reasons, in the immediate postwar calculations, for discussing the possibility of Eastern trade flowing to the West. The Marshall Plan, in order to get congressional approval, needed all the ammunition it could get. The idea that eastern Europe could contribute to lightening the American burden was born of economic minds. Politically, it was naive.

Nevertheless, it was seriously discussed.

The commodity structure of west European needs pointed to eastern Europe as the traditional and natural supplier. Coal, timber, and foodstuffs were high on the list. A study by the Committee for European Economic Cooperation shortly after the war, made some predications. By 1948, the committee estimated, Poland, for instance, would be able to ship about 16 million tons of coal to the West, and this amount would nearly double by 1951. The calculation was based on two premises—prewar Polish production of coal and the results of the first postwar years. In 1947 Polish production reached 97 percent of the prewar level. Poland planned to mine 80 million tons of coal by 1951, the year on which high hopes were put by the Committee. In her first five-year plan, Poland included the projected expenditure of $90 million for the purchase of mining machinery.

Timber, another important commodity, was to be found in the Soviet Union and in Finland, a country outside the socialist bloc, but close enough to be extremely careful about her political and economic decisions. For Finland to obtain Soviet timber, it would first be necessary to provide the Russians with tractors, timber-cutting machinery, and other types of modern equipment.

Imports of foodstuffs called for similar investments. Large quantities of fertilizer and farm machinery would have to be imported to make the Western flow possible, which, in turn, called for credits. Yet the hope was voiced that a flow of cereals and other food items equal to the prewar level would be secured before long. But it was a hope based on skimpy evidence.

Debate began in the West on the merits of the issue. Economists, wedded to the theme of the east Europeans being wise enough not to stop their Western trade, continued to speculate. The most effective way to spur the flow, they argued, was to make sure that exports of capital goods were secured for eastern Europe. Credits were also needed to create purchasing power for Western goods. It would be counterproductive for the Soviet Union and its allies to take strong measures in an attempt to frustrate the Marshall Plan. "So far the evidence is that the Russians favor continuance of our trade" wrote William Diebold in 1948.[4] "Should they adopt a different attitude in the future . . . they will incur the political onus of blocking trade, which the people at both ends of the transaction want to continue."

That onus was indeed incurred. It did not make much difference to the Russians. Their decision was made, their road selected, their attitude firm. Few in Moscow cared about, or even considered at that point, political blame by outside powers.

The importance of this lack of mutual understanding cannot be overemphasized. The Soviet Union made a major move by creating COMECON. She was explicit in her inner economic approach and in creating interbloc dependency, away from, rather than closer to, Western markets. Some statistics from the period are available. In 1947 the Soviet bloc accounted for 4.1 percent of total Western exports; imports accounted for 2.7 percent. The downward trend manifested itself during the period, reaching an all-time low four years later—1.9 percent of exports and 2.1 percent of imports.[5] In the case of the United States, in 1946, these tiny percentages were translatable into $102 million of exports and $141 million of imports. The volume dropped during the next seven years, to $2 million in exports and $46 million in imports.

No wonder the American business community was not worried when embargoes were placed on the overall trade turnover with the bloc. National security was easily invoked. There was little or no sacrifice involved. The ogre of communism was superimposed on the question of trade.

The Soviet political theory justifying the need for economic independence was taken seriously by the West, whose response was the Marshall Plan to save Europe from the type of chaos the Russians were predicting. Western theories of a possible reopening of trade channels and the securing of Eastern contributions to west European recovery met with disappointment. When COMECON was organized, the Western powers responded politically, not economically. The principle of cause and effect came into play, and there was no way to retreat. Both sides had locked themselves in their respective positions. In the editorial cited above, *Pravda* was, in a way, correct. There *was* a boycott of east European trade, but the reasons were different. The boycott was a direct result of Soviet policies, so it was largely of the Soviets' own making.

The American Embargo

On both sides of divided Europe a rigid frame of political and economic institutions was imposed. The moves and countermoves, the Marshall Plan and COMECON, were prompted partly by these institutions. In the West, reaction was predicated on the policy of saving western Europe from economic disaster. There were strong political bonds. The Marshall Plan was to provide a base for the creation of a similarly strong economic line. But in the East, the opposite was true. Economically, the east Europeans had no place to go—except east. What was missing was a political link. The new governments, composed largely of imported individuals, lacked native roots.

While being essentially economically oriented, COMECON was to perform an important political function. The consequent creation of the Warsaw Pact alliance, in response to NATO, was to add the military component and cement the mutual interest foundations. In the process, east European countries acquired new status, but they also lost their contacts with the West and suffered more than the Soviet Union when the Western reaction set in, a reaction led by the United States.

The strong, militant American strategic export embargo, combined with the existing legislation limiting trade with Communist countries, was the core of the new Western policy. Previous legislation included the Trading with the Enemy Act of 1917, the Johnson Act of 1934 prohibiting long-term credits to countries which had defaulted on payments, the Export Control Act of 1949, and others. In 1951 the Trade Agreement Extension Act furnished a legal base for withholding the most-favored-nation status from Communist countries. The policy of embargo itself created a new mechanism of control, reinforcement, and supervision.

A series of committees sprang to life. The Consultative Group, later to be known as the CG; the Coordinating Committee, to be known as Cocom, with the key assignment of preparing the list of commodities under the embargo policy; and a few years later, the China Committee (Chincom) were organized. All NATO countries, plus Japan, supplied committee members. The United States determined to prevent the Soviet bloc from rearming itself and thus concluded a series of about 50 bilateral agreements with other countries. These agreements were to extend the embargoes all over the world.

The United States was ready to enforce her policy by every available means. In view of her position just after the war, few countries openly resisted. Gradually, though, friction developed in the Western camp. America's European allies, accustomed to dealing with the East, saw in many of the embargo measures an excess of zeal.

The first problem the allies encountered was that of definition. What was a *strategic* item? What were the criteria for determining the definition? From the American point of view, the principal reason for putting an item on the embargo list was its potential importance and usefulness to the military economy of the Soviet bloc. The next consideration was the production level and trade capacity of the bloc's producing country. All of this was spelled out in the basic document known as the Battle Act Report issued in 1951.

This document was an extension of earlier legislation. Congress attached an addendum to the Foreign Assistance Act of 1948, which permitted the termination of American assistance to any country trading with the Communist bloc. For years, the move was cited as proof of the Soviet contention that the United States' approach was political and strategic.

But this definition of The Battle Act Report did not satisfy everyone. A diversity of national interests were involved. There was a difference of opinion between the Americans and the British regarding steel. It could obviously be used to make weapons, but at the same time, the British argued, it had many peacetime uses—the rebuilding of shattered cities, for example.

Another difference between Britain and the U.S. lay in their opinion of the strategic importance of rubber. Britain exported rubber, America imported it. For the British, it was a currency-earning commodity; for the United States, it was a scarce, highly strategic material. Preoccupied with the development of a synthetic rubber, Americans found it difficult to sympathize with the British. But England could be stubborn. The export of rubber permitted the import of Soviet agricultural products, the British argued, which, in turn, helped feed British workers employed in munition industries. What could be more strategic to the West?

But there was a more pertinent question. How *effective* was the embargo? How badly was it hurting the Soviet Union? How much damage had it done to the Western countries that had been deprived of east European markets?

It would be rather difficult to provide definite answers to these questions. During the crucial embargo years—1947 to 1953—the embargo list was long and detailed. Prepared by Cocom and circulated under highly restrictive and confidential labels, it was applied rigorously. In a preface to a book published in the late 1960s, about the effects of the embargo policy, Gunnar Myrdal claimed that it hurt the Allies as much as it did the Communists.[6] In his capacity as executive director of the United Nations Commission for Europe, Myrdal spent a good deal of time trying to fight or by-pass the embargo.

The main target of the embargo was overall Soviet economic growth. It was construed to introduce a process of retardation to that growth. In a way, that objective was accomplished. According to various calculations undertaken by Western, as well as Eastern, sources, the retardation rate amounted to about 1 percent of the Soviets' annual gross national product. The figure was impressive, but not decisive, in the attempt to shift Soviet priorities.

Economically, many critics asserted, the embargo helped the Soviet Union define her production goals. Although they were classified, the embargo lists were available to the Soviets. Their stockpiling of embargo items, and special efforts to catch up in production, were some immediate results. The lists were excellent economic indicators for the Communist planners. This belief, that the embargo inadvertently helped the Soviet Union, is still held by some economic historians.

The embargo provided another justification for the Soviets' go-it-alone policy. It added push to the Soviet effort to integrate east European economic policy. Some economists maintain that the retardation process was matched by a speeding up of the effects on the inner workings of the Soviet sphere of influence.

This argument might be valid, yet the Soviet Union acted as if the embargo was hurting. In the early 1950s two organizations were formed to try to by-pass the embargo. Trade and commercial offices, with considerable powers, were set up in various Communist embassies in western Europe. In Berne a special, secret purchasing office was established. It reportedly had large funds at its disposal and handled its transactions through a Swiss bank in Zurich. An office was also established in Sweden.[7]

Considering that neither Switzerland nor Sweden was bound by the Cocom decision, the Soviet activities seemed plausible. The Soviet Union particularly, but also the entire east European area, were hungry for Western products. Embargo or no embargo, they had to have access to it.

The embargo policy started to weaken shortly after Stalin's death. Events in eastern Europe in the mid-fifties, such as the Hungarian and Polish uprisings, changed many Americans' views. The Soviet Union and east European countries appeared as two different political entities. Punitive policies toward each had to be revised. Western Europe pressed for a change, a relaxation, a more realistic approach to using an embargo. One telling argument for a major policy change was the launching of the Soviet Sputnik, which demonstrated to everyone that Soviet technology was moving ahead in spite of Western efforts to slow it down. The drama of Sputnik's voyage had a direct influence on the revision of Western thinking regarding the embargo's effectiveness.

A forceful British move (Prime Minister Winston Churchill's statement in Parliament) caused Washington to agree to a revision of the embargo list. By the time the revision was finished, it went much further than the Americans initially were willing to go. It also turned out to be the beginning of the end of the embargo policy. The only American inflexibility was that regarding China; while Great Britain unilaterally abolished her own Chicom list, the United States refused to do so.

The policy of embargo was coming to an end. While its immediate consequences for the Soviet Union were disputed, it had left its mark on eastern Europe, whose dependence on the Soviet Union was increased. There the process of growth and development had slowed. The juxtaposition of the policy toward eastern Europe, proclaiming an eventual restoration of national independence while at the same time forcing the east Europeans into the Soviet economic orbit, was all too obvious.

A Divided Europe Becomes a Reality

The east Europeans were changing their patterns of economic thinking, as well as their patterns of working. Highly dependent on the importation of raw material from the West and on foreign trade with the West, they were forced to turn to the Soviet Union. The internal policy of the bloc, complicated by the hostility of the West, left them no other choice. These early developments were to seal their pattern of external economic relations for years. Only the subsequent periods of economic reform—to be initiated much later —altered the pattern, and then only slightly.

Numerous sectors felt the impact of the new situation, of the gradual calcification of the new intangible European boundaries.

Eastern Europe was short of primary sources of power. It was short of sources of energy, principally oil. As time went by, the Soviet Union emerged as the principal supplier of power for Poland, Czechoslovakia, Bulgaria, and East Germany. Crude oil was even shipped from Russia to such oil-producing countries as Romania.[8] The Soviet Union became the supplier of more than a third of east Europe's iron ore, cast iron, grain, in addition to about half of the rolled steel and nonferrous metals.

That was not, however, a one-way street. The East European exports to the Soviet Union and other nearby countries became an equally important aspect of economic development (which later became a problem when reorientation toward the West was acceptable). The initial structure of east European production was geared —not unlike it was in the Soviet Union—to heavy industry. Traditional foreign trade-oriented approaches were only marginally important. More solid industrial infrastructures emerged in a number of countries, a distinct benefit. This was achieved at the expense of advanced technology from the West. Export-oriented east European industries shipping their products to the Soviet Union and other socialist states were meeting Soviet needs and adhering to Soviet standards, which were lower than the West's standards.

This situation influenced the early economic system of the east Europeans. Shut off from the West and looking inward, they did not exert themselves to be export-oriented. The Soviet Union was willing to accept relatively inferior products. She was also willing to bend her demands to the requirements of centralized economic planning. Eastern Europeans, previously geared to a private-enterprise economy, were faced after the war with the requirement to retool and adapt. Central planning replaced the diversity and the multiplicity of previous methods. It meant the inclusion of foreign trade in long-term planning and the necessity of following decisions, regardless of the fluctuations of foreign markets and changing demands. As it turned out, central planning required immediate change once the reorientation of exports occurred.

The system had been also suffering, as a result of some of these conditions, from the lack of ideas. In technology, for instance, the number of registered inventions emanating from eastern Europe in the early postwar years was only about one-eighth that of west European inventions.[9] This helped perpetuate outdated production methods. There was abundant evidence that, in many countries, agriculture was taking a back seat to the industry. The lack of technological innovation was also due to a lack of basic research and incentives. Independent research was dominated by institutions. Like foreign trade, basic research and development were centralized. In the Soviet Union the Council of Ministers supervised foreign trade operations through the Ministry of Foreign Trade and the State Committee for Foreign Economic Relations, and the east European countries followed this pattern. Various academies of science conducted research and development and reported to their respective ministries and special party committees. The east Europeans also adopted this pattern.

Nothing better illustrates the problem of innovation under socialism than Nikita Khrushchev's order in the mid-fifties telling his technicians to look into the manufacturing process of synthetic fabrics, which by then were standard items in the West. In the field of pure science, the long and rather painful episode in the field of Soviet genetics, with Trofim Lysenko playing the role of prophet and later of witch doctor, is another example.

A new, artificially divided Europe had to adjust itself to a new role. The Western part, operating with a powerful injection of the American economic assistance, took off rapidly. Eastern Europe had different problems. One was that of retaining national identities; another involved the compromise between the membership requirements of the bloc in economic terms and their individual efforts to continue and increase the process of normal growth. Foreign trade figured prominently in these problems; it was important—in some cases, vital—to national development. Several east European countries depended heavily on trade with the developed countries. The new division of the continent forced them to make special and determined efforts to reconcile economic dependency on the Soviet Union with their Western links.

These efforts were not always understood in the West. The communication lines were rusty. The political psychology of the situation pushed the two European halves apart, something the United States, in the early days, contributed to.

Eastern Europe emerged from the ordeal of intervention by the big powers confused, weaker, less equipped to deal with her immediate problems, and politically insecure. It took time, patience, and a combination of native determination and a feeling of political frustration to snap out of the postwar slumber.

Outside changes of attitude, as well as political and psychological evolution in America and western Europe, led to a period of east European economic reforms. Changes in the West have also influenced the attitudes of the Russians. Both sides thus contributed to the emergence of a slightly less divided Europe of the latter third of this century.

CHAPTER 4

The Nature of Gradual Change

Rhetoric versus Facts

There was little doubt in the West that change had to come, but the timing and nature of it were impossible to predict. At stake were two elements, the considerable differences between the two systems and the political overtones. The capitalist and the socialist systems had evolved differently. Their convergence was easy to understand but difficult to anticipate, as to where and when. In addition, the rhetoric of the would-be partners defied prediction.

"We value trade least for economic reasons and most for the political purposes," Nikita Khrushchev stated in his usual blunt fashion to a group of U.S. senators on a visit to the Soviet Union.[1] He was convincing, for there were several in the group who felt the same way. A few years later, Dean Rusk echoed this theme when he said to the Senate Committee on Foreign Relations, "Eastern trade . . . should be an integral part of our overall policy toward international Communism . . . trade with the Communist world cannot be effectively used as a blunt instrument. It must be flexibly adapted and flexibly applied. . . ."[2] Lenin had predicted at the outset that the capitalist world would not be able to survive economically without trade with the Soviet Union.[3]

The prospects were dim, yet, aside from the rhetoric, there were needs, desires—and some illusions. They all pointed to better communication and eventually to more trade. The embargo, as a method for denying east European countries access to Western technology, was of dubious success. While both the Soviet Union and the United

71

States were ready to discuss the matter, their approach was distinctly political. The East requested the removal of restrictions and granting of most-favored-nation status. The West asked first for proof of movement toward détente, including a Soviet willingness to discuss military subjects. But the question of timing remained unresolved. Détente first and removal of restrictions second, was the Western message; removal first and détente second was the reply.

In both the old and the new rhetoric, facts were few and far between. Shortly after the worst period of mutual exclusion was over, the volume of business increased. In the West a series of studies were undertaken to explore the possibility of greater economic cooperation. In the East there were various economic plans calling for bold industrial expansion, plans which could not be carried out without help from the West. In the Soviet chemical industry, for example, plans called for increased output of plastics, fertilizers, and synthetic fibers. The estimated capital outlay would be about $2 billion. Projected production goals couldn't possibly be reached without annual foreign purchases of about $300 million, on the average.

Other Soviet industrial sectors were also busily planning for growth and greater productivity. Modern oil refineries would be built and synthetic rubber and textile plants modernized. An unusual number of Soviet orders had been placed in the West in the early 1960s. Several fertilizer plants were purchased in the United States; a complete paper mill was imported from Sweden, and 20 fish factory ships and refrigerator ships were ordered from Japan, to cite a few of the more important examples. The volume of trade grew, while the usual rhetoric suggested just the opposite.

The post-embargo period—or rather, the period in which the process of American denial grew weaker—saw significant changes. The Soviet Union became a more important partner than before. During the difficult period, 1956–62—a period punctuated by the Hungarian revolt, the Polish internal détente followed by retrenchment, and the tense Kennedy-Khrushchev encounter in Vienna— Soviet imports from the West tripled, rising from $236 million to $600 million. In the Soviet Union these years represented an extraordinary concentration of national resources on space research, specifically, in the launching of Sputnik I.

It was also during this period, and spilling over into the later, post-Khrushchev years, that Western imports played a part in fulfilling earlier economic goals. Diversification and expansion of chemical and petrochemical industries were directly assisted. Equipment and machinery were imported for the iron and steel industry. Through increased mechanization and automation, productivity rose. Technology imported from the West was sufficient to save the Soviet Union considerable research and development funds of her own. The time normally required to move from the drawing board to full production was reduced considerably.

This extensive change was never articulated; it just happened.

The Preliminaries

Both sides approached gradual change soberly and deliberately. A process of serious rethinking was undertaken in the West, which was more political than economic. In the East the rethinking was crucial; it had to find a place within basic Marxist doctrine for expanded trade with the capitalist West. "The main features of the Soviet Union's planned economy are determined primarily by the basic economic law of socialism," stated the authors of *Fundamentals of Soviet Economic Planning*, "which expresses the essence of the socialist mode of production—the continuous expansion and improvement of production on the basis of advanced technology for the purpose of the maximum satisfaction of the constantly growing requirements of society."[4] The authors mentioned the need for economic ties with other countries. Since Soviet foreign trade is based on stable and planned principles, they said, such expansion would offer considerable benefits to the Soviet new trading partners in the West. These benefits came under scrutiny when commissions, associations, congressional committees, and others looked into the matter more deeply. What some concluded was just the opposite of what the Russian writers of *Fundamentals* had proposed. Stability and planning often spelled lack of flexibility. In the West this was *sine qua non* to a successful foreign trade program. Adjustment to world price fluctuations, shortages, and surpluses of specific commodities, as well as the viability of distribution systems, was required.

How to reconcile these two points of view was the problem. Looking at the Eastern markets—limited yet exciting, constrained yet offering future possibilities—the Western business community was free of political and moral qualms. Traders followed their respective governments, which were ready to soften their earlier, intransigent position. Politically, this was all that was required. The only link remaining was the economic viability of the proposition.

Toward this end, a look into the business potential was required, and several prominent, scholarly institutions were asked to undertake studies. The U.S. Senate asked Library of Congress specialists to furnish background information on East-West trade. Business International in America, the Committee for Economic Development in Europe, Deutsches Institute für Wirtschaftsforschung, and others were consulted.

On the Eastern side, the mechanism of central planning was used to prepare for change. There was hardly anything else, any other important instrument that socialist planners could use in the early stages of East-West evolution. Within this centralized planning, an opening here and there was possible, an occasional phrase which would give a hint as to the needs of technology, of changing some patterns of production. It was too early to spell out these needs (as clearly as they were spelled out a decade later), but a small beginning had been made.

The two sides thus gradually adjusted their positions—but not in a vacuum. There was a slow, steady growth of East-West trade. During the three years, 1958–61, the relationship between the socialist bloc and the European Common Market was limited, to say the least. Trade with the bloc amounted to about 2 percent of the total foreign trade of the Market. Six years later, the situation was quite different; the Soviet Union alone increased her exports by an average of 10 percent per year, with Italy playing a leading role on the Western side. In Asia, Japan picked up much of the Soviet trade. The interesting point here was the growth of Soviet exports, but a relatively slow increase in her imports. The explanation probably lay in Soviet efforts to earn hard currency, which was reflected in her export items. Aside from crude oil, iron ore, and raw cotton, the Russians began to export such items as watches and cameras.[5]

To any observer who might inquire about the socialist position of economic independence, the Soviets had a ready answer: the bloc's independence will be better preserved once it acquires needed technology and industrial know-how. The capitalist West is ready to provide these tools for a monetary consideration, which only proves that Lenin was correct in asserting how badly the capitalists need Eastern trade. Without it, they would wither away.

The preliminaries to expanded contact were approached in the usual way. Illusions were mixed with hard economics, psychology with trade. Mutual confusion was sure to survive.

Western Studies

Western studies, which were numerous and diffuse, had a common denominator: find out how trade and commerce could be increased without political embarrassment. In terms of business, how viable were the socialist countries? How far would Western businessmen go in adjusting to the peculiarities of state-controlled economies?

One of the studies was done by the research committee of the Committee for Economic Development; on this occasion, an American group was joined by its European and Japanese counterparts. The purpose of the study was to find ways to expand trade. Judging from past experience, such expansion was possible. In 1963 Eastern exports to members of the European Communities (OECD) were $3 billion, four times the volume 10 years earlier. But the same did not hold true for the United States, for reasons which did not always have to do with the Communist countries. Total OECD exports to the East were three times as high in 1963 as they were in 1948. American exports showed a down trend, with 1963 figures representing only 40 percent of their exports 15 years before. Lend-lease pipelines could still have been counted in 1948, but not to any significant degree.

The group's recommendations were addressed mainly to its participating countries rather than to the East. Great flexibility was required, flexibility dictated by rapidly fluctuating political and economic conditions. Close Western cooperation and synchronization of approaches was needed, and toward that end, the Committee for Economic Development suggested establishing an intergovernmental committee on East-West trade. Out of such a coordinating effort, a common Western policy could evolve. Once this was done and the entire range of Eastern trade had been coordinated, the likelihood of internal policy clashes within the Western group would be greatly reduced.[6]

The recommendation of the group was not endorsed by the Americans. Evidently memories of earlier differences regarding the strategic embargo lingered. It was left to the French, Italians, and Germans to issue a call for unity.

The influence of the Americans appeared elsewhere in the report. In the section dealing with pricing, credit regulations, arbitration, and marketing opportunities, a warning was issued to avoid the accumulation of debts by the east European countries. Credit should be kept to a minimum, the Americans suggested, to provide an incentive for the east Europeans to produce for export and to earn enough to pay for their imports. But the suggestion was not well received. To produce for export, eastern Europe needed tools and equipment, and to acquire these, credit was necessary.

Bilateralism versus multilateral trade—a future problem area for eastern Europe—was touched on briefly. Bilateral negotiations and trade agreements were suggested, with a provision requiring payment in hard currencies of balances due by either party. The west Europeans, like their American partner, missed the point when they recommended fewer barter deals. Once again, the national interests of the Europeans were evoked. Bartering was detrimental to the development potential of export-oriented commodities and therefore should be avoided when possible. It was essential for the east Europeans to try the new, more effective, methods of marketing. In effect, barter agreements would kill such incentive.

The east Europeans, starved for Western goods and beginning to look into the possibility of relaxing their political requirements as well as their centralized economic planning, very much needed to barter. But they were not equipped to export the required quantity of goods, and for what they could export, service follow-up was not available. In addition, the barter method offered a way to by-pass hard-currency requirements.

The Committee for Economic Development made an *economic* judgment without first looking into the economic and political circumstances of the east Europeans. East and West kept talking *about,* but not *to,* each other. It was to be many years before they began to listen to one another.

Two other voices were raised during this period, regarding the potential of East-West trade. A British outfit known as the Political and Economic Planning Group and describing itself as a "bridge between research and policy-making," produced its own analysis.[7] The other was the United States Council of the International Chamber of Commerce, whose efforts were centered on providing badly needed support for the new legislation concerning trade with eastern Europe. In 1966 the East-West Trade Relations bill, which was being considered by the Congress, needed strong outside support.

There was a touch of realism, as well as hope, in the British approach to the entire subject of trade with eastern Europe. There was no need to make a big issue of it, they said. Trade would be relatively unimportant unless certain steps were taken, and even then, the volume would not greatly affect the Western economies. One way to earn hard currencies was through licensing, subcontracting, and joint production.

Both East and West could make an effort. For instance, Westerners might organize the means for a swift exchange of data on deals, practices, payments, and the like. One possibility was that some countries would benefit from less stringent Western restrictions. Another was the eventual granting of MFN status, a possibility that was initially linked with a wish (or perhaps a request) that, in order for an east European country to be granted MFN status, she must show that she was evolving toward a market-type economy. This request, if it ever was that, was later dropped by the Political and Economic Planning Group. Either we are willing to consider MFN status, some members of the Group reportedly said, or we aren't. There was no use in making it sound good by attaching unobtainable clauses.

Some aspects of the practices of the east European countries should be mentioned, though. For example, it would help trade if the traditional Eastern request for counterpurchases, as partial payments, were removed. Also, Western trade suffered from restrictions imposed on the movement of Western buyers and sellers inside the Communist bloc. The main suggestions touched some raw nerves, however. The pricing system could stand reforming, and individual enterprises should be permitted to participate directly in foreign trade. The bureaucratic layers hindered rather than assisted the flow of trade.

Most of the subsequent economic reforms concerned these points. Pricing was made more responsive to supply and demand, and in the countries with a record of successful reforms—Hungary, for example—individual enterprises were given access to foreign transactions. The British study undertaken in the early 1960s, was remarkable in its insight and realism.

Congress and the President: Trade Issues

In the United States, aside from private and semiprivate efforts, the executive and legislative branches of the government played a major role. Congress was challenged by two successive presidents to relax East-West trade restrictions and to see what could be done to increase the flow without appearing to appease the Communists. Small steps at a time were suggested and progress was slow and not always successful.

In 1962, a trade expansion bill contained a minor provision for increased East-West trade, which, if enacted, would remove fur skins from the list of restrictions, a provision that was particularly important to the Soviet Union. But Congress rejected the bill, and in doing so, struck another blow at the trade expansionists. A more stringent bill was passed, which contained discriminatory provisions aimed at two countries which had been treated liberally before—Poland and Yugoslavia—and which had MFN status.

The next year, President Kennedy countered by adding an amendment to the Foreign Assistance Act of 1963, which permitted trade concessions already accorded to continue if the President determined that they were in the national interest. In order to pacify the congressional opposition, *national interest* was defined: it was to be in the national interest whenever the President thought that expanded trade would promote eventual independence from the domination or control of international communism.

In 1964 President Johnson used this yardstick for Poland and Yugoslavia. The definition struck home both ways. It was accepted by the Congress and it was viewed in the East as an open admission that America viewed trade as a political lever and not as a normal commercial undertaking. While the Communists had always considered trade as a political weapon, their tolerance for others doing the same was limited.

It was at this time that the U.S. Council of the International Chamber of Commerce went into action. The momentum for closer trade relations with eastern Europe began to be felt. The Administration introduced new legislation known as "the East-West Trade Relations Bill of 1966." The bill failed after long, protracted debate, but it did indicate a changing national mood in the United States. "After years of careful study," said Secretary of State Rusk, "the time has now come for us to act, and act we should and act we must."[8]

Rusk's call for action was based on the assumption that a significant change had taken place in the East, both internally and in the East's relations with the West, a change that offered the United States an opportunity to move and to work for "the cause of freedom." He called for removal of the existing discriminatory tariffs on imports from Communist countries and appealed to Congress to adopt a more flexible and purposeful trade policy. He underlined the potential benefits to American producers who would find new markets for their exports. Reference was made to American copyrights, the possible settlement of lend-lease obligations, and the prevention of trade practices injurious to U.S. labor and industry.

Once again, political considerations intervened, this time in a form even more difficult for east Europe to digest. A paragraph in the bill, linking trade expansion to a potential diminishing of eastern Europe's dependence on the Soviet Union also included a reference to Vietnam. "We are reaffirming in Vietnam," Secretary Rusk stated, "our determination to aid free and independent nations to defend themselves from Communist aggression or subversion. But determined resistance to such force is only a part of our strategy to maintain a peaceful world." Trade, of course, was the other part of this strategy. Rusk concluded by saying: "We need to make unmistakably clear to all the Communist nations of Eastern Europe that their best interests lie in economic development and peaceful trade, not in support of futile attempts to gain advantage through the use of force."

It is difficult to imagine that an act of Congress that contained such language would be welcomed by the Soviet Union and eastern Europe. While it might have been premature to move from politics to trade, the Americans' lack of subtlety was difficult for the East to accept or understand.

The U.S. Chamber of Commerce gave support to trade with eastern Europe when it looked as if the Congress was opposed. The Chamber represented a different part of American public opinion, a part which, theoretically, would benefit from expanded trade with eastern Europe. The East-West trade relations bill of 1966, the Chamber said, should be enacted immediately. A document prepared by the Chamber's Committee on Commercial Policy (issued April 21, 1967) echoed most of the provisions of the trade relations bill and added some of its own.

Further liberalization of the Export Control list, the removal from it of items freely available elsewhere in the world, and the extension of Export-Import Bank credit guarantees to buyers in eastern Europe were among the Chamber's major recommendations. But there were others even more daring. Admission of some east European countries to the General Agreement on Tariffs and Trade (GATT) would be of considerable benefit to the West, the Chamber stated. Western countries doing business in eastern Europe would have their work and the security of their investments more regularized by east European compliance with GATT's regulations. Connected with the GATT suggestion was one stressing to the Soviet Union and its allies the benefits of a convertible currency. Such convertibility would make it easier to transact business and would be more realistic in terms of payments. It was this realism that was feared in the East, a realism which at that time would bring their currencies, if convertible, closer to their real worth.

The realism of various U.S. presidents has not been fully shared by the Congress, and skirmishes between them continued. It did not help when President Johnson tried to reassure Congress about his intentions when the East-West trade relations bill was introduced in 1966, nor did it make any dent when he pleaded with Congress to look at his legislation as being in the political and economic interests of the United States, saying that the bill "provides for trade, not aid. It does not affect the system of controls on the export of strategic goods. It does not lower our guard."

In the disagreement between the President and Congress, the Vietnam war, at that time in its early stages, did not help. A confrontation over Vietnam was already in the making, and Soviet assistance to North Vietnam was certainly no incentive to congressional leaders. Through the device of the executive order, the President had some maneuverability, but it was of limited value in matters of trade. The mere fact that a confrontation with Congress was visible indicated change, which was duly noted on both sides of the Atlantic.

The Significance of the Change

The issue of trade with Russia and eastern Europe had been revived in the 1960s when a realignment of power in the East was suspected. Trade itself was not a particularly significant issue (the volume of trade was miniscule); but the political implications were. The White House engaged in a new policy of building bridges to the East while recognizing its earlier failures to build tunnels in the same direction. Overt, rather than covert, approaches were needed, and there were sufficient signs of movement within the socialist camp to encourage a new approach. The period of violent unrest in the East appeared to be passing; economic tactics were gradually replacing political ones. Thus the West began to change its mind.

The significance of the change lay in the period in which it occurred. The Vietnam war was entering its fiercest stage. Talks with the Soviet Union were restricted more to the spectaculars—the summit meetings—than to specifics. Verbal duels between the U.S. and U.S.S.R. continued with monotonous regularity in the United Nations. Americans were as strongly anti-Communist as ever. The anti-Vietnam war movement, questioning America's motives, was just beginning.

Several explanations are possible. The postwar policy toward eastern Europe had failed. The final division of Europe awaited one more signature to become a fixed geopolitical entity. Relations between the Soviet Union and the United States were entering a more workable, more realistic stage. While politicians still referred to the "national interest," the restoration of human rights, and similar points, other issues were being weighed. The rapidly expanding American economy was eager for new markets. New technology and its application now permitted a much better standard of living in eastern Europe, if only it could seize the opportunity. The opportunity was seized with the eagerness of a child given a new toy. The child was old enough to have the toy—but only if it did not endanger the nursery, a fact the toy's manufacturer had to learn quickly.

In an effort to translate this mood of change into reality, a series of industrial cooperation agreements were worked out, which permitted a gradual transfer of technology, with a resulting increased production capacity of some east European industries. The agreements included the transfer of technology and equipment, thus permitting savings on research and development. Occasionally, they also included special provisions calling for the development of follow-up services such as a network for sales and related activities in the markets of the Third-World countries. Their economic and political neutrality permitted a more efficient, more profitable operation.

These agreements represented an important shift in attitude. In the West, fear of contributing to the rebuilding of the war-making capacity of the Soviet Union was gradually replaced by a more relaxed mood of commercial cooperation (in the United States the change took place more slowly and with more difficulty). The willingness and ability of both East and West to accept the transference to a state-controlled economy of modern technology designed and built by the West was a major step. As has been true throughout Soviet-Western relations, the change was possible only because of a changed political climate. In Vietnam the two superpowers were engaged in a war with strong ideological overtones, but in Europe, they were sitting down at the trade-negotiating table. Such inconsistency wasn't new; it had happened many times before, under tzarist and Soviet regimes alike.

Eastern Reflections

The very slow, very gradual change in the attitude of the Soviet Union and eastern Europe was quite different from that of the West. In the East there were no public debates, no examination of their relations with the West. Foreign trade, as an integral part of the socialist economic structure, simply evolved along with the rest of the economy.

A centralized system of Soviet economic planning, one that served as a model for other socialist countries, was at the center of the issue. Planning traditionally was a joint product of the socialist societies. Economists played a part, but the Communist party played an even larger part; political considerations were therefore mixed with economic ones. In foreign trade, which affected many domestic economic sectors, political considerations were at the forefront of the planning.

Yet the changed circumstances, the new needs that had arisen in Europe, made it imperative that the Soviets' economic thinking now be flexible. Some Soviet leaders admitted this publicly. In 1965 the new Soviet premier, Alexei Kosygin, deplored the lack of modernity and the low level of production in Soviet industry which had been unable to produce modern machinery and equipment and which was behind in applying modern production methods. A U.S. congressional study published about this time concluded that the overall level of Soviet technology in 1962 was behind that of the United States by about a quarter of a century.[9]

There remained the problem of how to increase their technological capabilities, while retaining socialist principles in their planning. "The scale and structure of the Soviet economy, with its numerous independent sectors, are such that it can be organized only on a nationwide basis," concluded the authors of *Fundamentals of Soviet Economic Planning*[10] in the early 1970s. This policy should be applied to the entire socialist bloc, as well as to trade affecting socialist economic development. The creation of COMECON was motivated by a desire to see a central approach extended to the whole socialist bloc, but the emergence of the west European community was, of course, also a powerful incentive.

This problem slowed down the rate at which the socialist economies could absorb Western technology, and presented the east European members of the bloc with more headaches. Their problem was compounded by greater dependence on foreign trade than the Soviet Union. But the problem was also a blessing: the east Europeans, hard-pressed and forced to devise methods that permitted economic growth within the existing political framework, set out on their own separate road toward economic reform. This step appeared at about the time the first signs of Western liberalization appeared.

The first layer was that between state planning commissions and individual enterprises. It consisted of industrial associations, or trusts. The individual enterprises were members. The trusts were to replace various specialized ministries; their job was to deal with administration and implementation of the plans, while the state planning groups were confined to the planning itself.

Among the countries on this metaphorical road were Poland, Romania, Hungary, Czechoslovakia, and East Germany. The basic principle of centralized planning was retained, but there were differences in the planning process. At first, central planning units interfered in the administration of individual enterprises; later, the trusts and associations acquired more responsibility. One example was the Romanian effort to liberalize her foreign trade by creating "industrial centrals," independent groups of related enterprises to which authority was given to deal directly with foreign buyers and sellers.

Hungary and others liberalized their foreign trade even earlier. One of the problems they faced was that of pricing. How could centrally controlled prices be decentralized when the economy was not flexible enough to allow the transference of national resources to more productive and innovative industries? Price manipulation, within the narrow scope of individual enterprises, was the only answer; prices were to continue to be controlled centrally, with the result that incentives were eliminated or simply neglected.

The Soviet Union was not particularly concerned with centralized planning. She had other problems. Centralized planning was to continue in force for some time to come. No one in the Soviet Union was advocating the liberalization of economic planning. The Soviet Union was not in nearly the hurry that the other members of the socialist bloc were to develop better trade channels with the West. To her, more trade with the West was important, but not vital, not worth a special effort. Intra-bloc trade and the unity of the socialist economic bloc were more pressing problems. To do something about them, COMECON was created. In addition, the West's embargo helped clarify the areas in the East that required special attention. Finally, the political climate made it possible to reconsider the Soviet Union's earlier philosophy of economic self-sufficiency.

It took time for COMECON to become viable. When in the mid-1950s, it did become viable, it turned out to be a giant clearinghouse. The concluding of trade agreements between its members, the synchronization of economic plans, the effort to avoid duplication of lines of production—all were the function of COMECON. And so was distribution.

Some limited objectives were reached in the 1950s. Poland and East Germany signed an agreement on specialization in the heavy industries and the production of electrical equipment. Poland, Czechoslovakia, and the Soviet Union reached an understanding regarding shipbuilding. East Germany and the Soviet Union agreed to cooperate in such diverse economic sectors as agriculture engineering, the production of turbines, and the manufacture of diesel engines.[11]

The creation of COMECON was essentially defensive, a reaction to the growing unity of western Europe. But in addition, it was instrumental in making increased inter-bloc trade a reality, of pinpointing shortages and technological gaps and eventually in refocusing attention on the economic potential of the West. The function of COMECON was of modest proportion; it was primarily a pretext for the Russians to integrate the economies of the socialist countries.

COMECON

It was 1962. COMECON was 13 years old, with little genuine accomplishment. The general mood concerning trade was changing, both in the East and the West. A reorganized COMECON would play an important role, that of planner and coordinator for the entire socialist community.

The concept, structure, and agencies of COMECON were all important in the reorientation of the Soviet Union's policy toward the West. Its failures, rather than accomplishments, paved the way for greater interest in trade with the West. But COMECON also served as an internal catalyst and as a yardstick for measuring the capabilities of the socialist bloc. Its original, ambitious goal of integrating the economies of the socialist countries was soon discarded; economic reality impinged on the Soviet Union, as it also did on the other members of COMECON.

The Soviets strived to make COMECON work. Noticing its weaknesses in the early attempt to make it into a sort of Communist Common Market, the Soviet Union—supported by other socialist countries, especially Poland—proposed a bold plan for reorganization. The plan was simple: COMECON would be transformed into a major organization. Rather than being merely an outsized clearinghouse, it would be a supranational institution responsible for overall economic planning, allocation of resources, and distribution of investments. All members would have equal status; all would be subject to majority decision. As a regular member, the Soviet Union would have the same vote as the others, a radical departure from the past.

The idea unexpectedly ran into Romanian opposition. Romania argued that to elevate COMECON to a supranational level would interfere with the national suzerainty of each of the members. It was not the Soviet Union that Romania objected to; it was the strange notion of making socialism in one country subordinate to socialism in a nonnational institution. To this political objection, Romania added her own economic worries. Should the proposed division of socialist labor be universally accepted and COMECON empowered to act as an overall planner, countries such as Romania would be forced to halt their industrialization. They would be relegated to the position of suppliers to the more industrially advanced members of the bloc.

Romania's opposition was a surprise. She might have profited from the internal, dogmatic mood then prevailing in the bloc, a mood still firmly wedded to the belief in rapid industrialization (which, the Romanians feared, would slow down) and the principle of a national, rather than supranational, system of economic planning. The Soviets perceived, probably correctly, that these two economic considerations were too strong and too important to be challenged. The issue was therefore dropped.

A compromise was arrived at. Internal COMECON decisions would have to be unanimous; other decisions would not be binding —thus skirting the issue. A member would be given the opportunity to vote against a move it considered wrong. Further, individual countries were charged with implementing decisions that were unanimous. COMECON was not given supervisory rights; in effect, it was reduced to a consultative and middleman negotiating role.

The debate, the Romanian arguments leading to a change of direction for COMECON, and the reemergence of a strong role for individual members all strengthened the East's preference for bilateral negotiations, a preference that lingered throughout the 1960s and into the 1970s. It was brought to bear on relations with the West whenever the European community tried to replace bilateralism with multilateralism. Western Europe viewed these attempts as further steps toward integration, while eastern Europe viewed them as a threat to its members' limited sovereignty.

Romanian-Soviet differences regarding the future of COMECON and the process of economic integration were only the beginning of COMECON's troubles. The Russian proposal for national equality within COMECON was not as selfish as it appeared in the early sixties. As time passed, the bilateral approach was used successfully by individual COMECON members to establish links with the

West. But inequalities developed. Economic flexibility and greater economic reform in some countries gave them access to the West, to the disadvantage of other COMECON members. Yugoslavia, an outsider but still a socialist country, was a noteworthy example; Hungary was another. Once more, the Russians faced a problem. They were interested in foreign trade, but it was not vital to them. The east Europeans, on the other hand, saw foreign trade as being crucial to their industrialization and economic development. It was only much later that the Russians came around to this view. In the meantime, they regarded COMECON as a tool for reinstating the inner balance of the bloc.

A number of organizations were built around COMECON. Iron and steel were put under one roof, as Intermetal. The chemical sector was grouped as Interchim. There was the Institute for Standardization and another organization for such specialized functions as the manufacture of antifriction bearings. One of the more successful undertakings was the founding of the International Bank for Economic Cooperation (IBEC). IBEC was to be the principal financial institution of COMECON; it was to create a substantial reserve of "transferable rubles," to be used as an internal, semiconvertible currency for financing intrabloc transactions.

But even IBEC had a marginal role in the mid-1960s. Various institutions that were supposed to coordinate COMECON operations became purely administrative organs. The only useful activities of COMECON were bilateral cooperation agreements between its members, similar to those of the fifties. COMECON facilitated trade between Poland and the Soviet Union, on one side, and Hungary, on the other. Clay derived from bauxite deposits was shipped from Hungary, in exchange for crude aluminum from Hungary's two partners. COMECON offices were also used for a Hungarian-East German agreement in the field of computer technology and for Poland and Czechoslovakia to coordinate production in the low-voltage industries.[12]

But this second great effort to move COMECON out of the artificiality of its institutional existence once again met with little result.

Various shifts within the structure of COMECON, various attempts to make it a more acceptable, a more workable channel of commerce, trade, and finance, only led to more studies. For instance, one of the problems COMECON faced during its first two decades was the price structure. The Soviet Union enjoyed a preference treatment through a provision favoring raw materials; she was COMECON's principal supplier. Inter-COMECON prices were set at a higher level than the prevailing world prices, thus creating an unfavorable trade pattern for eastern Europe.

The price structure was suspected—and rightly so—of being politically motivated, but there were economic advantages in this arrangement. Thanks to the price structure, Soviet deliveries were steady, thus assuring long-term deliveries of badly needed raw materials, including fuels. Payments were made either through barter arrangements or with nonconvertible rubles. The east Europeans did not have to stretch themselves to earn hard currencies; thanks to barter arrangements, they were guaranteed outlets for their manufactured goods.

Subsequent studies were concerned with the influence of world price fluctuations on COMECON's price structure. This was a problem for the Soviet Union. The issue surfaced in 1965 when the Russians sold oil to the Italians at about half of the amount they charged their own allies, the East Germans and the Czechs.[13] The only recourse of the other COMECON members was to diversify their trade and look for outlets and supplies outside COMECON. This led to a period of economic reform, reform that was caught on the horns of potential economic benefit and the political limits. The situation also led to the east European members of COMECON taking a new look at the Soviet Union as their principal source of raw materials, for it had become too costly for eastern Europe to purchase Soviet raw materials. The division of labor within COMECON was now ready for reexamination; at this point, there was an attempt to outline the future of COMECON economically rather than politically.

Eastern Studies

Some of the studies of the functions, aims, and purposes of COMECON, as an integrating force in the socialist bloc, accomplished much. They focused attention on the possible and probable areas of economic integration, as well as pointing to concrete steps which COMECON was ready and eager to take. Unlike the West, where studies were more scholarly, with little chance of influencing policy related to East-West trade, the East published studies that were practical guides. In the West, research was often intended to support or oppose proposed legislation. In the East, it was commissioned by decision-making bodies primarily to strengthen their position within the bureaucracy of COMECON.

In 1968 Poland and Czechoslovakia undertook an important study of economic integration. Written before the Soviet intervention in Czechoslovakia, the study was unusual in its bold recommendations. It also appeared to be a mixture of scholarship and semiofficial thinking. One of the authors was the well-known Polish economist Z. Kamecki, who held various official positions and was a theoretician on foreign trade in general and East-West trade in particular. The Czech coauthor, V. Pavlat, was a specialist and proponent of an integrated socialist economy.

If implemented, the models would have changed COMECON into a genuine international economic body comparable to the Common Market. Unified planning and the creation of a planning center for long-term projects were at the top of the long list of recommendations. In a way, the study was a return to earlier Soviet-Polish efforts to make COMECON supranational. The coordination of long-term economic plans would also have included the investment plans of COMECON members, to be combined with a large documentation center which, among other tasks, would have a major role in monitoring the production of COMECON members.

Price structure was to be reformed. Common prices would be determined through decisions taken by national pricing authorities. (Kamecki and Pavlat rejected world market relations as a basis for pricing.) This would have eliminated the economic significance of national boundaries. The example of western Europe was cited. A common pricing policy was to be combined with a unified tax structure, a common denominator for structuring wages, and a common budget and currency. Major construction projects would follow, with the financing expected to create few problems; it would flow out of the large transnational funds created by unification.

These proposals seemed so grandiose and the optimism of the authors so vast that skepticism was voiced as soon as the study was released. Yet a number of recommendations were taken seriously by the policy-makers. The next Five-Year Plan, covering 1971–75, was being discussed when the study was released. Drafters of the Plan enlisted COMECON's assistance in deciding what recommendations of the study should be included. COMECON obliged with specific suggestions, one of the most significant of which was its outline of product specifications, intended to integrate socialist production. An indirect result of the study was the establishment of the International Institute for Economic Problems of the Socialist World System, which was to handle the integration of planning, the methods for economic forecasting, and comparison of socialist profitability among nations.

Shortly thereafter, a major integrating decision was taken by the East. The International Investment Bank of COMECON, established in 1970, was to provide financing facilities for cross-national projects. But the main reason for it was to finance exploration for raw materials in the Soviet Union. The bank's initial capital amounted to one billion rubles, with the Soviet Union providing almost 40 percent of this amount. Thirty percent was in freely convertible currencies or in gold.

Probably there was no direct link between the 1968 study and the decision in 1970 to establish the bank. Yet the role of the bank was crucial in the process of economic integration. The central issue was that of Soviet raw materials. The east European countries depended—and still do—heavily on Soviet raw material. Creating a new financing institution would allow more exploration and increase future mutual dependency within the bloc. The industrial development and economic progress of the members of COMECON required that two routes be taken. One led to the West, the other to the Soviet Union, in importing raw materials. The role of the International Investment Bank grew as the wave of economic reforms swept eastern Europe. But when certain reforms went too far, the Russians marched into Czechoslovakia. The others learned their limits. The Bank, while financing exploration for new sources of raw materials in the Soviet Union, was a factor in assuring economic interdependency. It also provided a stable base for exercising political leverage, if necessary. After Czechoslovakia, the Soviet Union was determined to continue keeping in check a too-liberal approach to her allies, but she had learned the lesson of the unpopularity of direct military intervention.

The studies in the socialist bloc looked for a way to accomplish economic integration without sacrificing the national sovereignty of the Soviet Union's east European allies. They also indicated a potential for mixed economies within the bloc. What was not foreseen were the different ways the various members would proceed. With the coming of extensive reforms, the race was on. Some COMECON members were distinctly in front, while others were left behind, a trend COMECON failed to stop.

The Growth of Trade and the West's Dilemma

The COMECON group, whether integrated or fragmented, kept growing in economic and trade significance in the 1950s and 60s. The volume of trade between COMECON and the West registered a phenomenal growth rate of 10.2 percent per year in the 1960s, while the figure for world trade for the same period was much lower—0.1 percent.

These figures indicated movement. The earlier turnovers were insignificant, and the total share of the bloc's countries in world exports, for instance, was a mere 6.8 percent in 1950; it jumped to 11 percent in the early sixties, to drop slowly, due principally to the upsurge of west European and Japanese economies.[14] Eastern markets represented little for the United States. Early in the 1970s, after the embargo policy or at least after its principal thrust, trade with the bloc diminished considerably. Even after the period of change had clearly affected American political thinking, the volume of American-Soviet trade was small. It was barely 0.7 percent of the total figure of American foreign trade in 1971.

Yet, even with such small amounts, the issue itself presented difficulties. The mutual dependency of various COMECON institutions signified the mutual dependency of its members. The new investment bank was in the process of cementing that interdependency. Soviet raw materials—precious, important, and irreplaceable —were an additional cementing factor. The Soviet Union, in turn, needed more technological input from the West in order to use the bank's resources and to put the raw materials to good use. Should Western powers contribute to the already considerable interdependency? Should the United States be an active part of it? The Soviet-American agreements signed since the thaw carefully spelled out the

Soviets' and Americans' exclusive and mutual economic interests. But for domestic consumption, the socialist countries were vocal in attributing to the closer links with the West, a political rather than economic, significance.

The question asked and posed does not require an immediate answer. The conflict between the political implications—of rather limited value—and the economic benefits was to be resolved in favor of the latter. There was no other way, no other road, once it was decided that the two halves of the European continent had to coexist.

The dilemma persists, no matter what rationale is used. Economic reforms in eastern Europe have provided a little more elbow room to the smaller countries. The reformers need Western trade, Western technological imports, and Western markets for their products. The Soviet Union has been moving gradually into the mining of minerals and various sources of energy, which could be of great economic value. The flow of capital from the West in general and the United States in particular, is needed for exploration and production. Would a major Siberian discovery of oil contribute to a higher degree of COMECON's interdependency or would it slow down the reforms?

The problem is complex. In the past, only about 6 percent of the Soviet GNP has been derived from foreign trade. A substantial Western involvement in exploration for gas, oil, coal, and other fuels could change this percentage, however. In the United States, the GNP portion of foreign trade is about one-fourth that of western Europe. What remains unresolved is the extent increased trade with the socialist countries would change the pattern. The Soviet Union— probably groping with a similar doubt—moved forcefully to explore the Siberian areas. But the Soviet Union alone cannot produce as much as some geologists and oil experts think is feasible. Huge capital investments have been made in Siberia since the end of World War II, and they continue to be made. But the technology of the Soviet Union is inadequate for achieving the desired results. The cost of the undertaking is high. Assuring the stability of fixed structures erected on frozen ground adds at least 20 percent to the construction costs. Labor is more expensive. Material has to be hauled from faraway places.

But Siberia continues to intrigue and lure Westerners (and Japan). The Tyumen region is the one on which Western attention has been concentrated. A severe climate, ice nine months out of the year, fierce mosquitoes, and a sparse population made up of the descendants of political and criminal deportees make Siberia uninviting—yet it is still considered a future bonanza. The Soviet Union has claimed that there is an oil basin there with 100 billion cubic meters of gas annual yield capacity. The Russians have also added an investment price tag, which supposedly guarantees everything needed up to the actual extraction: $2.85 per thousand cubic meters. Ferrous metals, coal, and timber are in abundance. The only thing needed is Western and Japanese willingness to invest.

Aside from the economic risks, there are the political overtones. While these projects dangled in front of an energy-hungry world, the observable change in East-West relations brought changes in trade. What earlier was a sin gradually turned into a virtue. Communist markets became attractive; Western goods became acceptable.

A Searching Look, A Set of Discoveries

The attractiveness of these markets and the gradual acceptance of Western goods was just a beginning. It was a notion more than a fact; it was a change of attitude more than a cold business analysis. The movement of trade across the ideological frontier required a number of ingredients. Westerners were interested in such factors as profitability. They were wondering what kind of risks they would be taking if a substantial flow of credits began. They also asked for some kind of feasibility study, which would make it possible for them to make a judgment. The Western business community was, and still is, a creature of its environment, a prisoner of its own philosophy and procedures. Approaching the socialist world, the West was forced to bend, to change, to adapt, and in some cases, to dispense with what has always been considered normal precautions. A sixth sense was called for. It was a new and exciting game. Part of the Soviet attraction for the West was the prospect of dealing with a society about which little was known.

The first discovery the West made was that the two things most needed were unrelated to each other—modernization of the Soviet economy and a détente with the West. Business was thus politicized and politics—domestic or international—has never been considered a comfortable environment for business to operate in. The attractiveness of Eastern markets made Westerners bend to this requirement, too, and they dived into international politics.

Those who survived continued to look closer, piercing impenetrable walls of Soviet secrecy in an attempt to analyze the unknown continent. This mutual attraction began to produce results. During the 1960s, the flow of trade more than doubled, still representing a modest figure—$2.3 billion in Soviet exports by 1970—but a growing one. The commodity composition was steady and reliable. Russia exported oil, coal and coke, wood and wood products, metals, cotton, diamonds, and a number of semifinished goods. The Soviets were eager for Western machinery and equipment, various metals, and all kinds of consumer goods.

Outside the Soviet Union, the east European countries' voice began to be heard. East Germany was the most dynamic, but even countries such as Romania, one of the economically weakest members of the bloc, moved forward. The Western business community's efforts to understand, to read the economic signs, to relate them to their own capabilities, to react, all grew.

The industrial and agricultural sectors of any economy—socialist and capitalist—depend heavily on productivity. This is where the Soviet Union was clearly behind. In the mid-sixties, the period of change in approaches and change in mutual reappraisal, the amount of output generated per unit of capital and labor input in the Soviet Union was about one-third that of the United States, a discovery that amazed and shocked Western businessmen. In industrial production, the Soviet proportion was 41 percent of the American amount. But in agriculture, the backbone of Soviet economic life, it was only 11 percent. Yet there was a time when Soviet wheat had been high on the list of export items.

An understanding of this phenomenon was lacking in the West. Explanations multiplied, with the political structure a vital element in almost all of them. The fact remained: the Soviet Union, with her vast territory, tremendous natural resources, and large labor force, was behind. What complicated the attempt to understand was the factor of growth. It was there, and in some cases, it was ahead of the American growth rate.[15]

During the two postwar decades, 1950–70, the Soviet Union achieved an average 8 percent growth per annum, which looked impressive. The growth rate, however, was calculated by combining the growth of numerical labor and the capital input. The results dropped to 5.9 percent. Pure increases in productivity took only 2 percent of the share. When there was a downturn in the 1960s, it was attributed to a decline in labor efficiency and capital-use efficiency, rather than a slowing down of input.

This was deciphered rather late in the West and caused a stir only among the economists. It made them observe even more closely the early Soviet fluctuations, because, statistically, during the fifties, it appeared that labor productivity in the Soviet Union was forging ahead of its American counterpart. The Soviet rate of labor productivity growth surpassed that of the United States—3.3 percent in Russia and only 2.3 percent in the United States. The overall outcome, however, came on the side of the capitalist economy, not because overall production was greater, but because capital productivity was declining in Russia. The increase of the GNP unit of fixed business capital input, known as capital productivity, was steadily declining. The rate of Soviet decline was estimated at about 2.2 percent per annum. At the same time, there was a growth of about 1 to 1.5 percent per annum in the U.S.

The combination of the two worked to the Soviets' disadvantage during the 1950s and 60s. The productivity growth rate of the Soviet Union was about 80 percent that of the United States.[16] The gap continued to grow, until it reached a proportion that called for a larger rate of exchange with the West, an exchange that would contribute to a higher rate of production—in other words, importing technology, combined with the knowledge needed to use it. This became clear to the business community. It had the technology; it wanted to use it.

Western attempts to understand different economic cycles in the Soviet Union rarely included Soviet agriculture. Later, it turned out to be important. Russia's massive purchase of grains from Canada and the United States involved Western and socialist economies in serious problems. Soviet agriculture was even more complex, more politically motivated, than the industrial sector.

Soviet Agriculture

There is an asymmetry between the two superpowers in the field of agriculture. The Soviet Union has about twice as much land as the United States. America's arable land is 70 percent of the Soviet Union's. Most of this land, in both countries, is located in the north temperate zone. Both countries consume a large proportion of their agricultural products domestically—about 85 percent. Both process about an equal proportion of livestock and livestock products.

This is where the similarities end and the differences begin. A Western exporter of agricultural machinery, of livestock, or any other item considered essential to the growth of the agricultural sectors must look beyond the statistics, for they tell only part of the story.

The low proportion of agricultural productivity in the Soviet Union, compared with America, continues in spite of the gradual shift in the Soviet Union from agriculture to industry and in spite of a fairly rapid pace of mechanization. In one decade—1960–70—the Soviet farm sector's contribution to the GNP dropped from 29.4 to 22.4 percent. The proportion of the total labor force employed on the land decreased from 42.1 to 29.3 percent, a significant change. It has been hailed as a great success and is considered the beginning of a new economic trend.

But the gap between the United States and the Soviet Union continued.[17] By the early 1970s, the comparable figure in America was 3.5 percent GNP contribution by the agricultural sector and 5 percent of the labor force. America has been preoccupied with the problem of overproduction, the Soviet Union with shortages. Earlier Soviet predictions of surpassing the West in various economic sectors suffered the greatest disappointment in agriculture. In addition, it turned out that during the biggest boom in American agriculture, the Soviet Union added 157 million acres to the area under cultivation, while the U.S. took out 35 million acres.

What was behind this difference? There was a lot of farm machinery in the Soviet Union; grain production was almost entirely mechanized. It could be argued that maintenance of the machinery was the root of the problem. But the problem was more than that. One of the more plausible theories advanced by socialist economists observing the Soviet Union from within the bloc but from without the Soviet Union, links the agricultural failures to the early days of Stalinist economic planning. It was at that time that heavy industry received top priority. Jobs were available, pay was attractive, and workers were needed. Within a few years, the best, most enterprising, and most intelligent left the farms for industry. In the villages, only the less industrious remained. The quality of farm labor today is poor. It is unskilled and untrained. There is little use of machinery and fertilizer; upkeep is neglected. Instead of learning how to use chemical fertilizers efficiently, farm workers use them indiscriminately—damaging rather than helping the soil.

Stalinism caught up with the problems of the seventies. The damage turned out to be of lasting duration.

There is little doubt that the poor results in the agricultural sector in the Soviet Union contributed to a renewed interest in purchases abroad. There is also little doubt that these purchases have been viewed as Soviet admissions of failure. It was on the land that the new economic system begun by the Revolution was to be a showcase of communism. It was there that the state ownership of the means of production was as important a factor as industry.

The West's response indicated the changed political climate. There was little or no rejoicing. Instead, there was a sober readiness to comply with the Soviet desire to use the existing Western surpluses to feed the Soviet people. Large purchases of wheat were made. The Soviet Union, through grain transactions, was invited to reenter the world markets.

The agricultural scene cannot be left without mentioning another intra-bloc difference which surfaced in the early seventies. Poland, where collective farming was rejected by the farmers, turned out to be a socialist country with an affluent farmer class. There are still problems with the internal distribution of food, but producers managed to do well, and the position of the farmer class and the outside appearance of the Polish countryside have changed for the better. Hungary, another bloc country, where farm land is collectivized and where the standard of living is considerably higher than that of the Russians or the Poles, began to market its wheat abroad in 1972. That year, Hungary exported 100,000 tons of wheat. Some of the sales agreements were concluded with American companies, which needed it either as payment or for resale to their European clients.

Fiat Enters the Socialist Bloc

The East-West dialogue, as well as East-West business transactions, bridged legal and conceptual differences between East and

West. It was not a great waterfall, with waters rushing to a dam generating huge amounts of East-West energy. Rather, it was the thin trickle of a slightly shy stream, uncertain in a large body of water. Nikita Khrushchev started the trend. His successors changed the style of approach, but not its thrust. There were signals that the Soviets' interest continued, with bilateralism the preferred form of cooperation. Multilateralism was feared by the Russians because of the strong economy of western Europe. It was feared by the other members of the socialist bloc, who wished to maintain their own ties rather than be submerged in the collectivism of the bloc.

Among the steps taken by the Soviet Union to follow up her declarations were international and binational agreements. She signed the International Patent Agreement, which opened the way to sell Soviet patents and licenses in the West. In bilateral approaches, the Soviet Union traded gas deliveries for pipes and other equipment with Austria, Italy, and France. A Franco-Soviet group was formed to implement scientific, technological, and economic agreements. Treaties and memoranda of understandings were signed with Belgium, Sweden, and Denmark. A Soviet-Japanese Committee was formed to study economic cooperation in the Far East.

Nothing, however, was more significant than the entry of a major automobile manufacturer into the socialist market. For generations the name of Ford in the Soviet Union had been equated with the automobile. Yet it wasn't Henry Ford II who managed to introduce a car-oriented economy into the Soviet Union. A comparative newcomer captured that trophy. Fiat of Italy brought into such countries as Poland, Romania, and the Soviet Union new dimensions of consumer-oriented products. In Poland, where the total production of autos was about 100,000 units a year, Fiat installed satellite industries, forced the economic planners to shift priorities, and assisted in the post-Stalin transition from heavy to light industry. Fiat also had a significant social impact. The affluent Polish farmer class surfaced as the greatest buyer of this luxury item, priced at the level of two years' salary for a highly paid government executive or five years' salary for a skilled worker.

In the Soviet Union the impact was different, but equally significant. After the initial political decision was made by the Communist party to permit construction of a major automobile factory, Soviet-

Italian negotiations began. For a long time to come, these negotiations will be a prototype of how to negotiate across national, political, and economic frontiers.

The first decision that had to be made was the type of vehicle Fiat was to build. The dimensions emerged after a long period of negotiations. The Soviet Fiat had to be simple, easy to maintain and to operate. It had to be sturdy enough to withstand the Russian climate, poor roads and long distances. It had to be adaptable to limited servicing and repair facilities and to a lower grade of gasoline. It also had to be durable; changing cars every two or three years would be impossible for Soviet buyers.

The type of factory to be built was another major decision. Its location, production capacity, and supply of raw materials had to be well planned. The outcome was a shop capable of producing 2,200 units every 14 hours, totaling 660,000 cars per year. This was a drop in the bucket compared to the potential absorptive capacity of a country the size of the Soviet Union. The factory was to be a vertical production line, housing smelting, ironworks, presses, mechanical and body works, and principal accessories under one roof. A work force of 60,000 was anticipated.

Training shop managers and foremen presented a major linguistic problem. For instance, Russian standards of unifications had to be prepared, which took a team of 100 translators four months to accomplish.

Transferring technology on a continuing basis was another problem. The Soviet Fiat had to be modern, yet immune to technological changes occurring in the West. Making changes, transferring new technology, and eliminating obsolete parts would create sizable production and bureaucratic problems. Italian engineers had to solve such problems as designing a body suspension system that would be resistant to Siberian cold without having to substantially change it when newer designs appeared in the West.

Bureaucratic Soviet apparatus was another problem. Italians, accustomed to their own bureaucracy, were still flabbergasted by the Russian bureaucracy. Due to the flexibility and helpfulness of the lower echelons, tasks were often accomplished and shortcuts discovered.

The decision to build an automobile factory in the Soviet Union and other socialist countries has not been regretted in Turin. Taking

into consideration the overall change in attitudes in East-West commercial relations, the move was of great importance. Whether an
automobile entering the developing—and rather, backward—
economy of the Soviet Union will rival the revolution Henry Ford
started in the United States remains to be seen. There is little likelihood that it will. The Soviet government continues to restrict the
mobility of its citizens artificially. A truly popular and accessible
automobile could make such mobility possible and may force a relaxation of existing rules and regulations. Further, the entry of automobiles into the economy of the Soviet Union could bring about a
change in priorities. But first the Soviets must overcome the problems of a lack of roads, service stations, and other services required
by an auto-oriented society.

The Change of Trade Patterns

Fiat was just the beginning, but an important one. It alone was
not decisive in clearing the lines of communication between the two
new partners. East and West were moving in several directions at the
same time. There was growth in both, but a different kind of growth.

The 1960s saw the East-West trade total volume surpass for the
first time the total foreign trade of the COMECON countries. The
fact that the overall East-West volume, including non-COMECON
states, increased so rapidly was especially significant.

Relations with western Europe have indicated a new, congenial
atmosphere. However, the basic Soviet opposition to the idea of
European unity remained, as well as fears that the new, enlarged,
self-centered community would constrain trade and economic exchanges with the East settled in the subconscious of socialist economists. The fears centered on agricultural commodities such as Polish
bacon and ham and Hungarian wines, whose marketability could be
curtailed. While these fears persisted, theories of all kinds were offered as to why European trade tactics were directed against the East.
These were merely theories—not facts. It is true that the cohesiveness of the European community stimulated the more inward-look-
ing EEC trade. In the field of imports alone, the share of intra-EEC

economic turnover increased from 31.3 percent in 1955 to 48.6 percent 15 years later.

East European volume grew, but not significantly, from 2.6 percent in 1955 to 3.8 percent in 1970. Food items, tobacco, fuels, nonferrous metals, and agricultural raw materials were the principal import items. Community exports to the East increased more significantly—from $1.2 billion in 1963 to $3.5 billion in 1970. The increase was hardly indicative of the wave of discriminatory tactics which the East feared.

These statistics alone are inadequate for making a thorough analysis. There were other indicators. One of the biggest obstacles for expanded economic relations was that neither capital nor labor were included in the commercial exchange plans; goods and services formed the bulk. The influx of capital was limited by the political differences on the definition of its role. Labor mobility was an almost unknown quantity in socialist planning. Yugoslavia —a very special case, standing apart and outside of this consideration—at some point later, introduced it fully, making Yugoslav workers a major force in the country's foreign currency reserves. The limited commodity structure of the East was also hampering the normal trade increase.

In spite of all this, volume grew, interest increased, and Western companies continued their talks with state-controlled socialist enterprises. Economics was linked with East-West détente and the problem of security. The old idea of an all-European conference was revived and came to fruition. Trade and economic issues figured prominently in the agenda. European politics were gradually being meshed with Europe's economics. The United States did not escape involvement.

It was not a new link, nor was it unexpected. As long ago as 1966, the two principal Soviet newspapers, *Pravda* and *Izvestia*, floated the idea of linking détente with an increase in trade. In 1965 the Warsaw Pact nations had proposed the European Security conference, and the two papers outlined its purpose as "strengthening of economic and trade ties, multiply contacts and various forms of cooperation in the fields of science, technology, culture and arts. . . ." The time was not yet ripe for favorable Western reaction, but the idea was tried and shortly thereafter, repeated; eventually it would become a reality.

Reforms Follow Change

The 1960s, therefore, were significant. Some kind of new, subtle set of relationships began to emerge. There was nothing conscious, nothing deliberate, about it. It just happened. It emerged in spite of the American involvement in Vietnam and in spite of Soviet invasion of Czechoslovakia. Progress in economic relations might have been a direct result of the growth, development, and spectacular change wrought by modern technology, but it could also have been triggered by a greater belief in global interdependence. Whatever the reason, the change was here.

In the West, the new attitudes were not entirely new. Fluctuations of mood and attitude had been noted before and after the Revolution. Once the shock over Czechoslovkia had worn off, the Western business community was ready to move. Western observers watched for signs of a Soviet thaw.

The Russian reaction was predictable, and politically shrewd. The immediate post-Czechoslovakia period demonstrated the Soviet capacity for waiting. Then another momentum was added to their desire for an all-European security conference. The conference was conceived in a way which would permit it to separate political and military groups such as NATO and the Warsaw Pact from purely economic entities such as the Common Market and COMECON. The idea of the conference was probably also rooted in Eastern efforts to weaken the European unity impetus, which had reached the point of genuine economic concern for the socialist bloc.

The European community was viewed as an example of a closed economic entity, bound to go through a long period of protective policy. Open-ended institutions such as COMECON were, in the Soviet view, much more acceptable and flexible. But in line with the Soviet pragmatic attitudes toward centers of power—be they political, military, or economic—the observable change in the 1960s also affected the Common Market. There were suggestions for COMECON and the EEC to establish direct links. This ran counter to the mood inside the socialist bloc, and it found few interested parties in the West. Direct lines of communication could affect the reform movements in eastern Europe. They would call for payments in hard currencies rather than for industrial cooperation agreements, including barter arrangements. They could conceivably affect credit arrangements. Finally, COMECON, in which the Soviet Union predominated, could conceivably diminish the only area in which east European countries felt comfortable and free—their foreign and domestic economic policies.

There was also a marked change in the East's attitude toward the United States. Japan, with its emerging economic power, formed on the Soviet and socialist horizon as a new economic power. The West followed the traditional pattern of a dynamic business sector looking for new outlets. In the East, change occurred more swiftly, perhaps less obviously, but nevertheless, importantly. The socialist countries —including the Soviet Union—began to examine various ways to achieve economic reforms. The more orthodox the individual country's policy, the less inclined it was to initiate economic reform. Consequently, in the Soviet Union, the ideological backbone was more calcified than elsewhere. But the issue was joined: how to absorb steady transplants of foreign organs within the Marxist-Leninist body? Would the body reject them—the Fiat transplant was perhaps the most telling example—or accept and change its habits and way of life, accordingly? How flexible—within the new circumstances—is the system itself? Reform in the socialist countries has been one way various groups of socialist states have attempted to absorb the transplants without losing their Marxist personality.

CHAPTER 5

Eastern Europe Undertakes Reforms

Roots of the Reforms

Economic reforms in eastern Europe emerged as a series of compromises. They were an absolute necessity in making the area more acceptable, more competitive, and more attractive in an interdependent world. The reform of production, responsibilities, methods of exporting and importing, and planning were to satisfy those who wanted change. Economic evolution was the most that could be expected. Economic reforms were the only changes which were acceptable to the East, including the Soviet Union, and which permitted even a slight opening to the West.

Reform was also of a particular kind. Most reformers start out full of dreams; they are often angry about what they wish to change. Some act and think like missionaries. Perhaps this is truer when political, rather than economic, reforms are being considered. But economic reforms are equally important. When a Labour government was elected in Britain after World War II, it reshaped her social fabric.

The economic reforms in eastern Europe were different. They were more subtle; their claim of accomplishment was more subdued. After all, the socialist states were born just about the time the Labourites took power in England, and they were imported. For years, this importation has been declared perfect, or nearly so. There was practically no room for error. Reform—meaning a change for the better —had to be muted.

The outward appearance of the transplant was one of success.

The new socialist states started with almost nothing, and moved rapidly. They quadrupled their national income, increased their industrial output sevenfold, and upped their share of the world's industrial production from 18 to 30 percent. It took them barely 20 years to do it, an accomplishment in which the Soviet Union participated. It was evident that reforms were to be applied, but not with any notions of past weakness.

Since weaknesses did exist, it was necessary to gloss them over, to make them appear invisible, but repairable, even when they were visible.

The socialist leaders (some of whom were as much of an imported nature as the system itself) wished very much to succeed. Their newly established regimes were shaky, their acceptability not yet established, their popularity tarred by their known subservience to the Soviet Union. There was hope in the early postwar period that a different economic system, a better distribution of income, and a more equitable use of national resources would make the people realize the benefits and convert them to supporters of the regimes. This was one reason why the Hungarian and Polish reforms were difficult for the Soviet Union to support. Brezhnev regards Kadar and Gierek with disdain. Their goals are different, their perceptions diverse.

The socialist governments looked to economic forces to accomplish political objectives. When the first phase ended in failure, instead of abandoning the method, the second generation of socialist planners simply refurbished it. Economic reforms were to accomplish the same thing. Paralyzed within the political structure, which was not to be touched, the east Europeans had only one way to go —that of economic improvement. The first phase saw the growth of output, production, and national income, but a high price was paid for it.

A lower standard of living followed. In some cases, the estimates indicated a drop as drastic as 40 percent. Artificial limits were imposed on consumption, low priority was given housing and transportation, and general services were inadequate.

This period also saw uneconomic use of raw materials and their consequent depletion. It witnessed an extravagant use of labor, one of the most unpopular policies. Long hours, frequent appeals for voluntary overtime, and the use of women laborers regardless of their family obligations created an atmosphere of social tension and resentment. Motivation, a vital factor in genuine national growth, was gradually vanishing.

Central planning was an important part of the reforms. It could be argued, as it has, that central planning was a necessary prerequisite in the formative stages of a socialist economy. Two prominent east European economists, one of whom, Oscar Lange, returned to socialist Poland after spending the war years teaching at the University of Chicago, has defended this approach. Lange felt that within the framework of revolutionary change, centralized control had to be exercised over the allocation and utilization of basic resources.[1] His Hungarian counterpart, G. Varga, echoed this. Varga felt strongly that a highly centralized system was required under postwar conditions in order to reach the social goals of the new regime.[2]

Toward that end, a well-designed chain of command was established. A state planning commission was set up in each socialist country, with the power to set production targets for each and every enterprise. And that wasn't all. It was also up to a commission to determine economic priorities and to be responsible for implementing economic plans. The lower echelon units—the ministries, branch associations, and enterprises—were simply recipients of predetermined goals.

The system was borrowed from the Soviet Union, for it was there that centralized planning worked efficiently; it had gotten the Soviet Union through the war, it was often pointed out. The Soviet economy operated on the basis of central decisions affecting the allocation of resources, the structure of production, output, pricing, wages, and the settlement of accounts. The problems that arose in the newly created socialist countries were lack of experience in central planning, differences in size of the economy, shortages of raw materials, and the like.

While the comparison may have been valid, central planning did not prove useful. The differences outweighed the similarities. Aside from a few Communist-trained economic planners, there was little enthusiasm in the smaller socialist countries.

The reasons were not difficult to find. Managers of individual enterprises were not allowed to make decisions, so they were easy targets for blame. The hierarchy of decision-making called for each manager to go through branch associations to an appropriate ministry, which, in turn, would send him on to the Planning Commission. A manager could not appeal a decision. He could not ask for a different production quota or for needed supplies. Even direct communication with regular suppliers was denied. Furthermore, decisions were legally binding. The shorter the period covered by a given economic plan, the more detailed decisions reached the company level. At the top—the Commission and the ministries—economic plans were undertaken to meet production goals in accordance with political, as well as economic, objectives. Top-level officials expected results from below. Blame for failure was uneven. The first ones to be singled out were the managers, whose careers, and often personal freedom, were in jeopardy.

There was also the physical balancing, which made the system cumbersome. Physical units serve as elements of accounting. Postulated outputs were the guiding principles, with prices used for the purpose of aggregation. They were not used as guidance for the allocation of resources.

The theory of socialist development dominated the entire system. The basis for future economic reforms was there, but the theory ran head-on against practices which produced results in the growth factor, but failed in its application to actual economic needs. Later attempts to change, reform, and preserve the theory included one in which there would be decentralization of planning and competition. Another was much milder. It would leave central planning intact, but would partly decentralize decisions. Both were revolutionary in their own way.

One Way to Move

It is possible, even probable, that economists like Oscar Lange —in spite of his long exposure to capitalism in America—were correct. They might have been right, that centralized planning was needed after the war. The political situation alone would have dictated this. The Soviet Union was next door to Poland. There was also the example of France—victorious but chaotic—unable to control her economy or her politics.

With the passing of time, there were calls for change, but change had to be gentle. It must escape the revisionist label. It must follow in letter, if not spirit, the initial concept of a Marxist-oriented economic system. Above all, whatever changes were to be introduced had to be politically acceptable.

The principle of economic self-sufficiency was challenged. It was doubtful that it could have been achieved without continuing, and even growing, economic denials. Then there was the belief that the Communist countries should compete with the capitalist states. The urge to demonstrate the superiority of socialist methods of economic development over the free-enterprise countries became almost an obsession when Khrushchev ruled Russia. The notion was based upon the socialist high level of social justice, the eventual attainment of a socialist society, and their economic dynamics. The theory had difficulty surviving in face of the realities of the two systems.

There was another factor which at first acted as a brake, but later as an incentive. A new postwar generation of men and women, wedded to the party, fully convinced of its rightness for their countries, longed for economic success. Immediately after the war, when devastation and a general lack of social cohesiveness made a political base the first order of priority, the economy had to wait. The assumption was Marxist: a political system, established within a series of countries and spreading westward, would carry with it an economic boom. When this failed to materialize, the new generation turned to economics. They contended that the way to move was to use whatever tools and channels were available to get their countries out of economic Stalinism.

Politics and economics merged at that moment. The new generation was shaken by the post-Stalin revelations. It had been decimated by Stalin's dictatorship. It clung to Marxism as the goal, in spite of all that had happened. This generation had grown up under socialism. It had to find reasons for continuing its confidence and allegiance. A successful experiment in national economics could have created a new base, restoring the new class's faith in its own intellectual integrity. After all, the class banked on the socialist system.

An interesting thing happened. The way out of the dilemma, the most effective way to introduce change was not to bemoan the past. "The reforms have not been aimed at tinkering with the old system," wrote Hungarian economist, G. Varga. "The *sine qua non* of further rapid development in the long run is a comprehensive overhaul of the previous system, going far beyond merely removing its obvious failures." The search for alternatives—by the new class and its adherents—at first centered on evolution which would leave untouched the principles of the system. Aside from ownership of the means of production, the concept of central planning should also be saved. It was tampered with, but gently and quietly. It was much later that the untouchable became changeable.

The 15-year period, 1956–70, from the Hungarian revolt to the Polish uprising, has been a history of efforts to preserve the old ideology. It was also a period in which the Soviet Union and the rest of the socialist bloc inched toward more trade with the West.

Banking and credit practices were changed, to ease the flow of foreign capital. The law of supply and demand, a law alien to a state-controlled economy, reentered the picture. A greater trade turnover, particularly in imports from the West, followed. Some incentives were reinstated, which, in turn, triggered greater work motivation, resulting in better products and a competitive edge for Eastern goods in Western markets. Their quality rose, their market selectivity became more planned, earning capacities increased. The admission that this was the way to move was difficult psychologically. What was developed received a different label. It was not a reorientation toward a market economy; it was a more sophisticated socialist system.

The principle had some merit. It depended on what angle and perspective one looked at it from. A fairly complicated network of foreign trade organizations was developed, each with a specific assignment linked to a given line of products. Each product had its own niche in the bureaucratic strata. An additional, important, novelty of the system was the ability of the new administrative units to deal directly with their Western counterparts. These could be individual concerns or state organizations when a state economy was involved.

Each group was responsible for outside agreements. Each was authorized to negotiate and establish prices, quality, delivery, and payments. In some cases (rare to begin with, and then confined mostly to Hungary), individual enterprises were permitted to conduct their Western transactions directly, without asking for higher approval. This was the outer limit of decentralization.

Finally, the nature of some of the changes developed a set of common denominators transcending national borders. The Poles, after the turbulent year 1956, were able to legalize workers' councils, a move that brought representation into the economic planning process. In Hungary, where events that year were bloody and heavy with political consequences, the process was slower. Yet a few years later, the Hungarians outdistanced the Poles. The only area in which Poland stood fast and the Hungarians were unable to move was agriculture. Collectivization, rejected by the Poles, remained in Hungary.

These attempts were just a beginning, but later changes were easier because of them.

The Pace of Change in the Soviet Union

It would be misleading to say that change in the Soviet Union had not been coming, but it was different from the change that occurred in the other socialist countries. In the Soviet Union, decentralization was approached more warily. Regional economic councils replaced some industrial ministries. The councils, a lower administrative echelon, were given authority to make decisions affecting production, distribution, and even certain aspects of regional planning.

But there was another important evolutionary aspect. In the mid-1960s, in the process of planning, profit criteria were discussed and seriously considered. This was combined with more independence being granted to individual enterprises, as well as to selected state and collective farms.

The economic councils did not prosper, and they disappeared in a few years. The ministries were reinstated. There was some indication that this was due to inner disagreement within the upper economic hierachy of the Soviet Union, a concession to the more conservative elements. But there were areas of moderate change, in spite of the general signs of retrenchment. For example, commercial accounting was introduced into agriculture, which led to a pricing system that was much more responsive to market fluctuation, thus bringing a gradual commercialization of the collective farm economy.

Soviet resistance to change persisted, however. Some years later, complaints were voiced by the official Soviet press that government-initiated reforms were being paralyzed by industry. To be sure, the reforms were not the most revolutionary ever. They had been prompted by the slow growth of the economy, slower than what had been envisioned in the five-year plans. Labor and capital were still the two most significant factors, making any improvement of the Russian standard of living even slower. The reforms were confined to procedural changes in the planning, administration, and management of the Soviet economy.

Opposition to even this moderate change came from the traditional, well-established bureaucracy, which was totally unprepared and unwilling to yield. One aspect of the change which caused particular concern was a proposal to create a system of government associations. These associations, not unlike large American corporations, would absorb and consolidate the production of smaller production units. But not all sectors of the Soviet economy would be affected. The purpose of consolidation was to promote high-quality products for export. In its new détente with the West, the Soviet Union was making an effort to enter competitive world markets. Soviet licenses were sold, and Soviet industrial machinery was advertised in the United States and western Europe.

The reform—or rather, approach to reform—is of recent origin, much more recent than the reforms in the east European socialist countries. The reform announced early in 1973 in the form of a decree passed by the Central Committee of the Soviet Communist party, was limited in scope but still quite important in the context of East-West trade. As many as 50,000 industrial plants were to be removed from the direct supervision of individual ministries (there were similar moves elsewhere within the bloc) and combined into industrial associations. The associations were to be endowed with powers which, up to that point, were identical to those of the ministries. Not surprisingly, the ministries balked at that proposal.

The extent to which the bureaucracy will succeed in diluting the reform attempt remains to be seen. It is a complicated business in the Soviet Union, due to the requirement for statistical reporting, which makes new institutions cumbersome conglomerates which must fit into existing structures. It is complicated by the fact that salary scales are established by the government, which, so far, has not recognized the new echelons created by the associations. In announcing the new step, the Soviet Union recognized the need to revamp the archaic economic machinery. It has also recognized that consumer demand must be taken into consideration, as well as labor and social morale.

There are two other ways in which the situation could be improved somewhat. One is to shift more resources from defense to the civilian sector, and the other is to increase the importation of technology and equipment from abroad. Naturally, the latter is linked to the development of export-oriented industries—unless the Soviet Union contemplates a massive sale of her gold. There are no signs of her doing so and no indication that mining Soviet gold would permit such large-scale sales in the near future.

Aside from traditional sales of agricultural products and of such barter deals as trading Pepsi-Cola for vodka, there is the export of Soviet industrial equipment. The import potential in the west is highly dependent on the granting of MFN status, which has been withheld from the Soviet Union since 1951. The negotiations, which led to the signing of the lend-lease payment agreement and which were linked to MFN status, ran into political snags. Repression of dissidents in the Soviet Union has caused serious doubts to be raised that the U.S. Congress will grant the Soviets MFN status. Even if Congress did, the Soviet Union would still face the formidable challenge of competitive Western markets.

Soviet economic reforms may face a considerable problem once the United States is willing to treat Soviet goods the same way goods of other countries are treated. Russian exports to west European markets (where the Russians enjoy MFN status) have not been impressive. Products they would like to sell abroad include electric motors, metal-cutting tools, mining equipment, hydrofoil boats, transistor radios, plywood, and movie equipment. Some, such as plywood and movie equipment, have been marketed in America in spite of the lack of MFN status.

When we look at the current status of economic reform, the Soviet Union does appear to trail behind. MFN status, which appears to be a very important factor in Soviet planning, may force them to alter their domestic machinery. A denial of MFN status on political and moral grounds could easily produce internal economic retrogression. The pros and cons of a congressional decision, from the United States' point of view, is one thing; the advisability of the Soviet Union's reshaping her economic thinking under the pressure of Western competition is another.

According to one theory, MFN status is much more important to the Soviets for reasons of prestige than for economic reasons. This is only a possibility. The Pepsi-Cola Company, for instance, is interested in MFN status for the Soviet Union because it would affect Pepsi's sales there. Also, under the present arrangement, vodka imported in large quantities is costly. MFN status would help keep the price down. On the other hand, granting MFN status is likely to rekindle Soviet deliberations about the advantages of a change. The bureaucracy will not go as deep as to question the validity of rigid control of foreign trade, but it may look for a new economic mechanism which could, one way or another, enhance the Soviets' competitive position abroad.

Is the Soviet Union, the second largest industrial power in the world, willing to make changes that will make possible a higher level of exports? The question is unanswerable at the moment. Export-oriented industries usually combine built-in incentives with a structure for providing repairs and installation services. This approach implies vast internal rethinking and replanning. It is up to the Soviet Union whether she will participate in the world economy to a greater extent than she has so far. In 1972, the year the current détente began and at a time when there were loud declarations about the Soviets expanding their trade with the West, the ratio of foreign trade to the Soviet GNP was 2.8 percent. Comparable figures for the Common Market were 16.9 percent, and for the U.S., 4.3 percent.

If Soviet rhetoric begins to match Soviet deeds, there may indeed be a movement to introduce change. In a speech in the United States in mid-September 1973, Jermen M. Gvishiani, deputy chairman of the U.S.S.R. Council of Ministers for Science and Technology, declared that Soviet-American relations are entering a new phase. There will no longer be a sporadic series of commercial deals. Instead, a planned program of economic cooperation will be developed. Gvishiani added: "One can hardly underestimate both the economic and social implications of this tendency."[3]

This statement was significant. Its significance would be enhanced if the message were communicated to the Soviet policy-makers, and more so if to the Soviet people. But there is no escaping the import of Gvishiani's words. A planned, long-term, fully operative system of Soviet-American economic cooperation would have much deeper implications for the Soviet Union—if taken seriously—than for the United States.

Romania and Others

The economics of the Eastern bloc may be imagined as a flowing stream whose bed is solid political rock and whose water is sometimes muddy. Movement has been observed lately, movement which may indicate the gradual acquisition of power. But questions posed regarding the Soviet Union are adaptable to the rest of the bloc. For instance, can a basic Marxist society live side by side with a genuine economic reform movement which permits coexistence with a market-oriented economy? What are the goals of Eastern reforms? Should they be viewed as temporary phenomena or a permanent change in the socialist economic structure?

The only way to answer this question is to analyze some of the reforms. As in Hungary and Poland, some reforms went deep into the social fabric, and required a longer treatment. Others are significant but not nearly as revolutionary. Still others appear to be just a series of gestures, without much economic or political significance.

The semiindependent foreign policy of Romania does not necessarily suggest a parallel development in the field of economics. But Romania is an interesting proving ground for importing foreign capital and foreign technology, for preserving a free hand in foreign affairs, and for battling the general economic backwardness at home. It was Romania which opposed the Soviet-Polish proposal to make COMECON a supranational organization. It was Romania which in the early 1960s, published a significant political declaration. Shortly after the death of Togliatti, the Italian Communist leader and release of his testament, the Romanian Workers Party issued its own declaration. In a document called "The Declaration on the International Communist and Workers Movement," Romania called for the establishment of normal links with all states, regardless of their social and political structure. Not long thereafter, the Romanian government made it clear that in its efforts to modernize and progress, it will turn westward. A clear-cut approach was fully covered by the restatement of Marxist-Leninist principles. Romania was not deserting the socialist camp; she was determined to stay in it, but develop a better Romanian society at the same time.

What was at stake and what Romania was trying to accomplish was greater independence and national autonomy within COMECON's economic system. She has managed to achieve that goal—to a degree, but a degree greater than others—in the field of foreign policy. Her goal is to become a developed economic country by the 1980s. In order to do so, Romania cannot go it alone. Western capital, technology, and cooperation are needed. This, in turn, requires readjustment of the economic structure and the creation of form and substance which will make Romania attractive to others. Where there is determination, results usually follow. Romania became the first COMECON member of GATT in 1971, and a year later joined the World Bank and the International Monetary Fund.

Earlier Romanian decisions touched the field of foreign trade and investments in a number of ways. A new legal framework was set up to encourage such investments. Enacted in 1971, the new law was called the Law on Foreign Trade and Economic and Technico-Scientific Cooperation Activities. It was followed by a constitutional decree on joint ventures and a companion one, describing regulations governing taxes and profits.

Unlike some other socialist countries, there is in Romania little correlation between the liberalized, rather aggressive, foreign economic policy and its domestic counterpart. In Hungary, for instance, the economic reform system cuts deeply into the entire structure. One is hard put to discover a similar link in Romania. Almost identical asymmetry exists in Romanian foreign policy. It is white on the outside and red inside; it is flexible, progressive, and highly independent, without its domestic counterpart following the lead.

The new law regulating Romanian foreign trade, enacted in 1971, sets a series of specific objectives. It spells out the need to create a modern technological and industrial base, "on a par with world standards"; it gives priority to the organization of production designed for export. It establishes incentives for production units and foreign trade organizations which exceed their planned quotas of foreign currency receipts.

The direct connection of the new foreign trade law with the rest of the economy is contained in the state planning. Several articles of the foreign trade law spell out their dependence on the two basic plans included in the overall state plan. One deals with foreign trade and international and technical cooperation, and the other with the balance of payments. When the two plans are approved, the Council of Ministers must act by assigning implementation tasks to each ministry, central body, and people's council.[4]

Joint-venture companies are to play a particularly significant role in the new scheme of things. The law provides for Romanian joint companies with foreign participation in the fields of industry, agriculture, construction, tourism, transport, and scientific and technical cooperation. There is a requirement for 51 percent Romanian ownership, but only for joint ventures inside Romania. The provision does not apply to similar organizations set up in third countries.

These Romanian steps were taken after more liberal actions were evident in the West, but also in anticipation of some move, especially from the United States. In May 1971 Romania, along with Poland, was placed in a less restrictive control group by the U.S. Department of Commerce. During the same year, President Nixon exercised his authority in permitting the Export-Import Bank to help finance U.S. exports to Romania through the extension of partial credits.

A flow of credits followed. Eximbank had extended some $53 million in loans and guarantees as part of the financing for over $83 million of Romanian imports of American-made commercial jet airplanes, construction material for a tire plant, and an offshore drilling platform. In April 1973 another major step was taken to boost Romanian imports: the Overseas Private Investment Corporation (OPIC) agreed to provide insurance and help finance United States private investment projects in Romania.

The example of Romania illustrates how action triggers reaction and how genuine efforts on both sides bring results. It also is indicative of the political nature of foreign trade. Romanian independence within the socialist bloc made her move more boldly than the others. This boldness is limited in two respects: politically, because Romania is not considered a major threat to the Soviet Union or to the cohesiveness of the socialist bloc, and economically, because of Romania's early stage of development. In both cases, the rigidity of the government assures calm and uneventful transition from developing to developed stage. The nervousness of the Soviet Union, as demonstrated in Czechoslovakia, starts when the socialist calm seems to be endangered by the social implications of economic reform.

Other socialist countries made courageous efforts to emerge from the economic stagnation. East Germany, Bulgaria, and Czechoslovakia, in addition to Poland and Hungary, took a stab at various facets of possible change. The Czechs managed to introduce banking and credit reforms in spite of the events in 1968, East Germany followed the same line and added a reform of the system of industrial pricing. Bulgaria made an effort to liberalize and decentralize her state planning system.

Forecasting Economic Reforms

It is both human and predictable that an attempt to create a new tool, a new theory, or a new structure provides a good setting for optimistic predictions. The reform movement in eastern Europe, which suddenly appeared on the socialist horizon after Stalin's death, started a series of such predictions. Marxist superiority over the non-Marxist entities had been artificially arrested by the Stalin period, so the new theory went. Release mechanisms provided by Khrushchev in the Soviet Union and other leaders in Communist eastern Europe were to make possible a new boom, a new height of development. There was also to be a considerable increase in East-West economic cooperation.

An example of such forecasting was provided by a prominent Polish economist in a paper presented at an international gathering of economists, Western investors, and businessmen.[5] It was symptomatic of a highly trained Marxist academician who saw no basic contradiction in comparing noncomparable statistics and drawing conclusions from numbers rather than from the visible economic dynamics of western Europe. His first assertion was that the eastern Europe of 1971 already belonged to the developed part of the world. Growth was rapid and would continue to be so. At the time of the paper's presentation—it asserted—the GNP of the socialist countries had attained a level about 10 percent higher than the comparable level of growth of the members of the west European community. This finding—of significance once the base of statistical calculation is examined—led the author to another assertion, that the socialist countries already represented (in the early 1970s) large markets with a large demand capacity and equally large export possibilities.

Predictions for the future followed. By about 1980, the gap between East and West will grow more dramatically and more to the East's advantage. At that time, the socialist bloc will attain a level 28 percent higher in GNP growth than will the Common Market group, calculated as six, not yet nine, members. In relation to the United States, the Eastern bloc will move up and measure its GNP as only 35 percent lower than that of America.

It is not entirely clear whether these predictions were construed in order to boost the desires for more reform, more modernization and government support of foreign capital and equipment, or whether they stemmed from a truly Marxist rationale. GNP is calculated differently in the East; it does not include such services as public administration, justice, education, science and culture, health and social welfare, local government, and housing. The accounting is limited to purely physical production. So it is difficult to make comparisons, to weigh the dynamics of the two economies.

The United Nations yearbook of statistics, based on the data provided by its members, lists the average annual growth of the eight socialist countries as 8 percent. The period covered includes almost two decades—1951–69. The same statistical compilation lists a series of Western developed countries—Japan averaged 10 percent, the United States 4 percent, the European community 5 percent. The worldwide average was also 5 percent. On the evidence of purely statistical compilations, the optimistic predictions for eastern Europe stand. The method of calculation tells a different story. The results observed in western and eastern Europe cannot be ignored either.

There is little doubt that in eastern Europe there is a new birth of firm economic desire to move forward. There is little doubt that this desire, translated into concrete results, is bound to spur the growth rate and make eastern Europe a more attractive and perhaps even more accessible market for Western exports. It is much less clear to what extent the social and political implications of these changes will be acceptable and tolerated.

In the meantime, thanks to the reform movement, there is change. Modern production units are under construction. A sharp increase in demand for capital equipment is on. It is hoped that the modernization process will contribute to greatly increased foreign trade, principally with the non-bloc countries. It is also anticipated that the reforms will alter the traditional east European commodity structure. The Soviet Union is eager to secure markets for her machinery and technology and is actively marketing her own licenses. A similar trend may occur in some of the more advanced, smaller, socialist countries.

Reforms are also aimed at securing better credit. The Romanian case is a good example. Some Eastern economists are willing to descend to the realities of everyday economics. They plead for changes in basic investment policies, in planning and management systems. They call for what some have already built into their new legal systems—more incentives to be granted to export-oriented industries. The Poles and Hungarians—especially the latter—lead in this respect.

CHAPTER 6

Economic Reform—Hungary

The First Step

Someday historians will puzzle over Hungary under socialism. In less than two decades the country went from despair to revolution, from revolution to submission, and from submission to economic creativity —all on her own. She moved into the slippery area of economic improvement and political dependency, an area in which others have fared poorly. It undertook a major assignment calling for change with the appearance of stability. Prague is not far from Budapest.

The Hungarians ventured into reform probably without fully realizing its implications, without knowing how successful they would be. They may have asked themselves how far they would be allowed to go, assuming that they were successful. Permission would be forthcoming from their ideological big brother who was watching the experiment from afar. But since the first step and the first set of goals were limited, political fear was not noticeable at first. The New Economic Mechanism (NEM) was born with at least tacit Soviet consent.

NEM was to be the first step in a new policy of national economic development, an attempt to liberalize the system, a departure from the earlier years of economic semi-stagnation. NEM was also a step toward recovery, economically and politically. The Hungarian regime, still suffering from its loss of credibility in 1956, decided to make a drastic change in order to restore balance (as well as some credibility). NEM was to inject new life into Hungary's economic engine; it was to act as a source of energy for managers, directors, and workers, for whom there had been little incentive in the past. It was to inaugurate a new method of socialist planning.

It was a big gamble, risking the shaky balance that had existed for some time. The revolt in 1956 had been the biggest yet in the socialist bloc. It was a gamble in view of subsequent events in Czechoslovakia, where proposed changes included economic liberalization. Internally, it was a dangerous gamble if it should fail. It was even a gamble vis-à-vis the West, for NEM offered the West new potential in a small, insignificant, socialist country. Failure would doom East-West trade efforts for a long time to come.

NEM's beginning was actually the second such effort by Hungary since it had become a people's republic. It was right after World War II that the first effort was made, the first framework built, permitting one of the greatest transformations in her history—from a capitalist to a socialist economy. The attempt was fairly successful. When the 1956 revolt shook the country, bringing with it Soviet troops and years of uncertainty, economics was relegated to the back burner, to be brought to the fore again when the political existence of the country became more of a reality. In Lenin's writing, the Hungarians found that even under socialism, there must be a market, and from this premise, the concept of NEM emerged.

The reform has been described in various ways. It was a shift of centralized responsibility from the owners of capital (the state) to the producers, or enterprises. The plan for NEM was to operate as a general directive, but no longer be in full control of the country's economy. The plan was to be an instrument of economic policy for determining the rate of growth, with a limited period of time (usually the traditional five years), in order to insure equilibrium within the economy. One of the most revolutionary aspects of NEM was the new pricing system. Pricing would no longer be based on a fixed approach. Price mobility permitted, as the first step, a free bargaining process between buyer and seller.

Explanations of NEM (such as the goal of economic equilibrium) implied a balancing. NEM had to include an equilibrium between the requirements of the socialist nations and the mixed features of reform. It had to include elements of planned and market economies. But first, it had to anticipate criticism and make certain that the Soviet Union would have no reason to object.

In several official publications, the basic features of NEM were spelled out. The most recent one was contained in a volume issued by the Hungarian Academy of Science in 1972 and made available in an English edition a year later. It sets forth some of the goals clearly and describes the outstanding successes of NEM.[1]

The Academy, concerned about "misunderstandings stemming from certain publications abroad," set the framework of the reform within these points:

The system of economic control and management—also its reform—constitutes an instrument for implementing (planning) objectives of economic policy.

The economy continues to be centrally planned. The principles, methods, and major measures of economic regulation are determined in compliance with the national economic plan and the mutual correlation therewith.

The goal of the reform is to link the central plan to the operation of the plan-regulated socialist market. The market is to have a direct influence on the producers. The main trend of development, however, will continue to be determined by the plan.

The state is to retain the right of decision in problems associated with the major trends in the national economy. For instance, the growth rate is to be determined by the central planners rather than by the market's reaction.

Individual enterprises have the right to determine the volume, trend, and composition of production and realization, as well as the utilization, of the enterprise's resources.

Other aspects of the Hungarian reforms have been underscored in the debates and literature. In most cases the wording implies adherence to the concept of central planning and the development of "economic regulators." In most of this language, what is carefully covered are the liberalizing aspects of the change.

There is an interesting interaction between the "economic regulators" and central planning. The former implies indirect influence of the economic activities by the central bodies; the latter refers to the central planners acting as the direct instrument of state regulations. Somewhere in between, the principal issue of the new forms of economic growth and development is lost. It might even have been lost on purpose. The evolving economic regulators are supposed to set limits on the sphere of the enterprises' authority. While the managers are given a free hand, they must still remember the goals of the national plan. This is what is called "indirect regulation." The essence of it is to connect national economic interests with the personal interests of the managers and lower-level enterprise directors. If the system of regulators operates properly (as the Hungarians keep saying and writing), it must take into account the contrasting interests of the interacting enterprises, making their results parallel with the interests of the national economy.[2]

In plain language, this means creating a contradiction in terms and purpose. An individual enterprise is asked to perform in the best possible form, for itself and for the national economy. When facing a competitive enterprise, it should keep competing as long as the plan outlining the national goals is not in danger. The wisdom of the competing managers is then called into action. They will look at their results, examine them, and stop competing. They may even be expected to join forces. At that point, the national interests take over. In theory, indirect economic regulators would now come into play. Competition would cease. The spirit of socialist solidarity and adherence to the plan would theoretically reenter the scene.

Reform and Foreign Trade

From the beginning, NEM has stressed its interest in foreign economic policy. It has talked about contributing to the dynamic development of international economic relations, about improving the efficiency of social production, thus linking the two—a crucial element in the thinking of the reformers. NEM has also been anticipating some of the consequences of the fourth Five-Year Plan, which covers the 1971–75 period. This plan requires that by 1975, 40 percent of the national income be derived from foreign trade. It is also anticipated that every percentage of increment in the national income be accompanied by an annual average of 1/14 percent increment in foreign-trade turnover.

The post-1968 results showed that NEM was working well. The economy grew 6 percent a year, compared with 5.3 percent before the reform. Foreign trade continued to increase, rapidly approaching an average of 12 percent. Productivity and efficiency grew. But what kept developing with almost unpredictable speed were various processes of democratization within the economy as well as outside it. The participation of workers and managers in the economic development, their involvement in the foreign-exchange earnings, made it possible to open up other areas. Eventually the social fabric of Hungarian society, in spite of the presence of the Red army, felt the pressure of change.

Naturally, foreign trade—the ruble as well as the dollar—has been influenced by the domestic evolution. The reentry of the law of supply and demand into the Hungarian economy made a difference in the production and marketing of goods. There was more diversity. The system of distribution of supplies was revised. In many instances, sales increased faster than production, which permitted the liquidation of stockpiles. The decrease in inventories was one of the goals of the proponents of NEM.

But there was no shortage of problems affecting domestic and foreign trade. The relatively low level of managerial talent has often been cited as one reason for this. How could NEM instill in the minds of technicians, men whose past responsibilities were limited to reacting rather than doing, who did not take risks, the new idea that they now, indeed, had responsibilities? This was most important to conducting foreign trade.

Efforts to increase exports were often hampered by the bulging bureaucracy. Speedy consummation of agreements and business arrangements was difficult. In addition to that, when the managerial class was finally given the authority to make decisions and take responsibilities, some balked. They were afraid of losing their previously stable positions. Under the new system, the managers were being asked to decide not only what to produce and what lines of products to market more aggressively, but also where to buy raw materials, the number of workers to hire, and whether or not to market their products abroad.

This was a change with psychological as well as economic dimensions. Each manager had to make decisions on the basis of his own financial resources. Preplanned instructions, or what in the NEM vocabulary were called "economic regulators," were introduced. In applying that vocabulary, Hungarian economists outlined the instructions vaguely. Foreign trade had to be adjusted. The formal text which applied to foreign trade stated: "to the complex development of our planned economy."[3] Also, the trade and political interests of Hungary were to be observed in import and export activities.

Whatever the language and bureaucracy, the new system meant a change for the better for outside traders. Instead of dealing with a faceless bureaucracy, foreigners could now deal with individuals.

The volume of foreign trade—its composition and functioning— also moved forward. Some unexpected areas showed growth—for example, exports in the machine-building sector. The composition of trade indicated a gradual increase in imports of materials and semi-finished goods from both sides, the ruble countries (COMECON) and the dollar countries. In the future, more machinery and equipment are expected to be imported from the West. All in all, a fairly healthy evolution was gradually settling in. NEM was playing a positive role in an attempt (with good results) to increase trade with the West, trade that was essential for Hungary's economic prosperity and progress in general. In the beginning, the lag in technical development and a cost-quality factor had been instrumental in slowing down needed changes in the composition of Hungary's exports; but the trend was now in the right direction.

There were, however, the ever-present "political interests" of the state, which had to be observed. This is where NEM, as a function of Hungary's foreign policy, had to be considered.

NEM and Foreign Relations

At one point, there was a brief exchange of views between a well-known Hungarian political figure and his American friend. The conversation, relaxed and private, was an excellent summary of the delicacy of the Hungarian situation as well as the realities of her approaches to the West. The Hungarian politician, a man of impeccable Communist credentials and total devotion to the ideas of socialism, saw little possibility of an East-West agreement, with a 100-percent guarantee of its being implemented. Both sides could sign papers, pledge themselves to keep commitments, and then renege on the grounds of technicalities. In other words, Hungary could simply refuse to grant visas to businessmen who needed to visit Hungary. Or the U.S. Secretary of Commerce could refuse to grant import or export licenses. Signed agreements remain, but, in themselves, they are not worth the paper they are printed on.

Hungary's connection with the Soviet Union came up during the conversation. That it was a strong connection, no one had ever doubted. That it was strongly influencing the domestic decisions of Hungary was evident. Economically, the Soviet bloc countries had played a major part in Hungary's foreign-trade turnover. After the introduction of NEM, problems arose in maintaining the level of socialist imports; with the abolishing of nearly all restrictions on imports, the West took the lead. This had to be corrected. After all, the Hungarian economy was not only connected with her own foreign policy, it depended on it. Human and economic factors were involved. Hungary had a shortage of labor, one of the few socialist countries that did. Since the end of the war, sizable Hungarian minorities who were living in the territories taken over by the Soviet Union had wanted to emigrate. In 1972, for the first time, 60,000 Hungarians were given exit visas and permitted to leave Russia. There is hope that as many as 30,000 more will be allowed to emigrate soon.

The conversation between the two friends ended on this point. All of a sudden, the American saw the full dimensions of the Hungarian economic reforms. They were dimensions not ordinarily encountered in the West, dimensions studded with economic potential, political dangers, and deep human emotions.

NEM, a typically Hungarian invention, a methodology conceived to fit Hungary's conditions, has been explained to the outside world in a manner acceptable to all. It has been strongly tied to Hungary's foreign policy. It has been deliberately linked with Hungary's place in the Soviet bloc. It has been conceived in a manner which would neither change that place nor provoke suspicion on the part of the other members of the socialist family.

Hungary's past has not been forgotten. She has had her share of revolutions during the past few centuries. Like the Poles, always considered the unreformed romantics of eastern Europe, the Hungarians have sobered up to political reality. NEM may be one of the best examples of this new sobriety. Instead of fighting impossible political odds, Hungary has resolved to create for herself a better way of life. Neighboring Yugoslavia has been an excellent example of socialism with a smiling face. The grayness and grim determination of an East Germany or a Bulgaria were enough of a deterrent. Hungary chose to live and to live better—but within political bounds.

As a result, prescribed terms, acceptable concepts, and carefully chosen methods make up the rhetoric of reform. Common ideas about foreign policy in the rest of the bloc—socialist ownership of the means of production, central planning, and state monopoly of foreign trade and foreign exchange—are all part of the official pronouncements. One small, seemingly insignificant deviation concerns the individuality of each of the socialist countries' economic requirements. This is where NEM comes in, a purely Hungarian entity. The decentralization of the decision-making apparatus has created trusts and enterprises. The umbrella of economic regulators has been spread over the area in case of an anticipated rain of socialist criticism. So far, it has worked.

The umbrella works in other ways. The pronouncements aren't devoid of belief that the only way the new Hungarian socialism can survive is to combine Marxist principles with the cooperation of non-Marxist societies and non-Marxist concepts within Hungary herself. Whenever the basic economic structure of the state is affected, decisions are made centrally, something that has been underlined in the literature. Janos Fekete, deputy director of the Hungarian National Bank and considered one of the most knowledgable persons in Europe about monetary problems, stated it plainly in an article: ". . . in such cases . . . decisions are in the hands of Governmental organs . . . partly through the medium of direct measures derived from the state's position as owner and partly through central economic regulators exercising an indirect influence on enterprise."[4] The language may be slightly obscure, but the message is clear.

Fekete was not alone in his reaffirmation of faith in the principles of a centrally planned economy. Rezso Nyers, secretary of the Central Committee of the Hungarian Socialist Workers Party, added this:

In the central plan we have to decide, and do decide, such important questions as the ratio of consumption to accumulation (stockpiling), the principal proportions of investments, the main proportions of production and consumption, the development of participation in the international division of labor. . . . Economic regulation is based on these decisions and determines the framework and operational conditions of the market mechanism.[5]

No matter how much of a protective umbrella was spread over NEM, its political implications were unmistakable. It was contemplated as almost a natural fallout as early as 1968, when it was officially launched. In an editorial shortly after the experiment began, *Nepszabadsag*, a leading Hungarian daily, stated: "The new concept of economic management demands similar concepts in the social superstructure as well . . . [Although] such a process requires . . . the absolute leading role of the Party . . . it demands primarily a free atmosphere in which well-meaning critics are not the targets of arrows of suspicion."[6] The editorial read almost like a repetition of the intellectual unrest of the mid-1950s. Yet the new line was accepted, legalized, and followed. As predicted, the new reforms would not have left other sectors of national life untouched. Constitutional guarantees were publicly aired, the abuse of power by the party—which "has never forgotten the lesson of 1956," in the words of one of its leaders—was discussed, and a desire for more open, more accessible government and party was expressed.

The change created a highly favorable climate for Western trade. But the climate had to be nursed along. The idea of communicating to the West the precociousness of their economic and political situation was difficult. There were also other, wider, more complex relationships which Western businessmen had to understand or at least accept. Hungary was very much dependent on her trade with members of COMECON, and she had to emphasize publicly her intention to lessen her dependence on the capitalist countries.

So the dual approach started on its way as soon as, or perhaps before, NEM had been created. A rapid increase of imports brought about a situation calling for an increased export effort. Both the industrial items and the agricultural products that were exportable were highly sensitive to business fluctuations. NEM had to take them into consideration. In attempting to rationalize a more diversified industrial output and to influence the commodity composition of exports, Hungarians evolved another theory.

The theory ran along simple lines of semi-traditional Marxist dialectics. Recession was to be expected in the West; a slower rate of growth in demand for investment goods can be expected among the socialist countries. Thus new economic regulators were needed to guide the trend. They were to improve the competitiveness of export items and increase the efficiency of production, especially of goods produced for export. Internationally-oriented enterprises had to be helped more than the others; more had to be created. Strong motivation to export must be developed, and resources must be made available to export-oriented enterprises. Finally, the foreign-trade regulators were to include income differentiation, according to the progress of development. While this was not new in the West, it certainly was in a socialist economy. The vocabulary of NEM was adapted to the current ideological posture, and foreign trade was subordinated to foreign policy.

This is where the relationship with the capitalist countries comes into focus. It was stated over and over again that the reduction of the dependency of the developing countries on Western nations is in the political interests of the socialist countries. Therefore, the bloc's export effort ought to be diversified and imports regarded as developmental and not only economic channels of relations. The Hungarian machine industry, for instance, has often been mentioned as having a good potential to export to the Third World.

This amounted to a call for a competitive approach toward Third World markets. It was a curious, yet significant approach, considering that at the same time, the West—the competitor—was being wooed elsewhere. Third World joint ventures were promoted, and Western credits to Third World countries were sought.

There are two possible explanations for this development. A purely political explanation held that the approach was just another slogan aimed at easing potential Soviet fears of Hungarian movement toward a market-oriented economy. The other, more devious, explanation was a mixture of economic needs and political shrewdness. Hungary, as much as most of the smaller socialist countries, had become dependent on Soviet raw materials. Looking to Africa and Asia partially to replace these raw materials through barter and other deals, Hungary and the others could accomplish their economic objectives, satisfy Marxist politics, and, at the same time, gradually loosen their dependence on Moscow.

It makes sense from all points of view to diversify the sources of supply; it makes sense to cooperate with the nonaligned Third World. No one could object; only Hungary could gain.

The Hungarian View of the United States' Role

The reform movement in Hungary was considered by many of its creators as something that ought to arouse interest abroad. Yet very few signs were observed in the U.S. that would support this. The American attitude was disappointing, in the eyes of the Hungarians, on two counts. It was inefficient, and it was ultimately a failure. The inefficiency was attributed to the fact that Washington had been looking at east European trade from a political rather than an economic perspective. This was surprising, considering that the entire socialist bloc had always viewed trade as an extension of state politics. The explanation lies in a different set of standards, in which socialist states are fighting for their lives and capitalist countries are fighting for the status quo. Dialectically, there is no contradiction. Only a warped Western logic, in the socialists' eyes, could see it that way.

The United States kept saying openly that the purpose of trading with the East was to gain economically as much as possible, while contributing as little as possible to the technical and economic development of the East. Who wants to trade on those terms? Hungarian politicians asked. Is this an example of Hungarian realism? Years before, Lenin had suggested that Russia could learn from the realism of the Americans. Would he repeat his advice today in the circumstances surrounding East-West trade?

Apart from the political situation, the lack of realism in American policy has been demonstrated by the economic success of the socialist countries, in spite of the American policy of embargo, as well as other Western measures. The Hungarian NEM is only one example. The reform was a sign of economic dynamism. It was also a signal to the outside world that Hungary was willing to enter into a series of special agreements with the capitalist world.

The country's new trade policy was directed toward financial and industrial cooperation. Bond issues were offered on the international money markets. Long- and medium-term credits were used to finance Hungarian imports, a novel approach after long periods during which only short-term loans had been available. Import-incentive industries—as indicated earlier—received priority. They included chemicals, motor vehicles, automation, electronics, agricultural products, and processed food. In the biggest gesture of all, Hungary opened her doors to joint-venture agreements, over 250 of which were concluded in the first three years of NEM's existence. These agreements were a form of co-production with foreign countries, including some Western ones. It disappointed the Hungarians no end that American companies did not take advantage of the opportunity. At the end of 1972, there was only one Hungarian-American venture.

Joint ventures have been considered by the Hungarians as the highest form of cooperation. The first step was trade agreement, in which mutual barriers had to be tested and broken. The next step was to be an agreement on cooperation. A joint venture established between the two sides had to be built on a solid foundation of mutual trust, backed by solid, mutual experience. For the Hungarians, the obvious advantages were the adoption of up-to-date manufacturing methods and payment in the form of goods produced by the partners. The West had different goals in mind: supplementary investments in their own plants, through product-sharing, and gaining new markets. In addition, a Western company joining forces with a Hungarian one was establishing a foothold in one of the most economically dynamic and imaginative countries in eastern Europe.

The American company was Chicago-based Corn Production System, Inc. (CPS). Complex arrangements were made, with Switzerland the base of operations and with CPS acting as the principal supplier. Modern agricultural machinery, as well as special methods of farming, were included in the plan. The system introduced mechanization and modern sowing techniques into Hungary, with the result that by mid-1973, over 600,000 acres of corn were under cultivation. An elaborate import scheme for procuring machinery was devised. CPS's method of procurement was successful enough that it was able to expand its services to other COMECON countries, including the Soviet Union. In the immediate future, Hungary plans to import as many as 8,500 tractors and trailers, 250 self-propelled harvesters, 1,600 combine grain harvesters, and sugar beet, potato combine, and onion harvesters. CPS was in charge of the entire program. It was a success.

One sparrow does not signify the coming of spring. The Hungarians are still disappointed with the apparent American reluctance to view Hungary as a good market. On the other hand, they realize that a too-successful NEM could create problems on their eastern flank.

NEM'S Record

There is little doubt that the whole foreign trade policy initiated by the New Economic Mechanism has turned Hungary's eyes toward the West. It has brought about the beginnings of a much more significant, much more dynamic policy. As mentioned above, the Hungarians themselves see in the new approach to international economic relations a dynamic change aimed at the improvement of social production. Foreign trade is thus directed toward economic changes and social improvement—a highly significant approach by a faithful member of COMECON.

NEM has provided Hungary with practical economic and trade instruments for increasing and strengthening her links with both close and distant neighbors. It has also made possible the growth and prosperity of individual enterprises by taking over the risk involved in planning investments, in planning local production, and in calculating labor and other costs.

The risk run by individual managers was considerable. They had little experience. Inbred fears, as well as the system's past inclination to place blame on the shoulders of the managers, lay heavily on the Hungarian industrial consciousness. Yet the risks ultimately were taken by the majority of the people; reforms were implemented.

From a national perspective, one of the biggest assets in the situation was the ability to pinpoint weak links in the system. Enterprises that turned out not to be viable were isolated and closed down (the first major intrusion of the market mechanism into a socialist economy).

In addition to providing the tools, Hungarian authorities, as a consequence of their reform-minded, pluralistic approach, decided to enter more energetically into trade relations with the developed West. At the inception of NEM, a series of actions supporting foreign relations were taken. A formal resolution on cooperation was adopted by the Economic Committee that had initiated NEM. The Interdepartmental Committee on Cooperation was established, and the Hungarian Foreign Trade Bank Corporation was set up to coordinate the financing. This was done jointly with the National Planning Board and the National Technical Development Committee.

The Hungarians took their decision seriously. The new mechanism was indeed created to make sure that the flow of capital, know-how, goods, and services from outside would continue and even increase. The socialist countries, as well as the capitalist world, figured prominently in the planning.

In 1971 another body was set up exclusively for promoting cooperation with the West. The Inter-Cooperation Share Company was chartered to initiate proposals for cooperation with foreign companies in joint ventures and other types of agreements. ICSC was also to act as a clearing house for proposals received from abroad and to act as middleman by bringing together Western and Hungarian companies with comparable interests.

The most striking characteristic of the new organization is its degree of independence and freedom to initiate concepts and make recommendations. ICSC is authorized to work out trade-development schemes, to establish production-sharing enterprises, and even to work out policy recommendations in cooperation with the Ministry of Foreign Trade. It is allowed to take the initiative in promoting individual business transactions. This means a change from the position of an agent to that of a principal—a decision of weighty social and political significance for a socialist country.

There have also been considerable economic consequences. Hungary's trade with the outside world has risen, but the Western share of that trade has grown more slowly than has Hungary's trade with the other members of COMECON. Statistically, the increase in exports to the West rose from 26.9 percent in 1965 to 29.8 percent five years later. On the import side, the figures are 23.1 percent and 28.7 percent, respectively. With this increase in imports, trade deficits also grew. Toward the end of the 1960s, the negative trade balance with the capitalist countries amounted to $785 million.[7]

To the considerable disappointment of the Hungarians, the United States has played a minor role in this trade. The yearly foreign trade turnover in 1972 represented the substantial figure $6 billion, but most of it was inter-bloc. The American figure was an embarrassing $50 million. Official American figures published by the Commerce Department show an even smaller figure—$12.7 million in Hungarian imports and $22.6 million in American exports.[8]

This is where NEM succeeded to a lesser extent, perhaps, than the Hungarians would have liked. But the American interests, centered much more on the larger socialist countries, have not, as of the early seventies, concentrated on the Hungarian market. Elsewhere, prinicipally in Europe, Hungary has been more persuasive and successful. Numerous agreements, covering a variety of fields, have been concluded—automobiles, machinery, building products, and research and development components among them. The following examples indicate the trend:

The Swedish firm Byggingto agreed to introduce into the Hungarian building trade a device which reduces the cost of erecting tall concrete structures, something that is normally done only in a highly developed economy. Also, Renault, Volvo, and German MA concluded agreements for industrial cooperation with the Gyor Hungarian Wagon and Machine Works to produce diesel engines. Western partners provided manufacturing licenses, while Hungarian plants manufactured certain components. There was a dual East-West approach in these agreements. The Gyor Works, the most important manufacturer of its kind in Hungary, plays a key role in the production of buses and trucks for the COMECON market.

Other important agreements covered such ventures in Third World countries as the construction of an electric power plant in Turkey. The Fiat Works and the Hungarian Transletro Enterprise agreed to cooperate in the delivery of the necessary equipment for the plant. Direct connections have been established with about 50 French firms. In the field of machine tools, the dependency on Western imports has grown steadily. Western imports include forging machines and presses, shears, plate machines, single-purpose cutting tools, and fine drills.

Hungary's imports and exports in 1972 are outlined in a statistical analysis, indicating a continued high dependency on the Soviet Union.[9] Of the Western countries, West Germany leads. Over 100 countries are now included among Hungarian foreign trade partners. But the imbalance persists. Hungary imports about 34.7 percent of all her products from and to the Soviet Union, and exports 36.1 percent. This is as much out of economic necessity as it is political necessity, but it is neither healthy nor desirable.

Hungarian dependence is evident in numerous areas that are unrelated to economics. At the All-European Security Conference, the issue of Hungary came up several times. The theme of a political and military détente was linked with successful economic cooperation, and the Hungarian delegation closed ranks without ever mentioning Soviet troops stationed on its soil. At the more complex and difficult negotiations affecting the Mutual Balance Force Reduction, the Russians suggested eliminating Hungary from consideration in order to leave their troops there. Nothing was heard from Budapest. Publicly, Hungary did not take notice of the contradiction. The line between what was possible and what was permitted was never crossed. The foreign policy of Hungary remains outside Hungarian jurisdiction.

But NEM produced a new climate, introduced a new economic vitality, and lifted Hungary from the morass and depression of the post-1956 period. It is a unique institution; it lives side by side with Soviet troops. It creates a better material existence for 10 million Hungarians.

A new philosophy has emerged on the banks of the Danube. Its architects have been for the most part the Hungarians themselves. But the Hungarians couldn't have done what they did without the silent acquiescence of the Russians and the active cooperation of the West. It appears that the one country that is unable to understand this process and is therefore left behind the others, is the United States.

CHAPTER 7

Economic Reform — Poland and Others

The First Ally of the U.S.S.R.

The story of foreign trade between East and West is different when Polish economic reforms are analyzed. The difference is not only in terms of failure or success—and the latest Polish reform is not entirely a success story—there is a difference in psychological and political climates, in the traditional Polish-Soviet relationship and in the different temperament of the Poles. Yet it would probably be fair to say that the Poles are trying; they are trying to follow the road the Hungarians took, but in a different way. The Hungarians have acquired, principally through Janos Kadar, a degree of trust and respectability with the bloc, which the Poles possess to a lesser degree. Hungarian reforms flourish under strict Soviet scrutiny and are judged by the Russians not to be dangerous politically. Similar moves in Poland would be interpreted differently. The long-standing animosity between Poland and the Soviet Union, and the traditional contempt the Poles have for the Russians, make the difference self-explanatory. Finally, the importance of Poland as a buffer state for the Russians is far greater than that of any other east European ally of the Soviets. "Our goal," Polish Communists repeat endlessly, "is to be always the first ally of the Soviet Union." Goal or not, the issue is well put: they had better be the first ally. Otherwise, they will be forced to be one.

The Polish case in some ways is more significant than the Hungarian one. It underscores the new flexibility within the Eastern bloc and demonstrates the new permissiveness under the Soviet-

American umbrella. Usually considered the least reliable ally of the Soviet Union, Poland is gaining some ground in her struggle for economic betterment. The example of Poland also contributes to the possibility of more permanence in East-West relations.

Like most east European countries, Poland has adopted the Soviet system of planning and economic management, which is aimed at rapid industrialization, regardless of the cost. It is autarchic, with firm rejection of outside involvement, which results in decreasing the volume of foreign trade, particularly with the developed countries. Stockpiling has increased at the expense of consumption; investment in heavy industry has been increased in a way that has damaged other sectors of the economy. Poland's basic raw materials have gone into development of the metallurgy and machine industries. Coal, one of the most valuable Polish raw materials, has been exported to the Soviet Union in large quantities and at prices below the world level. During the period 1946–53, Poland reportedly suffered a net loss of $740 million due to coal shipments to the Soviets.[1]

Later events—the workers' Poznan uprising in 1956 and another outburst in 1970 among the dock workers in the Baltic seaport of Gdansk—made the Polish economy a principal element of political stability in Poland. Yet somehow, the results of various attempts to institute reforms fell short of expectations. They were half-hearted; they lacked the ability of the Hungarians to demonstrate that their economy could be improved without jeopardizing the political structure. In Poland, the differences were internal, more mechanical than substantive.

The Post-1956 Reforms

In the post-1956 period when a genuine wave of liberalization swept Poland and a brief period of intellectual permissiveness made many Poles euphoric, Polish reformers tried to improve the economy by turning it loose. Perhaps a better description would be that they attempted to make it less immobile. Formulation of goals was vague; there appeared to be a lack of understanding of the links between a decentralized economy and democratization of political life; the reformers wished for the first and feared the second. They failed, consciously or unconsciously, to see that a truly decentralized economic system must inevitably lead to sociopolitical consequences. When decentralization was introduced soon after Wladyslaw Gomulka came to power in 1956, it was aimed at developing more efficient, more flexible, more dynamic economic forces which, in turn, would lead to a higher standard of living through emphasis on consumer goods. Individual enterprises became independent in theory but not in practice. They received their central plan targets from the State Planning Council, which included the volume of goods to be produced, the volume of output of most important types of production, the size of profits (or losses), profit levies for the state budget (or subsidies), and subsidies for investment.[2] The narrow gauge of self-management was especially frustrating to worker self-management bodies that had been created earlier by the reform.

When there were food riots 14 years later, riots even more deeply rooted in the economic problems of the working class than they had been in the 1956 events in Poznan, the party examined the past and concluded rather bombastically that: ". . . the most important lesson to be learned by the party from the events of December 1970 is that in the future it must always aim at preventing any conflicts with the working class. This requires . . . that we should pursue such an economic policy that is fully consistent with the objective social needs of the working people . . . and which stems from the Marxist-Leninist ideology of our party."[3] The rhetoric, as usual, did not change. Some factions within the party were blamed for being incapable of following the party line. What followed was only logical.

A repetitious cycle of history can hardly be overlooked. Similar voices were heard in 1956; similar charges were leveled, similar resolutions announced. But before the events of 1970, the Polish economy was slipping badly. There wasn't much indication that the post-1970 change and growth would continue to satisfy both the party and the country's economic needs. The conflict lay in plain view; one or the other had to give. Apparently, even in the mid-1970s, the party is not yet ready to make such a decision. There is no indication either that the workers are satisfied. Early in 1970 they were treated better; their free time was respected, their needs met. Three years later, things were back to normal. "Social contributions," meaning free weekend labor, were made mandatory. In order to buy meat, a housewife in Czestochowa had to get up at two in the morning to get in line for the store to open.

The point of sharp economic deterioration was reached in Poland in 1968. It was then that various decisions introduced by reform-minded leaders created chaos rather than contributing to improvement. Enterprises caught in the web of conflicting decisions were unable to adapt their output to the different pattern of industrial and consumer demands. Many managed to increase their output, only to see their products end up in warehouses. During 1970 the inventory of unwanted goods increased at twice the rate of retail sales. By the end of the year, the value of the inventory had reached unbelievable proportions. It was estimated that it represented about half the value of Poland's GNP.[4]

Shortages of food and mass unemployment plagued the country. Once again, political, rather than economic, elements prevailed. Early in 1970 the party leaders decreed that 200,000 men had to be laid off. The economic reason was the party's eagerness to speed up the changeover from extensive to intensive methods of promoting growth. Perpetuating this approach was a provision in the 1971–75 plan which anticipated a dramatic increase in the unemployment figure by the end of the plan—5 percent of the total nonagricultural labor force.

A Mandate for Change

Food shortages and massive unemployment were coupled with a wage freeze introduced under the guise of new material incentives. When a new regime took over in 1970 after a period of riots and bloody government reprisals, it was given a mandate for change by the workers. The mandate wasn't optional; it had to live up to people's expectations if those who had been instrumental in starting the disturbances would not do it again. Therefore, there is a theory among observers of Poland that Edward Gierek's regime was born with a prescription for new economic policies clearly defined for it. The regime had to try a new and different approach to foreign trade and take into consideration the fact that Western imports, licenses, and technology were required for modernization. But this need was not high on the list of priorities for some time. At first, the more pressing issues were those involving domestic ills.

A declining growth rate was one. During the 1966–70 period,

labor productivity suffered a drop in growth from an annual rate of
4.3 to 2.5 percent, according to the Central Planning Commission.
An increase in the share of investment in the national product was
also noted; but at the same time, a sharp decline in the share of
individual consumption (72 to 62 percent) occurred. The aggregate
consumption fund—individual and collective—fell off seven points,
from 79 to 72 percent. The machine industry, for instance, was concerned primarily with manufacturing machinery for capital-produc-
ing industries, which resulted in neglect of the consumer goods sector.

There were efforts to stop this process. In March 1970 the Central Committee introduced a new incentive system for linking wages
and salary increases to the individual output of each enterprise. The
incentives were detached from the annual planned targets. The performance of each enterprise was to be judged according to the improvement in the unit cost of production. At the final cost level, the
profit and the ratio of profit to total value of capital stock were to be
calculated. The stock was defined as the sum of the values of fixed and
circulating assets.[5]

The idea was good, but its execution was faulty. An upper ceiling
was set for wage and salary increases, regardless of the enterprise's
performance. Then, frightened by inflationary pressures, the government decided to postpone implementation of its March 1970 decision
for two years, which was correctly interpreted by the workers as a
two-year moratorium on wage increases.

To add another dimension to the problem, Polish farmers had
prospered under the pre-Gierek regime, due to the fact that collectivization had been abandoned after 1956. Private landowners
managed not only to create out of the Polish farmlands a booming
supply of food for domestic consumption, but turned Poland into a
major food-exporting country. Meat and meat products, butter, bacon, and eggs (to mention the principal items) accounted for about
a third of Poland's total exports and more than 60 percent of her
hard-currency earnings.[6]

Ideology in the post-1956 period interfered with normal economic progress in Poland. The fact that farmers were becoming
prosperous, that the countryside looked better, cleaner, and more
affluent than the urban and industrial centers, drew the fire of some
of the more dogmatic groups in the party. While there was little that

could be done effectively—such as reintroducing compulsory collective farms—there were other methods that could be used. One was to use the pricing system to lower the profitability of breeding animals. At a time when adverse weather had settled in for one or two summers, after a period of excellent harvests, Polish farmers discovered that they had to pay much higher prices for fodder, while state procurement prices remained steady. Pig-breeding, a major source of hard currency, was affected immediately. In one year alone (1969–70), the number of hogs dropped by nearly a million. Poland, a large exporter of food, was suddenly faced with an acute meat shortage. There was no better way to adversely affect the Polish balance of payments, while at the same time incurring the resentment of the farmers.

Efforts to Restore a Balance—The Role of the U.S.S.R.

When Edward Gierek took over after the December 1970 revolt, one of his first steps was to restore the balance of prices, to freeze retail prices, and to decontrol wages and salaries. There was also an immediate provision to increase the statutory minimum wage level and to grant retroactive pay increases for workers who had made less than the minimum level before. But the problem remained centered on food prices, which were still at the level established by the previous regime. When Polish workers did not stop striking and protesting, the authorities lowered food prices to the level of December 13, 1970. Characteristically, the announcement of the decision gave credit to the Soviet Union: "Thanks to the credit obtained during the last few days from the Soviet Union," said Prime Minister Jaroszewicz in the Polish Parliament on February 13, 1971, "it was decided . . . to lower the prices."

Another bit of history had been made. A working class, striking for the first time against the regime on purely economic grounds, had won. It was a double victory. It managed to topple one group of party leaders and replace it with another, and it forced the new group—in spite of their own inclinations—to roll back prices.

Jaroszewicz's announcement was not a diplomatic gesture. Throughout the crisis, the Soviet Union had acted as mediator. Possibly the events in Czechoslovakia were still uppermost in the minds of the Soviet leaders. The Soviet Union may have been eager to avoid the spreading of their problems in Poland. Soviet leaders were vocal in defining them in proletarian terms, seeing in the worker dissatisfaction a genuine working-class movement. Substantial credits (amounting to about $100 million in convertible currencies), large grain shipments totaling about 2 million tons, and special arrangements for the use of Poland's credit balances at the COMECON Bank for Economic Cooperation were some of the tangible evidence of the Soviet Union's influence.

The economic policy of the new regime emerged later. It had to be reoriented in order to convince the people that the old system had been abolished, that new reforms would take into consideration the standard of living of the working man. Real wages and their relation to the price scale and the ability to satisfy consumption goals of the people were the cornerstone of the new economic policy. The new rulers found a new vocabulary for redefining their objectives, while at the same time they avoided steering off the socialist course too much and too far. What really mattered, they maintained, were not economic results as such, but the principal social objectives which the party intended to achieve by following a given economic policy. This policy, which was publicized in speeches and articles, reflected the social background and economic thinking of Gierek, a former coal miner and a dedicated member of the Communist party.

When the 1971–75 Five-Year Plan was introduced in Poland's parliament, its principal aims were described by the Prime Minister as being "a substantial acceleration of the rate of increase in living standards." This was a reversal of traditional economic priorities. Key target figures reflected this change: a drastic increase in individual and social consumption, raising real wages at an average rate of 3.4 percent annually, the creation of additional work for nearly 2 million people as a safeguard against unemployment, and a drastic increase in housing construction.

The Essence of the New Plan

These decisions meant something else in terms of Marxist doctrine: a new priority in allocating raw materials and taking investment funds away from heavy industry and shifting them to such consumer goods sectors as the construction industries, food-processing, and so forth. It also meant making special provision for export-oriented industries and shipbuilding.

In the planning, the stipulated growth rates of real wages and consumption were treated as primary basic data for the rest of the plan—the reverse of the way it had been done before. This approach was spelled out by one of the leaders of the new group in an interview published by an East German weekly in November 1971: "Our policy is based on the fundamental idea that the highest goal of socialism lies in the constant satisfaction of the material and spiritual needs of the people on the basis of a dynamic economic development."

Agriculture figured prominently in the new plan. A special package of social and economic concessions was offered by the regime to reassure the farmers that their interests were being kept in mind by the regime, that its long-range planning and the farmers' investments were going to pay off. Private farmers—who held about 83 percent of the land under cultivation—were given a new agricultural policy program. Its most important feature was the abolition of compulsory deliveries and, instead, the introduction of a graduated land tax. This had been a major demand of the farmers ever since the Communists had taken over in 1945. The earlier pricing system was designed so that compulsory deliveries had eroded almost half of the farmers' earnings.

Another major concession was the government's willingness to grant legal deeds of title to farmers who had no formal property rights. There were about one million of them, and their feeling of insecurity and dependence on the whims of the authorities had been major psychological and political problems in the past.

The bold new agricultural policy bore fruit. A year and a half after the new regime came to power, stock cattle production was up and the production of hogs (earning through bacon and hams a considerable amount of hard currency) in 1971 grew by 22 percent over 1970.[7] Farmers were buying more tractors and farm machinery, and farm products were once again major export items, after having been declining for a brief period.

Solutions and changes were less visible in the industrial sector, where the problem of central planning, as a political issue, was hard to reconcile with the obvious need to decentralize the decision-

making process and enlarge the scope of lower-level individual responsibilities. The solutions that emerged from the Hungarian experiment did not appeal to the Poles, for some reason. The latest
indications are that the state planners may retain their overall responsibility but will surrender their operational function to lower
echelons. Hopefully, this kind of solution will reduce the incidence
of errors being made by the central team, such as the decision to raise
prices, in addition to introducing a new incentive for initiatives to
come from below.

The Impact on Foreign Trade

The impact of the change on foreign trade and on Poland's
ability to maintain her level of exports and imports has been considerable. Foreign indebtedness has increased. Aside from Soviet credits, a substantial increase in the balance-of-trade deficit has also been
brought on by the new policy. In the past, such indebtedness would
have been dealt with by drastically cutting nonessential imports. The
new regime has provided a boost in the purchasing power of the
people, but is far from achieving its goal of a matching level of
production. As a result, it has been necessary to increase imports. But
they didn't just increase. Food imports jumped 36.7 percent over the
1970 level, with consumer goods rising 16 percent. Poland's trade
deficit reached a record level of $162.3 million in 1971. Later, in-
creased production of meat and agricultural products was instrumental in bringing down the deficit.

Foreign trade in general was given a larger role in the dynamics
of the Polish economy. The desire for modernization and greater
technological sophistication caused the planners to anticipate a
higher volume of imports. It was thus necessary to adjust economic
planning to take into account a longer period of trade deficits than
is customary in socialist societies. The importation of machinery,
equipment, and raw materials has been anticipated. Cooperation
agreements, as well as joint ventures, are considered to be the most
valuable form of partnership with the developed countries. In addition to increasing her rate of agricultural exports, Poland has discussed the potential of exporting electrical machinery and of increasing the export of services, principally for maritime transports, and
scientific and technological research.

Poland, however, remains a planned economy. The economy is perhaps less planned than it once was, but it is still sufficiently orthodox for her to have to subordinate her foreign trade to a general strategy of development. That strategy, as outlined by the new regime, has been assisted by a different approach to trade with the outside world. The increased importation of consumer goods eased the dissatisfaction of the people. This was made possible by abolishing a number of restrictions and shifting import priorities from industrial to consumer commodities. A new, active credit policy has permitted greatly expanded trade with the capitalist world, replacing earlier, barter-type agreements. The regime has eliminated the embargo on machinery imports from other socialist countries. The idea behind this had been to protect and encourage the domestic manufacture of machines, but it often worked to the detriment of the final productivity of Polish enterprises. Since 1971, these enterprises have been free to replace domestic machinery with imported machinery.

In line with the new policy, the commission specializing in restricting the imports was abolished. Broad cooperation with socialist and capitalist countries alike by all industrial sectors has been encouraged. A series of common industrial ventures was undertaken with COMECON. Thus, the strategy of post–1970 development has meshed well with the new approach to foreign trade.

The Results

It hasn't been necessary to wait long for favorable results. Foreign trade, considered a luxury in the past, and often branded as unpatriotic ("Why couldn't we produce better, faster, more efficiently, ourselves? What's wrong with the Poles?"), has been used to lower the cost of production and to extend some of the production lines that have been hampered by a lack of modern machinery. Suddenly, hard currency was discovered as a lever for growth, rather than as a commodity too precious to part with.

The 1971 figures told the Poles that they were on the right track. Exports increased by 9.2 percent, imports by 12.2 percent. The targets were exceeded by 10 percent. The biggest change was in trade with the West, slightly at the expense of the inner-COMECON turnover. In explaining this phenomenon, the official export journal indicated that the drop was inevitable due to the changing pattern of

Poland's needs, that the resolution passed by the meeting of COME-CON in Bucharest, calling for a rather complicated program of socialist integration, did not materialize; and that new institutions were needed to perk up inner-bloc trade. These institutions, according to the journal, may have to wait until the late 1970s to really get underway.[8]

Poland's trade turnover with the West changed for the better during 1971. Before that, annual increases were lower than the rise of Poland's global trade volume, so, for the first time, these figures were reversed. Exports rose by 11.9 percent, imports by 18.3 percent, with the result that the Western countries participated at the rate of 29 percent in Polish exports and 27.7 percent in imports—a substantial chunk of world trade.[9] The Poles have claimed that one of the items they have managed to export in larger quantities than before was machinery.

When the figures were released, there were calls for more centralized planning in the area of foreign trade, with the Ministry of Foreign Trade losing the power of making final decisions. New monetary and pricing systems, the introduction of more balanced cycles in foreign trade planning, and a greater degree of decision-making by individual enterprises were suggested. The Ministry of Foreign Trade was to retain its principal role of formulating foreign trade policy, coordinating and preparing foreign trade plans, negotiating trade agreements, licensing exports and imports, conducting market research, and promoting an efficient foreign trade structure.

The trend of Polish trade with the West growing faster than her trade with the East started in 1971 and continued into 1972–73. This may well go on. A study by the Institute of Business Research and Foreign Trade Prices in Warsaw estimates that Poland's rate of growth with the West in the future will amount to 9 percent in exports and 11.8 percent in imports. Should the prediction come about by 1975, the West's share of Poland's foreign trade may reach a level of substantial economic, as well as political, significance.

Western Europe retains first place on the Polish list, with West Germany occupying undisputed leadership. Great Britain is the biggest supplier of licenses, followed by Italy, where the license to build the Polish Fiat came from.

Long-term agreements with a number of Western countries, including the United States, assure the continuity of mutual economic interest. These agreements were signed with France in 1969, Italy in 1970, West Germany in 1970, and Great Britain in 1971. In addition, in December 1972, a 10–year agreement was initiated with Great Britain, following an important accord with the U.S. a month earlier. All of these agreements combine economic as well as scientific and technological cooperation, projecting coproduction as a way to increase trade.

Polish–Western Involvement: France and Greece

More specifically, Poland has begun to be an important customer and trade partner. France, a traditional ally and partner of Poland, but a country that went her own way after Poland became socialist, counts seriously now on reestablishing traditional trade links. There are plans for setting up Polish-French ventures in the Third World countries, and a credit amounting to about 1.5 billion francs has been opened by the French, to enable Poland to purchase French machinery and equipment. While France was unable to extend to Poland the MFN status because of Common Market and GATT regulations, she has undertaken to treat her partner as favorably as possible. After Gierek's visit to Paris, spokesmen in Poland heralded the new approach as an important step. Polish purchases of modern French technology, machinery, and equipment went up almost 40 percent. A nitrogen works near Warsaw has received a flow of French supplies, and an agreement has been signed with a French company, Berliet, for coproduction of a fleet of buses. Another French firm, LMT-CIT, has been commissioned to build a factory to manufacture telephone exchanges. The Polish knitting industry, a sizable hard-currency-earning sector, is looking to France for modernization and production of power looms. In the agro-food industry, as well as the milk industry, French firms have been invited to submit bids for building modern facilities for processing meat and fodder.

On the other side of Europe, Greece has begun to play a role, in spite of her political leanings and past history of being an anti-Soviet and anti-Communist bulwark. Here, Greece is used as an example of a symptom of a significant change.

The change in relations began when an agreement was concluded on the payment of reparations by the Poles for Greek property seized in Poland. This led to two agreements, both concluded long before the military coup of 1964, covering the delivery of Polish industrial equipment in return for Greek tobacco, and regulating the issuance of double taxations on profits derived from sea and air navigation. This is important to Greece when we consider that 65 percent of her total invisible receipt of the balance of payments with east European countries is composed of earnings by Greek ships. An additional factor here is the means of settling the shipping receipts through a clearing process. A considerable proportion of these payments is made by the socialist countries in "free" (convertible) exchange for sea freight.

Early in 1973, Greece and Poland signed a long-term trade agreement, with annual commercial protocols formalizing what has already been accomplished—a rapid growth of trade. For instance, exports from Poland to Greece rose from $11.742 million in 1971 to $15.729 million in 1972, an increase of 34 percent. Imports rose from $7.553 million to $10.976 million, an increase of 31 percent. Commodity structure in the turnover consists of Greece's imports of sulfur, machinery and spare parts, electric appliances, locomotives and other rolling stock, and synthetic fibers and timber. Poland imports Greek cotton, citrus fruits, tobacco, sultana raisins, hides, and fruit juices.

This pattern of trade is, therefore, different from Poland's trade with the more developed west European countries. It is plausible that part of the west European imports are used by the Poles to meet the demands of the trade with Greece, which creates a positive balance of payments and trade for the Poles, a goal that will be a long time in coming as far as trade with western Europe and the United States is concerned.

Special Needs: Hotels and Computers

There has been a good flow of foreign business visitors to Poland, who roam around the country looking for possibilities. Their interests are diverse, their hunting expeditions not always successful. But Poland welcomes them. The Poles, coming to understand more and more the competitiveness of international trade, including the socialist markets, encourage trade with the West. But however much the

Polish potential grows, some logistics of the process are getting wobbly. The lack of hotel accommodations is one example.

The story of Western buyers and sellers, investors and prospectors, who have fought their way through the maze of Poland's bureaucracy to get a hotel bed is long. The rates are often disproportionate to the quality of the accommodations. The reservation system doesn't work well. The double standards are irritating. A Pole staying in a first-rate hotel in Warsaw pays only a fraction of the price charged a foreigner. Yet it is the foreigner who is the potential carrier of foreign currency.

The Poles have recognized this problem and are planning to build 24 new hotels, with 5,700 rooms, in the next five years. The provision has been officially included in the current Five-Year Plan. In addition, renovation and modernization plans for existing hotels are underway, and several Western companies have been invited to submit bids for the work.

Some of them are already at work. A French concern is scheduled to build five modern 100–room hotels, including conference rooms, swimming pools, and other highly capitalistic features. The design will be French and the labor Polish. A Swedish company, Skanska Cementgjuteruet, has been commissioned to build a 750–room hotel in Warsaw. This project is a franchised arrangement between ORBIS, the Polish state-owned tourist agency, and Forum Hotels, a division of the Intercontinental Hotel Corporation, which, in turn, is a subsidiary of Pan American World Airways.[10]

Assuming that foreign businessmen will come, that they will find enough comfortable hotel accommodations to enable them to stay long enough to make some deals, the outcome will be industrial growth for Poland, which, in turn, will mean more technology for her. And more technology calls for appropriate equipment. Today, computers are the basis of any advanced—or advancing—society.

By the end of this century, many Poles estimate, their country will require 38,000 computers, based on their current rate of trade with the west. This figure does not agree with what the Polish National Data Bureau projects as a realistic approach. The current level of allocation of available resources for the development of computers will permit no more than 10,000 units by the end of the century. Ten thousand is about the number of units available in 1973 in such developed countries as the United Kingdom and France.

At the beginning of 1973, Poland's computer industry was rather small, consisting of machines for data-processing, numerical calculations, and technological process control—249 units in all. At that time, plans for the future called for about 550 new computer installations by 1975. By that time, 39 new pilot data systems and the training of about 15,000 additional computer experts and 40,000 executives is envisioned. But even if all this comes true, by 1975 there will be a gap between need and availability. It is hoped that this gap can be closed by importing American computers and computer technology.

A Look into the Future

Poland's prospects and plans for a substantial increase in her trade with the West offer possibilities for Western companies, including American ones. The forecast of the Institute of Business Research and Foreign Trade Prices applies three different variables to its projection of trade with the developed capitalist countries. Even at the lowest level, the minimum variable calls for Polish exports to increase by an average of 4.1 percent and imports by 6.7 percent in the next few years. Food and fuels, followed by machinery and transport equipment, are to form the bulk of Polish exports; textiles will also feature prominently, expanding by 8.7 percent a year. Imports of Western technology are to increase by 8.5 percent a year. The maximum variable provides, among other things, for imports of Western metals and ores (an increase of 12.9 percent), machinery (12.2 percent), and other industrial products by 12.1 percent. No matter how one looks at these forecasts, Poland's present administration is determined to move forward in the modernization trend started in 1970.

The Five-Year Plan that predicts this type of foreign trade growth anticipates an annual GNP growth of 6.4 percent during the 1971–75 period, with industrial output being especially dynamic in the field of chemicals (11.8 percent annual growth), electromechanics (11.2 percent), metallurgy (8.8 percent), and fuels and electrical energy (7.2 percent).[11] In fuels, where new demands and needs are bound to accrue along with industrialization, Poland intends to increase her oil-processing capacity by over 50 million barrels by 1975, for a total annual production of almost 100 million barrels. By 1980 Poland wants to have the capacity to process 170 million barrels of oil and 10 years later to be processing 550 million barrels a year. This figure may be a super-maximum variable, but it best indicates Polish ambitions and determination.

There exist, therefore, good signs that Poland appears ready to welcome Western technology. She wants to grow economically. She is also eager for a higher standard of living. But she is not Hungary; she needs to protect her political flanks. The introduction of a market economy into her social fabric must be slower, more deliberate, more political than that of Hungary. An example of this cautious approach was the new Polish leader's trip to France in 1973. Edward Gierek, surrounded by the euphoria of his aides and a delight of his hosts, sounded a note of caution before departing from France. In his farewell speech, he indicated that perhaps not all of his expectations had been fulfilled. Was this true, asked surprised Frenchmen, who had been told earlier that the visit was a huge success.

Of course it was true. Polish expectations were probably not capable of being fulfilled to begin with. They would have included much more reliance on France than would have been politically digestible back home. They would have meant much more dependence on the Western countries than Poland could afford. Gierek's carefully worded statement could have been a signal to all concerned that the Poles—willing, friendly, ready—remained on the other side of the line. Though their dreams were boundless, their ceiling was low. But in today's world, dreams can lead to national dramas, something the new secretary-general of the Polish Communist party, a pragmatist and a Marxist, wishes to avoid.

Epilogue I: Romanian Style

A firm political line has to be drawn in such distant and unlikely locations as Moscow and Bucharest. In each, it is for a different reason; in each, the situation calls for national efforts to change and improve the economy. In both capitals, the issue of economic reform brings forth a limitation of power. Each wants to change, to improve and to combine her own respective national status with slow, evolutionary approaches to bring about a higher standard of living. But both must stop short of their goals.

In Bucharest the level of economic development is one of the lowest in the bloc. The country's dependence on agriculture is great, the amount of industrialization lower than elsewhere in the bloc. There is, instead, a high degree of national identity. It is in Romania that nationalism has been elevated to official respectability. Elsewhere in the socialist bloc, this is not so. Socialist unity, cohesion within either the COMECON or the Warsaw Pact, is usually sloganized before any slogans appear which bear any resemblance to national pride. In Romania, the reverse is true. The preservation of this precious Romanian treasure calls for a price to be paid. The lack of meaningful economic reform is one price.

The national entity requires two pillars of support—the active support of the people and the benevolent tolerance of the Soviet Union. Popular support can be obtained on the basis of Romanian nationalism, which bridges differences between rural and urban populations, between farmers and workers, diffrences which are considerable. Pride in their independent foreign policy, in the role Romania played over the years within various international Communist bodies transcends regional and economic differences. The people of Romania, often dejected, often barely living at subsistence level, find a remedy and satisfaction in this policy.

The Soviet Union, which does not always look approvingly on the Romanian experiment with independence, nevertheless tolerates it. The Russians intervened in Czechoslovakia, which never proclaimed a desire for an independent foreign policy, but which was well on the way to instituting drastic economic reforms. Each reform the Czechs wanted and publicly declared their readiness to implement would have eventually brought a democratization of their internal political system. This, in turn, would have made a socialist country dangerously different in the Soviets' eyes, a country which might show that the liberalization of individual rights does not necessarily threaten the system itself. This would have caused serious implications for the Soviet Union.

Therefore, Romania, satisfied with her degree of international freedom, has shied away from internal reform which could annoy the Russians. The Romanians were afraid of being called revisionists by either the Soviets or the Chinese. After all, the relative amount of Romanian independence has been made possible by the government's clever use of the conflict betwen Russia and China.

Romania, in addition to the larger rationale against being refor-

mist, lacks an industrial and technocratic base for a reform movement. Should she attempt a decentralization of her economy, as the
Hungarians have done, she would have to have enough qualified
economists, engineers, and technocrats to run the enterprises and
make decisions. She does not have these people. Further, a market-
oriented reform presupposes pluralism, which would reveal internal
social and political conflicts. This would destroy the unity that has
been achieved on the basis of national entity. It could easily endanger
Romanian political independence, not only from without, but also
from within. As the present command system of the Romanian
economy is constituted, various groups in the population have access
to decision-making power. The National Association of Agricultural
Cooperatives is an example of an active body which represents the
farmers. Its elected officials help formulate work norms for agricultural cooperatives, reward forms, credit systems, and so on. The
association has at its disposal such tools as its own machinery pool, its
own production of fodder, and the ability to provide needed services
for land improvement and irrigation.

This is not meant to give the impression that Romania hasn't
moved economically because of political constraints. She has undertaken a number of steps in order to solicit foreign investments and
revitalize her foreign trade. Discussions about such problems as the
structural adaptation of Romania's exports to foreign market demands, ways and means to increase the efficiency of her foreign trade
have appeared in Romanian journals. More tangibly, the Romanians
have instituted a law which permits joint ventures with Western
firms and which stipulates that voting rights be included into stat-
utes. The new law is intended to make sure that minority participants—in this case, Western companies—will have decision-making
powers. The law calls for either a majority or a unanimous vote. Some
ventures were started soon after the law went into effect; they included Romaltex, a Romanian-French venture for promoting the
export of Romanian textiles to France and Third World countries and
to assist in negotiating industrial cooperation agreements in consumer goods between Romanian and French firms.

An interesting Romanian-Italian venture, the first of its kind in
Romania, was concluded in mid-1973. The partners—the Industrial
Center for Chemical Fibres of Romania and the Italian firm of
Romalfa—agreed to build a plant at Savinesti to manufacture acrylic

fibers. The capital investment is $2.3 million, with the Romanians contributing 52 percent and the Italians, 48 percent.Named REFIL, the new venture was organized on the basis of a general assembly, with each part having one vote, which means that the Romanians' vote will be decisive (a departure from the principles embodied in the law).

Epilogue II—The Soviet Union

Different circumstances make it difficult for the Russians to initiate full-scale reforms. The circumstances are different, but the reasons are equally political. Khrushchev went through a series of reforms, which were interpreted in the West as attempts to liberalize the system. In hindsight, it appears that his motivation was different. First, the Soviet had stagnated during his regime. Capital output grew dangerously, due to his attempts to develop the remote areas of the Soviet Union, including Siberia. The increased output was also due to the steady supplying of raw materials to east European countries, which resulted in tying those countries politically to the Soviet Union.

Second, Khrushchev had his own reasons for wanting to make a change—internal political reasons. He wanted to shift the economic responsibility from the state to the party organs. When he came to power, the state bureaucracy was powerful enough to acquire a degree of independence from the party. Khrushchev's power was rooted in the party; the republics and regions were his primary supporters. Therefore, a form of decentralization, giving more authority, was in his interest.

After Khrushchev fell from power, discussions about the economic reform system began all over again. The year 1965 marked semi-official recognition of the profit criterion, a concept first suggested by some prominent Soviet economists as early as 1962. But this was far from presupposing a shift toward a market economy. The Soviet Union, as much as Romania, but for different reasons, could not afford such a major shift, nor would she want to make one. As one observer of the Soviet scene put it, "marketization" of the Soviet economy may very well lead to the type of liberalization that was seen in Czechoslovakia in 1968.[12] Economic and political decentralization, in view of the multinational structure of the Soviet Union, would require changing the formal Soviet federal system. A federation of equal partners may be the only form that is acceptable to everyone. The individual Soviet republics would then acquire a genuinely independent status, which, in turn, would make the Soviet Union a different kind of world power. Internally, it would break up the monopoly of producers and strengthen the position of the consumers. The whole idea of a true market-oriented reform is therefore unacceptable to the Soviets.

While this theory may be only partially valid, it does point to a number of danger points which the Soviet Union, a status-quo power internally, cannot afford to touch. Soviet reforms, therefore, center on the plausible; they touch upon pricing. In 1967 a reform of producers' prices brought about an increase of oil prices by the 2.3 times factor, while chemical products rose only 5 percent. Cement rose 13 percent and coal 78 percent. All of this was instrumental in increasing the profitability and thus eliminating the need for planned deficits. At one time, a measure of decentralization was timidly introduced, beginning with the clothing industry. The industry permitted the planning of volume and content of production, according to the orders received from department stores. As an experiment, it appears small; as a departure from political principle, it was most important.

Regardless of the economic thinking of the Soviet leaders, however, Soviet society does have needs which require changes and advances in technology. The Soviet Union, drafting her latest Five-Year Plan in 1971, was ready to acknowledge a substantial gap between Western and Soviet technology. "When we compare our economy with that of the United States," wrote Soviet scientists, A.D. Sakharov, V.F. Turchin, and R.A. Medvedev, in March 1970, "we see that ours is lagging behind not only quantitatively but also qualitatively. . . .We are ahead of the United States in the production of coal but behind in the production of oil, gas, and electric power, ten times behind in chemistry, and immeasurably behind in computer technology. . . ."

Whether this is true or not, the cry of these three Soviet scientists reflects their genuine concern for Russia. This concern, in different forms and dimensions, has also been voiced by the official Soviet leadership, which, in turn, has been translated into a much more liberal approach to trade and credit agreements with the United States. The transfer of technology is one of the main common denominators in a number of commercial exchanges with the U.S., as well as with western Europe, still the principal trading partner of Russia and far ahead of the U.S. and Canada. This trade includes large-scale petroleum and gas extractions, transmission and distribution systems, management control, systems utilizing computer facilities, tourist systems, including hotels, roads, and transportation.

The central question, therefore, concerns the validity of economic reforms within the Marxist-Leninist system. The fewer responsibilities, the smaller the member of the Eastern bloc, the more room there is for reform. In the Soviet Union there has been a small amount of change. Should the Soviet-American polarization increase, the flexibility within each part is apt to diminish; should there be a convergence of interests, the flexibility will increase. It may be too early for the Soviet Union to move boldly in changing the system. The Soviet leaders may, justifiably, fear the contagiousness of doing so. For the Hungarians, Poles, Bulgarians, and others, the constraints were less rigid, and this is where the beginning of a permanent change is most visible.

In the Soviet Union, reforms can only be of a limited nature, not meaningful enough to make a difference, not daring enough to be dangerous. But the lack of reform does not preclude another road which could lead to social and political changes. This is the road that Russia has been obliged to travel, the road of technology imports. From the point of view of the West, this is a crucial change, one which opens potential trade gates wider and higher.

CHAPTER 8

Money and Credits:
Part I — A Change in Role and Goals

Money and Economic Planning

Money has played a special part in the emerging socialist economic system. Its role is linked directly to that of credits, which, in turn, have shaped internal socialist developments. Foreign credits have had a lot to do with the technological input. As it was with various economic reforms leading to a gradual change in the structure of the socialist societies, so it is with money and credits. The change could have far-reaching implications.

The role of money in earlier Communist societies was basically different from its role in the West. A person who had money did not have access to all available resources. He could acquire a few consumer goods and limited kinds of property for his personal use. Gradually a more liberal approach evolved, permitting small service establishments, artisans, and independent farmers to acquire goods. But this came much later and was more applicable to the newly created socialist countries such as Poland and East Germany than it was to the Soviet Union.

In the public, or state, sector, to which the role of money should theoretically be restricted, the role should be reduced, in traditional Marxist terms, to that of a passive recording and accounting device. It should be a tool to facilitate the administration and control of planned production and distribution. The theory even suggests that with the attainment of a full Communist environment, the tool would have outlived its usefulness. Money, then, like the state, would wither away.

157

In the meantime, as long as money was around, it should be used exclusively in conformity with the master economic plan. This is linked with the role of credit as an internal domestic force. Credit gives command over resources only if the acquisition of resources is foreseen in the plan. Conversely, an allocation of resources by the plan carries with it an almost automatic claim on credit. In other words, the power of money to influence real economic processes is limited by its subordination to planning. When there were attempts to use monetary incentives, as there were in the late 1960s and early 70s, it was considered an experiment, and great pains were taken to explain the essentially orthodox nature of the use. In fact, these attempts were a departure, permitting more flexible and dynamic economic developments. They were highly successful in a country like Hungary, less so in Poland, and even less so in the Soviet Union. The fact that the experiment was made and that some continue to be made is a telling indication of change.

Internal credits remained in the hands of the banks. There are no other credit-granting institutions in socialist countries. The main role of credits is to provide financing of inventories at various levels of production and distribution. Other types of credit—consumer, home-building, cooperative activities—have been introduced after some of the reforms took deeper roots. Only in Poland, where the agricultural sector retained its private character, were farmers eligible for special credits. After the changeover in 1956, some money was made available for both seasonal and long-term technological improvements. But this was a concession, an exception to the rule, which was tolerated only because of the special circumstances in Poland.

Five Principles of Credit

The rule—or the official doctrine of socialist credit—was based on five principles.[1] Credit must be planned, specific, secured, repayable, and with a fixed maturity. Official textbooks of socialist economics are careful not to mention the striking similarity between the above outline and the concept of self-liquidating loans that used to be applied in the West, but which were considered less functional than other types of credit.

Internal credits are used to supplement the working capital of state-owned enterprises. Funds are secured to finance current expenditures rather than fixed investments. Whenever projected targets cannot be reached because of a lack of capital, credit is provided regardless of the creditworthiness of a given enterprise or the profitability of its production. Since the entire purpose is the fulfillment of the plan, in some cases, credit can be granted to institutions operating at a loss. A *loss*, in the Soviet system, however, is not necessarily a loss in Western terms. Since prices are set to fit production into plans and do not reflect either the scarcity of a given product or its overproduction, it is not unusual for an efficient enterprise to show a deficit at the end.

But the deficit isn't the same economic problem that it is in the West. Often, when a planned loss occurs, it is eliminated by the decision of higher authority. The necessary capital is drawn from profits of other enterprises or simply from the national budget. Only when an enterprise fails to fulfill its production quota is it penalized. Planning, therefore, supercedes purely monetary considerations.

Another point to be made about the domestic use of credit in the socialist bloc is related to fixed investments. In the mid-1950s, for the first time, credit was extended for the financing of plants and equipment in the state-owned sector. The idea proved useful, and there was a shift from grant- to loan-financing. These were usually short-term loans for periods not exceeding three to six years. They were calculated for rapid amortization, with the Soviet Union leading other countries by amortizing her credits in one year on the average. At the beginning of this experiment with the role of money in a socialist society, short-term credits were available only for purposes that were profitable enough to permit quick retirement.

Loans for Unplanned Projects

The most significant aspect of these loan-credits is their purpose. They are for projects not included in national investment plans. They are used either for small technological improvements or for investments which have not been centrally planned. This is not only a financial, but an ideological, novelty. Provision was made for preventing abuse of these loans, such abuses as securing credits for projects that had been rejected by the central planners. One such provision is a stipulation that loans cannot be used for construction; the proposed unplanned investment may include construction funds not exceeding 15 percent of the total amount requested and granted.

In the Soviet Union, which experimented (without much success) with loans for small mechanization as early as 1932, there was new impetus in the early 1960s. Following the success of Czechoslovakia and Hungary, the Soviet Union in 1964 extended loans for small mechanization, amounting to 552 million rubles. Loans for augmenting production facilities for products of mass consumption, mechanization, and the acquisition of replacements for equipment were financed out of these loans.

Without being spelled out explicitly, the role of money thus underwent a major change, a change that has affected socialist lending institutions. The banking system in the socialist countries was created to distribute money for purposes that were predetermined in the central economic plans. A special investment bank, in turn, administered short-term credits. The system was effective in promoting economic development, based on the concept of rapid growth and the use of extensive resources. The banking was consistent with the centralized planning and with the goal that called for growth regardless of a profitable or economic use of raw materials and natural resources.

The change that affected the banking institutions has been, for the most part, a direct result of economic reforms. It was easier to bury some of the revisionist approaches to the role of money within the framework of an overall reform than it would have been in a separate approach to the issue of credit. Under the new system, bank credits have to play a much more active role. They are expected (to use the wording of an East German decree of 1968) to initiate an active credit policy "to strengthen Socialist economic relations and to shape the desired structural development of the economy."[2]

From then on, bank credits had to be used selectively and flexibly in order to facilitate changes in the economy that would favor the industries that were the most dynamic technologically. The emphasis was different, the goals the same. In the past, the policy of forced growth was indiscriminate, as long as there *was* growth. Now it was to be more selective, with the use of money as a specialized tool, regardless of preplanned blueprints. Furthermore, in line with the concept of decentralized responsibilities, banks providing loans were asked to supervise and police deliveries according to specification, quality, timing, and so on. Banks were also given sanctions. They could, if required, apply financial penalties against enterprises that failed to meet their obligations.

There is one important punitive element built into the credit provisions for purposes not covered by the economic plan—interest rates. Legally, they can be as much as twice the going rate. In countries such as East Germany, markups are allowed to be charged above basic rates, according to the degree of risk borne by the bank.[3] Further, there are stiff penalties levied on debtors who are late in their payments. In Bulgaria and the Soviet Union, they amount to 8 percent. Yugoslavs charge 20 percent, and the Hungarians between 14 and 16 percent. There has been much discussion in the Soviet Union about the need to raise the penalty rate to as much as 18 percent.

The Effect on Foreign Trade

The changed role of money and the different outlook on the credit system have also affected the socialist approach to foreign trade as well as foreign credit. High priority is given today to export financing. Economic plans include special provisions for supporting export-oriented industries. The October Revolution brought about a situation which has plagued both sides for years. In prerevolutionary days, Russia was heavily in debt. Between 1858 and 1914 she borrowed an estimated $2.5 billion to finance a network of railroads inside the European part of the country. This debt (on gold-clause bonds, denominated in British sterling, French francs, German marks, and Dutch guilders) was repudiated immediately after the Revolution. The repudiation also covered another debt of a completely different nature: $75 million borrowed from the United States to finance Russia's war effort. There were also several American companies,[4] banks, and other financial institutions that were affected by the Soviet government's policy. Their investments, bonds, loans, and numerous securities had been either seized or declared null and void. The issue remained one of the major bones of contention between the Soviet Union and various Western countries, particularly the U.S. There have been calls that, prior to repayment of the debts, no significant American investment or lines of credit go to the Soviet bloc. The Soviet government has made a number of gestures to appease the critics. The critics have been appeased but not satisfied. To respond fully to the criticism, the Soviets would have to repudiate some of their political principles. This would be asking too much, especially since Western and American critics are finding themselves more and more in the minority.

Looking at the Soviet Union, however, and trying to assess the importance of foreign trade and foreign credits, is misleading in terms of eastern Europe as a whole. Traditionally, Russia has been self-centered and independent. Her rich store of natural resources and her accumulation of gold have permitted a more secluded, more insular, economic development. Isolation from the capitalist world, interrupted by NEP, has long been a part of Soviet economic life. But this has not been so in the rest of eastern Europe. Countries such as Poland and Czechoslovakia, when they were absorbed into the socialist system, inherited national economies that had developed as a part of the totality of European economies. In spite of strenuous efforts to change their dependence on western European supplies, money, and services, and in spite of the dramatic switch to Soviet raw materials, eastern Europe has continued to be dependent on Western imports. These imports have to be paid for in convertible currencies. The intrabloc trade relationship was one channel, the outer relations were another. Trade with the West has always been based on prices established in competitive world markets and generally payable in hard currencies; there is no other way. The necessity of foreign trade for eastern Europe has manifested itself during the planning exercises; it has become a part—a crucial part—of economic planning.

The monopoly of the foreign trade and foreign exchange system was introduced in the postwar period. It was required for husbanding exchange earnings, in order to pay for needed imports. State trading organizations have been established which act as intermediaries between domestic enterprises and foreign firms. It was during the reform period that direct dealings were permitted between domestic producers and foreign customers. In some instances—notably, Hungary—specific amounts of hard-currency proceeds have been put aside for use by firms producing especially for export. In addition, foreign exchange loans were initiated, to permit selected export-oriented firms to purchase machinery and equipment needed to increase their export earnings. The Poles established a special fund for that purpose in 1963. It was administered by the Ministry of Foreign Trade, leaving the monopoly intact.

Banks and Foreign Trade: Financing Joint Ventures

Within the socialist banking system, separate banks perform the function of monitoring, sometimes financing, but more often administering foreign trade operations. In all the countries except Poland, where the bank is called the Commercial Bank, the name is the Foreign Trade Bank. Intrabloc trade relations have caused some of the countries involved to establish the International Investment Bank within COMECON. The initial capital of the bank (which was organized in 1970) was 1 billion rubles, of which 30 percent was in convertible currencies. The bank's function was to finance specific projects, including joint ventures promoting specialization and industrial cooperation among the member states. Short- and long-term credits were also made available.

The amount of Western investment capital is relatively small, and in most cases, is derived from joint ventures, a new and rather risky economic undertaking. It is risky politically for the Eastern partners (imported capital and technology are not always used in the public sectors) and economically for the Westerners. While there are no legal barriers to capitalist investors owning assets in socialist countries, the general rule is that a majority of the shares remain in the host country. One country whose joint ventures have blossomed is Yugoslavia, which has an atypical and very marginal economy, as socialist countries go. The Yugoslav parliament had to pass special legislation to protect Yugoslav interests as well as those of foreign investors. A substantial flow of foreign capital has necessitated the creation of a separate, international consortium of Western and Yugoslav banks. The International Investment Corporation was set up, with $12 million contributed by the International Bank of Reconstruction and Development, the International Finance Corporation, private banks in several countries, including the United States and Japan, and 12 Yugoslav banks. But this is a situation that cannot very well be compared with those in any other socialist countries. The Yugoslav mixed economy is neither typical in its relations with the outside world, nor does it fit into a study of the psychological changes in the approach to trade and financing. It is simply a totally different chapter.

Joint ventures, however, tend to become a permanent feature of a socialist system. They are evident in Hungary, and are beginning in Poland, Romania, and other countries. They are of different natures and compositions and are often devoid of financial participation in terms of direct loans to socialist enterprises, but they do bring in indirect capital investments in the form of loans and credits extended to Western firms which enter into partnerships. These partnerships are, by their very nature, a limited proposition. The term *trans-ideological corporation* was coined by a student of the problem, but it does not accurately describe the heart of the matter. Eastern partners are permitted to own shares in Western firms; Western businessmen consider themselves limited-liability partners with a minority share. They could not, even in the current period of détente, aspire to equity in the ownership of the means of production. As a writer on the subject has suggested, Western persistence in demanding true ownership would eliminate the concept of joint ventures from the east European scene.[5] And this is not likely to happen.

Joint Ventures and Mutual Gains

Both East and West have an interest in maintaining and expanding the joint ventures and cooperative agreements, but for different reasons. There are several motivating factors in the East. One of the principal ones, connected with the issue of capital investments, is the acquisition of hard-currency capital. For those east European countries, including the Soviet Union, which have an adverse balance of trade, this is a key point.

The acquisition of technology, a goal that is present in most Eastern dealings with the West, is another important point. Direct benefits include the development of management skills, access to Western markets that have been closed, and the construction of a more solid, more permanent industrial base. The political issue that remains is the acquisition of equity by Western partners. On more than one occasion, thoughts and ideas have been expressed in the socialist countries that the biggest incentive to be offered would be equity participation. This, however, remains politically unacceptable. The only possible compromise is to be found in the formation of joint ventures in Third World countries.

The main motivation of the West—accepting its inability to achieve equity—is the development of new markets and the profit to be derived from them. These markets can be inside as well as outside the socialist countries. A major American manufacturer entering an east European country as a minor partner calculates his investment according to several factors. He can sell his products to the host country; he can market them inside COMECON. He also hopes to sell them in countries, or groups of countries, which, for economic or political reasons, would not buy directly from an American firm. Soft-currency countries can pay in their own currencies to an Eastern partner, and part of the profits would accrue in the equity account of the American partner. Similarly, an Arab country which, for political reasons, would not want to purchase American products when an anti-Israel resolution is before the United Nations, could buy the same product labeled as having been manufactured somewhere else. There is no attempt here to be deceptive, since joint ventures are public knowledge. It is just another way of serving both partners. Without mutual interest, the likelihood of joint ventures being of a lasting nature is rather small. Joint ventures, however, are far from being widely accepted. For example, the Soviet Union is politically opposed to them. The Russians prefer coproduction agreements similar to their agreement with Fiat, or a multinational approach to a major development project, as occurred with the Kama Truck Company. A multinational enterprise requiring a substantial import of Western technology and lines of credit, the Kama project is still an entirely Soviet undertaking. There are no equity arrangements with any of the many foreign participants.

In the smaller east European countries, joint ventures are gradually being incorporated in economic planning, capitalization, and the importation of technology. A considerable number of joint ventures are being concluded inside the socialist bloc, but more and more Western participation is being considered useful and is, therefore, being sought. Special decrees were published in Romania and Hun-

gary in 1972, dealing with economic associations with foreign participation and regulating their operation and taxation.

Joint Ventures—Examples

So far, western Europeans have been most active in the field of
joint ventures. American and Japanese are getting involved but to a
considerably smaller degree. Typical joint ventures may include
marketing Eastern machine tools in the United States (Skoda in
Czechoslovakia and Simmons Machine Tool Corporation in the U.S.),
construction of automotive equipment (Gyor Wagon Works in Hungary and Renault in France), manufacturing of such heavy machinery as tractors and wheel cranes (Machine Building Association in
Poland and Jones Cranes in Great Britain), and handling trade between an Eastern country and Japan (Chimimport in Romania and
Ataka & Co. in Japan). The range is wide, the number of joint ventures growing, but there are cases when legal compromises must be
made in order to consummate a deal. There is seldom any public
explanation why compromises are needed; only the results are made
public. A case in point was the first joint venture entered into by Italy
and Romania, in mid-1973. With a capital investment of $2.3 million,
the two partners agreed to build a plant for manufacturing acrylic
fibers. The Romanian Industrial Center for Chemical Fibres subscribed for 52 percent of the capital, and the Italian company,
Romalfa, subscribed for the remaining 48 percent. There would be
nothing unusual about the agreement if it weren't for the fact that
the interpretation of the law was in favor of the host country. A
majority vote, rather than a unanimous-decision approach, was
chosen, with one vote for one part given to the members of the
general assembly, the joint venture's governing body.

This example brings forth one of the main problems faced by the
West: the majority shareholder in eastern Europe will always be the
state. The only way to insure some kind of controlling interest on the
part of the West is to rely on outside guarantees provided by binding
international agreements. Short of that, business decisions will always remain in the hands of east European governments.

Laws in eastern Europe are not precise enough to assure Western investors of a viable litigation process, should that prove to be the

only way out. In Yugoslavia, where the element of risk, both economic and political, is considerably smaller than in, say, Poland or Romania, there is a legal, compulsory reinvestment of 20 percent of earnings. Elsewhere, there are no such provisions. Some east European countries (Romania and Hungary) prefer to treat each joint venture on its own merits, without outlining in advance a legal framework to bind them together. It is, however, not easy for a Western corporation or a bank to go into partnership, or to extend a substantial line of credit when the terms of repatriation of capital and profits are vague, income tax regulations far from clear, and the regulations regarding import duties for critical components or raw materials have not been made explicit. While a flexible approach may occasionally be advantageous, experience has taught Western investors that the amount of time wasted and the efforts expended in getting a project through the bureaucracy are greater than anticipated.

Most joint ventures do not require direct participation of financial institutions. Many ventures are self-financing, with the east European countries relying on state funding or state guarantees. In the West, independent financing is sought more often, especially when international agreements and government guarantees are not specific enough. The risks are usually quite high in the West. When a Western bank is asked to provide a line of credit to an east European venture, it must evaluate the risks—not an easy task. In all of the east European countries, indebtedness is kept secret by the state, and data is little more than an educated guess. A change in attitude occurred recently in Hungary, as we saw; Hungary is the most reform-minded and economically daring country in the socialist bloc. The Hungarian National Bank published for the first time its estimate of the COMECON countries' outstanding debts to the West, a figure between $5 billion and $5.5 billion at the end of 1972. It may be a fair assumption that the Hungarians would not have published these figures without permission from their socialist allies.

Western Banks' Options

A Western bank can do two things in the financing of a joint venture. It can treat the Western partner as a separate entity and assess his creditworthiness, which is an easy, routine approach, or it can consider extending credits to the country in question or to the joint venture as a unit. In both cases, the appropriate foreign trade bank is the natural partner. How can it be assessed in terms of a credit risk? In view of its government ownership and its function within the centralized system, the bank must be identified with the political risks of the country itself. The lending process in the West —in connection with joint ventures, as well as with the process of direct lending for specific projects (socialist countries do not favor general Western loans)—comes down to a senior management decision. There are, however, a number of elements derived from past practices which can assist in making such decisions. They are primarily political, not economic.

The first is past experience. Most American banking institutions that have done business with eastern Europe would testify that the socialist countries have always met their obligations scrupulously. The other consideration, which is perhaps more doubtful, is that the Soviet Union, in case of a financial bind, would come to her allies' rescue. Two examples are cited by Western bankers in support of this thesis: Poland after the 1970 disturbances and a change of regime, and Czechoslovakia after the Soviet invasion. In both cases, large Soviet shipments of commodities were arranged and large lines of credit were made available. The argument appears to have limited validity when it is applied to lines of credit for small projects and when the international situation does not point to the emergency needs of Soviet rescue operations. However, it is apparently an element that must be taken into consideration when lending decisions are being made in the West.

There is another parallel trend of thought among Western bankers, who maintain that the socialist countries have every interest in maintaining an excellent credit record. In the future, they will have to use Western credits increasingly in order to build up and modernize their industries. As an indication of the east European countries' active interest in expanding financial involvement with the West, the number of new east European banking institutions in western Europe is cited. The Russians have pioneered in this field. They have had an office of the Moscow Narodny Bank in London since 1919, in Paris (Banque Commerciale pour l'Europe du Nord) since 1925, in Zurich (Wozchod Handelsbank) since 1966, in Frankfurt since 1972, and in Vienna since 1973. Further, the International Investment Bank, established in Moscow in 1971 and owned by all of the members of COMECON, is authorized to borrow abroad and to float bond issues.

The Attitude of East European Banks

On the other side of the coin, many Western observers fail to discover special aggressiveness or dynamism behind the efforts of east European financial institutions to be instrumental in financing and arranging either joint ventures or cooperation agreements with Western companies. In this, there is a traditional reluctance on the part of the Soviet Union (after all, she is the dominant partner in COMECON) to see too many close ties between the COMECON countries and the West. But occasionally there are exceptions. The Moscow Narodny Bank, for instance, has been involved in the private placement of Eurodollar notes used to finance the sale of American technology to Romania. In line with the rationale advanced by American bankers, the Moscow Narodny Bank usually relies on the guarantees of east European banks for financing imports and transferring technology. This reliance stems from the fact that the Moscow bank assumes that the credit of the Soviet Union stands behind each east European country. If this is so, Western bankers are correct in maintaining their assumptions, which are more political than financial.

The Moscow Narodny Bank has recently made a rather liberal move, from the Soviet economic viewpoint, by joining a syndicate of Western banks to finance the sale of Soviet equipment to Brazil. It is also expanding its activities all over the world, including Asia. Should the policy line regarding joint ventures change in the Soviet Union, the Narodny Bank and other Soviet banks in the West could play a major financing role. It would, of course, be a considerable push for the concept of joint ventures and an added incentive for Western partners. In the meantime, smaller east European countries are taking the lead.

The issue of joint ventures cannot be left without coming back to the initial matter of foreign credits by socialist societies. The change that has occurred, the ideological barrier that has been crossed, the new role that money is permitted to play, are all parts of the same psychological and political evolution that has been going on within the bloc for the past few years. Western willingness to join forces in joint ventures is testimony to a similar, though perhaps less drastic, less political change which has taken place on the Western side of the ideological fence.

The art of jumping over that fence is evident in the field of foreign trade financing, outside of joint ventures or cooperation agreements. Until quite recently—and in most cases, continuing—all payments related to foreign trade were and are being channeled through the foreign trade banks. These banks hold foreign exchange balances and are in charge of conversion into and from domestic currencies. In view of the price structure of the individual socialist countries, which bears no relation either to world prices or the prices in neighboring countries, exports may involve losses as well as profits. It is up to the foreign banks to channel profits into the budget and to distribute appropriate subsidies when losses occur.

There have also been efforts (during the economic reform periods) to create additional incentives for export-oriented enterprises. Bonuses paid in hard currencies, shares in foreign-exchange earnings, were some of the incentives offered. In Hungary, as was indicated above, this method was highly successful. In Czechoslovakia, where a similar approach was introduced before the 1968 invasion, success was short-lived, and it has been dropped by the post-invasion government.

Foreign trade banks are closely linked with the official state banks. In many instances, foreign trade banks have been an offshoot of foreign trade departments of state banks. As a general rule, the head of the foreign trade banking operation serves on the board of managers of the state bank. Both of these banks are the negotiating channels whenever foreign credits are being sought. They have made deliberate efforts to impress Western bankers with their commercial-banking approach and have successfully reestablished traditional banking relations. Foreign trade banks have also established an extensive network of corresponding relationships with banks throughout the world.

International Payments and Financing

The management of international payments is a complicated business, for reasons of a "socialist" making. Payments within the bloc are invariably channeled through the COMECON Bank for Economic Cooperation (IBEC). Intrabloc payments are handled so as to require little creativity, simply by balancing various operations. Financial dealings with hard-currency countries present a different problem. Here, there must be careful budgeting of exchange earnings and negotiations for the necessary credits, in addition to the preparation of special and separate foreign exchange budgets for countries with convertible currencies.

At first, it was a matter of policy to have the trade turnover with Western countries balanced the same way as inner-bloc trade is balanced among the bloc countries. The goal was to escape the development of a negative balance of payments. This did not last long, although there is still a tendency to do so. There have been serious attempts to balance trade exchanges. Within the last year or so, the Soviet Union has experienced especially severe hard-currency deficits, stemming primarily from huge grain purchases she has made as well as from increased imports of machinery and equipment. The deficit is particularly visible in the growing volume of trade between the Soviet Union and the United States.

A recent study by the legislative branch of the U.S. government outlines the ways in which the Soviets can finance their hard-currency deficits.[6] One of them is the sale of gold. In 1972 the official figure given was 250 metric tons of gold sold to the West alone. The output of gold during the same year was estimated to have been around 220 tons. The other two are Western credits and the decrease in imports of lower-priority goods. All three channels opened to the Soviet Union are easily accessible; they are also much more usable in short order than would be similar remedies in a Western country where no centralized monopoly of trade remains in the hands of the government.

The study maintains that since 1966 the burden of debt financing has rested largely on Western credits, thus creating almost certain prospects that foreign Soviet debts will be rising in the years to come. Gold sales were not significant enough in the past to offset these debts, and they are not expected to be so in the future. The only way for the Soviet Union to reduce the burden of debt will be to use credits for large development projects with a deferred payments clause, which would permit repayment of capital and interest with products developed by the project.

For instance, Austria, West Germany, Italy, and France have extended lines of credit to the Soviet Union for pipes and equipment for repayment in Soviet natural gas. In this type of contract, the U.S.S.R. has received large deliveries of equipment on hard-currency credits extending for five to ten years. There is also the Soviet-Japanese timber agreement, which includes development of the port of Vrangel Bay, to be financed by the Japanese and to be repaid with Soviet wood and wood-chip deliveries. These self-liquidating projects represent a total line of credit of $1.3 billion from the capitalist countries.

In rare cases, the Soviet Union extends credits and accepts payments in kind. The Iranian-Soviet agreement for the exploitation of Iranian natural gas is one example.

The Viability of Credits

Soviet banks operating in the West also play a special role. They finance some Soviet imports and occasionally, as in the case of Romanian technology, join forces with Western banks. Their limited resources permit mostly short-term financing.

Although long-term financing can be made available by Western banks, a couple of obstacles must be overcome first. One is technical and not difficult to negotiate: interest rates. The Soviets have always insisted on lower interest charges than is customary for large development projects. The other obstacle is more fundamental: access to information that is needed for assessing the creditworthiness and viability of a project. The Russians, with their mania for secrecy and suspicious attitude toward foreigners in general (and Americans in particular), make the problem sticky. Without solid on-site inspections, an independent survey of an area—as in the case of proposed major capital investments in Siberia—and a feasibility study, it is difficult to imagine any serious banking institution in the West undertaking the financing. The only exception might be the eagerness of Western banks to do business with the Russians. In the case of at least one developed country—Japan—this appears to be true.

Long-term financing and the future availability of Western credits are the key issues. Both are mixed blessings, to both the East and West. If east European economies continue to be unable to earn enough hard currencies to pay their debts, a semipermanent imbalance is likely. Should they want to offset this imbalance by selling gold or dumping unwanted industrial products on world markets, another disturbing set of circumstances may evolve. In both cases, the issue is crucial to relations between East and West, and not just in economic terms.

Banks Take Political Risks

The flow of credit between East and West continues, regardless of the larger issues. It continues partly because of the Western banking community's view that the size of the Russian and COMECON economies is so large that the likelihood of their being unable to repay their international debts is negligible. Further, as one American banking house put it in a recent report: "Since GNP and trading figures are not generally available, it is difficult to assess the economic risk of the USSR in particular. . . . we should view our risk as a strictly political one."[7] An optimistic recommendation followed, in which all that mattered politically was thrown in. Economic and financial considerations were simply left out after the preliminary statement which, in a way, absolved the author of the report from using the traditional, safe, cautious banking approach. The loan discussed in that memorandum was granted.

Other banks followed suit. Morgan Grenfell, a British bank, made an export credit agreement with the Soviet Union in 1972, extending a 25-million-pound line of credit. This was done within the framework of the ECGD (Exports Credit Guaranty Department) announcement made earlier, in which the ECGD said that it would guarantee financing of exports of capital goods to the U.S.S.R. up to the amount of 200 million pounds, at 6 percent interest. The time limitation was two years.

The credit was signed with the Soviet Bank for Foreign Trade, and shortly thereafter, two orders were consummated. A British firm, Wogau Machinery, agreed to supply the Soviet Union with a rivet plant. Another company promised delivery of another plant. There have been doubts in British industrial circles, however, that the Soviet Union will be able to use the entire line of credit of 200 million pounds before it expires in 1974.

The long-term financing problem came into focus when a syndicate of 20 Japanese banks agreed to supply about $1 billion to enable joint Soviet-Japanese development of oil reserves in Siberia. The loan is to be used to construct a pipeline from the Tyumen region to the port of Nakhoda on the Sea of Japan. The bulk of the funds is to be provided by Japan's Export Import Bank, Mitsui, the Industrial Bank of Japan, and the Long-Term Credit Bank of Japan. Because of its complexity and political implications, the deal is subject to the approval of the Japanese government.

Other British banks moved to extend lines of credit to Poland. National Westminster Bank decided to make a total of 18 million pounds available to finance exports to Polish buyers, with a minimum order value of 50,000 pounds. When the Westminster line of credit expired in early 1973, it was replaced by an identical agreement with Barclays Bank International. About this time, the U.S. Commodity Credit Corporation granted Poland a line of credit of $35 million for the purchase of agricultural products in the United States. And seven Japanese trade firms have combined forces to permit the Poles to purchase Japanese machinery and equipment in the amount of $200 million, repayable in eight years at 6.5 percent interest. Foundry equipment, licenses, and specialized equipment for the construction of an optical precision glass plant have been some of the first subcontracts under the loan signed with the Japanese.

These examples indicate a trend. In the meantime, Norwegian banks have extended their own lines of credit to enable Czechoslovakia to purchase Norwegian goods and licenses, and the first Romanian-American joint venture, involving the Control Data Corporation, has secured lines of credit for the purchase of equipment. This was included in a credit agreement negotiated with the Commercial Credit Company, a subsidiary of Control Data Corporation. The agreement, the first of its type, will provide the marketing know-how needed to develop the new venture's extensive trade projects with other, principally Western, countries.

Future Financing

This movement of money does not, however, solve the basic problem, that of the future financing of East-West trade. The Soviet Union, much more than the other countries in the socialist bloc, faces this problem. Will Western credits be adequate for meeting future Soviet needs? There appears to be a liberal tendency on the part of Western banks in general to take risks regarding the Soviet Union. When the American grain purchases were negotiated in 1972, the Soviet Union secured the approval of lines of credit up to $500 million from the Commodity Credit Corporation to finance the purchases. A number of American banks have indicated a willingness to grant commercial, nonguaranteed loans to the Soviet Union. Japan has moved in this direction also. Short- and medium-term, nonguaranteed credits can also be obtained by Russia in the Eurocurrency market. Further, some credits may be made available to the U.S.S.R. by the International Bank for Economic Cooperation, a COMECON institution. As a last resort, of course, there is the possibility of resuming sales of Soviet gold.

It seems that the complicated problem of moving into financial arrangements with the Eastern bloc, arrangements which must cross a conceptual and ideological barrier, is going to be with us for a long time to come. Multinational institutions dealing with international payments only barely touch the issue. There are only five east European countries which adhere to GATT, and the Soviet Union is not one of them. Czechoslovakia has been a contracting party since the beginning of GATT in 1947. Yugoslavia, Poland, Romania, and Hungary joined later. But GATT rules require adherence to the principles of the market economy. Yugoslavia qualified for normal membership. Poland acceded in a special agreement by which she undertook to increase her imports from each GATT member by a given percentage each year, in return for GATT members granting her most-favored-nation tariff treatment. Romania's provisions have been a little more flexible, permitting her to increase imports by amounts corresponding to the growth of her exports. The situation, which is far from satisfactory, has led a number of Western countries to suggest the creation of a new global economic organization which would represent both East and West. They have also suggested, in case the east European countries were willing to move toward multilateral trade and payments, to consider creation of a multilateral source of international liquidity.[8]

The Dilemma of Forced Growth

Despite the change of attitude toward the role of money, different conceptual approaches lie at the bottom of the financing dilemma. A double-layer factor illustrates this. On one side, countries like Czechoslovakia, East Germany, and Hungary run an export surplus with the Soviet Union, because of the Sovets' needs and for political reasons, while suffering a chronic shortage of Western-oriented export capacity. Incentives for them to adjust to the much more difficult Western markets have been increasing, but not enough to make much difference. On the other hand, or at a different layer of consideration, there is the socialist planners' inclination toward investments outstripping material resources. This is connected with the fact that, in most cases, production decisions are guided by producers', not consumers', preferences. "Producers" equals governments, and governments weigh political motivations heavily during the making of decisions in the planning stages. While in some smaller countries—for example, Hungary—decentralization has made some progress, the basic philosophy remains. Forced growth of investments, importing machinery and technology, exporting raw materials and agricultural commodities continue.

One school of thought among the economists feels that this situation will prevail, for reasons having little to do with a genuine economic growth, and that no matter how much capital is imported from the West, Eastern ability to earn hard currency will not increase significantly.[9] The increase can occur only if east European industrial output catches up with that of the West and becomes truly competitive in world markets. This is far from being realistic; some Western bankers and investors, assuming that that kind of a drastic change is at hand, are harboring dangerous illusions. Some east European countries have attempted to move in that direction, but they live in the shadow of the huge underdeveloped economy of the Soviet Union and have only limited flexibility. They are also being steadily pushed down in terms of product quality, a push that is difficult to resist and to readjust to when the recipient happens to be a Western, industrialized, sophisticated economy.

There is always the possibility that socialist banks, led by the International Bank for Economic Cooperation, will enter into the financing of East-West ventures and trade more forcefully. This would require a shift of emphasis from intrabloc to interbloc credits. It may also require more factual than merely planned integration of the members of COMECON in the field of banking and financing operations. A conflict of interest would immediately arise between Soviet and east European goals, but these conflicts wouldn't be a major hurdle for the bloc to overcome.

The Role of IBEC

Western money markets have lately been given greater attention by IBEC. The bank used to concentrate almost entirely on internal COMECON clearing accounts and transferable ruble credits. It granted long-term credits for such major socialist countries' projects as rebuilding the Tatra Motor Vehicle plant in Czechoslovakia and the Icarus Bus plant in Hungary and increasing the capacity of a Romanian plant for building railroad cars. The bank boasted of the stability of the common currency of the bloc—the transferable rubles —and pointed to its independence from the fluctuation of the international monetary system.

The move to Western money markets included taking a $60-million loan from a consortium of Western banks led by Crédit Lyonnais, consideration of placing a substantial bond issue on the money markets of western Europe, and considering a series of short-term bank loans to be used to finance long-term investment projects. This would be in line with the Soviet Union's keen interest in continuing to maintain close control of COMECON's credit policies. Greater integration of the financial activities of COMECON through the bank and the eventual introduction of a common, truly convertible currency would be one approach.

The other may be coordination of the activities of Western bankers who are particularly interested in East-West financing. This would require much more of a collective approach to East-West borrowing, making it possible to have a truly European approach to East-West economic cooperation. That would also require a different and more aggressive approach by the United States, where East-West illusions have often run head on into reality, causing discomfort, distrust, and retractions. West Germany has shown interest in involvement of the Community in East-West trade, but she has her own parochial political interests in mind. France looks toward EEC for support in her confrontations with the United States, and isn't particularly interested in any other arrangements. The possibility of widening the scope of the European Investment Bank to play a significant role in financing East-West trade should not, however, be dismissed out of hand.

Socialist Foreign Economic Policy

In the field of capital, credit, and money, as much as in direct trade, in which no credit is involved, the concept of the foreign economic policy of the socialist states is predominant. It is not being shaped according only to production and economic needs. Primary consideration is being given to the potential social and political consequences of any given contacts with the capitalist countries. The development of economic, monetary, and trade ties between the two world systems is a complex, internally contradictory process, as viewed by the U.S.S.R. and her allies. It also runs against conflicting sociopolitical forces.

Soviet needs are enormous. Her industrial dynamics are gradually transcending her own developmental resources. But as long as the present political framework remains, difficulties in contracting, negotiating, borrowing, securing data, and undertaking feasibility studies will continue. Western banks have been quite correct in assuming that their credit risks are purely political. They have been right also in waiving traditional conditions for granting loans in a number of cases. They may also consider the degree of political risk. This is a small and relatively minor risk. The considerations should also include the cyclical pattern of internal changes within the bloc in general and the Soviet Union in particular. These changes gravitate from orthodox to liberal attitudes toward the use of trade as an element of growth. It is true enough that current needs are vital for that growth, but it is also true that huge Western credits, in return for equally large Soviet deliveries of products and commodities, increase the political risks. Such deliveries, if substantial enough, could upset the economic equilibrium within the capitalist world. An example of large Soviet purchases which upset this equilibrium in a Western country was the Soviet purchase of U.S. wheat in 1972.

Conversely, large lines of Western credits for major structural development may lead to internal convulsions within the Soviet bloc. For instance, can Siberia be turned into a major oil-, gas-, and mineral-producing area without influencing the entire Soviet economy?

CHAPTER 9

Money and Credits:
Part II — Siberian Deposits in Need of Credits

A few days before Leonid Brezhnev's visit to the United States in 1973, the Novosti Press Agency in Moscow conducted an interview with the Soviet Minister of Oil Refining and Petrochemical Industry. The text of the interview was made available for worldwide distribution through United Press International. This was not a routine gesture in the Soviet Union. UPI, of course, complied with the request.

The gist of the minister's message was that international cooperation, pooling technological resources and providing a major chunk of Western capital, could produce wonders in Siberia. He cited the improved political climate and concluded that the time was ripe for meaningful cooperation. The U.S.S.R., he said, possessed unique resources of raw materials of hydrocarbon content.[1]

The minister knew his audience. He cited American specialized journals that had been emphasizing the problems the United States might soon face in the production of synthetic rubber. He suggested that an answer could perhaps be found in the Soviet Union, where organic synthetic products were being developed rapidly and a modern synthetic rubber industry was being created. He added that some aspects of Soviet technology in the field of polyisoprene rubber were being studied in the West. Perhaps a simple solution could be found. The Soviet Union was ready to sell synthetic rubber and rubber by-products, which were needed by the United States. In return, the Soviet Union would welcome deliveries of petrochemical refinery equipment, to be paid for with deliveries of refined oil and petrochemicals.

Thus the issue was stated openly and squarely. The technical and logistical problems of exploration in Siberia were not mentioned, nor was the form of cooperation. It was a matter of official record that the Soviet Union was interested in American participation in the Soviet development of Siberian gas and oil reserves. So the ball was now in the American court.

Brezhnev visited the U.S. and went home, but Siberia, as a potential golden egg of Soviet-American economic cooperation, did not capture headlines. It did stir up some discussion among bankers and industrialists about its actual potential, among some politicians concerned about getting into a venture which might, at some point, be used politically by the Russians, and among economists studying the entire problem. There was a sharp upturn of interest, which led to a lot of magazine and newspaper articles. Some businessmen were concerned that if the Soviet claims were even half true, Americans should get there first, before western Europe and Japan arrived with money and equipment.

The truth about the Siberian potential is much less dramatic. Gas and oil are definitely there, and Western interests are already involved, but the potential for development is limited. In fact, even a major capital investment and major transfer of capital goods to the area would not in itself satisfy Soviet needs. Developed for export, directed toward higher currency earnings, and viewed as a long-term project leading to eventual Soviet self-sufficiency in petrochemicals, the concept has possibilities. However, the time span must be measured in decades rather than years.

At the height of Western expectations, sometime in the last half of 1972, newspaper reports spoke of a giant deal that was nearly ready to be concluded between the United States and the Soviet Union, involving the purchase of $45.6 billion worth of Soviet natural gas. An initial expenditure of $10 billion would be made to lay a pipeline, to build the plants to liquefy gas, and to provide an adequate fleet of tankers. Such "minor" problems as laying 2,500 miles of pipe through the Siberian permafrost and other geologically tough areas were discussed. The building of a $750-million plant at the port of Nahodka, on the South Japan Sea, where the gas would be liquefied, and providing a fleet of 10 tankers capable of carrying liquefied natural gas, also entered the picture. A second pipe leading to Murmansk would provide an outlet for the American east coast. A fleet of 20 tankers would be needed.

The pipelines and liquefaction plants would be built by American companies but would be owned by the Soviet Union. The Export-Import Bank would finance part of the construction, and the rest would be financed by commercial banks and companies. The size of the project was measured in terms of the flow of Soviet gas, beginning in 1980, when the rate was expected to be five billion cubic feet of gas per day. The reserves would last 25 years. This would amount to roughly 5 to 7 percent of U.S. gas consumption at that time.

The entire venture was to be three-sided, involving the Soviet Union, Japan, and the United States.[2]

Soviet Domestic Needs

The Siberian venture had all the aspects of the situation in which the United States found herself a century ago, with a virtually unexplored region waiting to be developed. A huge flow of people looking for greener pastures walked, drove wagons, and rode trains to work, starve, and strike it rich in the American west. But this comparison is unfair to the Russians. The climate of the American west is a paradise compared to that of Siberia, a fact that is testified to by the labor forces that have been recruited to work on the oil exploration projects.

Yet the Siberian venture is badly needed. It is needed in terms of the new Soviet economic policy; but it is needed even more when one looks at domestic requirements combined with the expansion of Soviet industry. The two are linked. The expanding Soviet automobile industry cannot continue unless oil and lubricants are produced in the required quantity. There are other sources of supply, but they are expensive and not always politically sound (the Arabs, naturally, come to mind).

All available indications support the contention that the west Siberian venture will continue to receive high Soviet priority. The Soviet government is ready to take the risk of shifting the major production centers from Baku and other traditional sources to Siberia. The investment rate of about 16 percent annually in the Siberian area is high, but it has been fairly stable during the past decade or so. However, the Siberian region is not the only one included in the list of areas being considered for high investment rates in Soviet economic plans. The agricultural sector, the consumer goods sector, the nonferrous metals, and electrification programs are also on the list.

This does not mean that the Siberian project will be put on the back burner. It merely compounds the Soviet economic dilemma. While current supplies of oil are adequate to meet domestic and foreign requirements, continuing satisfactory arrangements will call on additional imports of equipment and technology. This is where Western help is needed. This is what the Minister of Oil Refining was talking about. This is why the Japanese and the Americans are being courted. There are times when the Soviet Union must have pangs of fear. During the 1967 Middle East war, the Soviet Union was faced with the problem of continuing deliveries of her oil to some of her Asian customers. Several emergency agreements were quickly concluded. The closing of the Suez Canal cut off the Far East from normal Soviet deliveries.

Considerable ingenuity is evident in the agreements. Shell and British Petroleum have provided 700,000 barrels of gasoline and gas oil from the Persian Gulf and Aden to the U.S.S.R. for delivery to Ceylon. In return, the two companies obtained a comparable amount of Soviet gasoline and gas oil in the Black Sea for their markets in western Europe.

Another swap involved Soviet crude oil originally destined for Japan. This was delivered to British Petroleum for disposal in western Europe. In return, the company undertook to supply an equal amount of Persian Gulf crude to Japan. Italy and France joined in similar swap arrangements.[3]

The 1967 war and the problems it caused the Soviets illustrate the importance of the Siberian project. Needed raw materials are there, technical capabilitiies can be developed, and credits can be secured.

Another important aspect of the Soviet Union's needs concerns her deliveries to eastern Europe. With Siberian exploration underway, the continuity of Soviet deliveries to her east European allies can be assured. If they aren't, problems may arise, problems not only of an economic, but of a political nature. When at one point during a discussion of oil supplies, a Polish spokesman suggested imports of Middle Eastern oil rather than Soviet oil, the figure of 630 million barrels of imported Middle East oil by 1980 was mentioned. Such a change would be a severe blow to east European dependency on Soviet oil deliveries. It could make the plans for a closer bloc integration even shakier than they have been so far. Deliveries of crude oil to eastern Europe were over a billion barrels during the 1966–70 period.

The total Soviet production of crude oil in 1970—to use some comparative figures—reached 2,436,000,000 barrels. Domestic demand was relatively small, only 1,617,000,000 barrels. Deliveries to other Communist countries, which included crude oil and other petroleum products, reached 329 million barrels, a figure almost identical to the 322 million delivered to non-Communist countries. The percentage increase, however, was different. Over the previous five years, Soviet deliveries to eastern Europe increased by 18.1 percent, to non-Communist countries by only 10.5 percent.[4]

Prospects for growth in the future are proportionate to the past. The 1971–75 plan calls for an increase of about 770 million barrels, to a total of 3,220,000,000 in 1975. The shift to Siberia, however, will call for installation of fully automated oil field equipment, designed with the extreme fluctuation of temperatures in mind. The logistics of importing and moving heavy drilling equipment, or providing a steady flow of supplies, and of making the entire project attractive enough to those involved staggers the imagination. As one American observer remarked, the Soviet search for oil in the Siberian wastelands undoubtedly will turn out to be the most expensive program in her history.[5]

Japan Looks at Siberia

Hungry for fuel, self-assured that her technology can overcome all obstacles, Japan has been eyeing Siberian possibilities for some time. When an oil mission was invited to the Soviet Union in June 1972, it came back with a conclusion befitting Japanese optimism: "Technically speaking, it is a project worth undertaking."[6]

But the amount of capital needed is too much even for the Japanese, and they have made a concerted effort to get the Americans to participate. A complication arose when Russian claims about the size of their Siberian reserves proved difficult, almost impossible, to verify.

Yet the idea is not defunct. The Japanese have watched carefully the Soviet-American political and economic dialogue, hoping that it will lead to a firmer commitment to the Siberian venture. After the American opening with China and the détente with the Soviets, reports were circulated in Japan (late 1972) that a triangular approach had been made toward Siberia. A memorandum was cited by one of the Japanese newspapers, suggesting that an understanding had been reached in several areas. They included Soviet permission for a Japanese survey of the Yakutsk development area, the supply of equipment needed to liquefy natural gas, transportation of liquefied gas, and, finally, provision for credits. The memorandum reportedly included a provision for participation by U.S. enterprises.[7]

If implemented, these agreements would permit exportation of about 44 billion cubic yards, of which half will go to Japan. In order to reach this figure, Japan is to provide total lines of credits of $2.5 to $3 billion over a 20-year period, beginning in 1978.

The background of Japan's willingness to take such a calculated political, financial, and economic risk involves various factors. Aside from pure economy and concern over the supply of fuel, Japan has been watching both China and the Soviet Union. A delicate balance of potential dependence must be preserved. Chinese suspicion of Japanese moves toward too close a relationship with the Soviet Union must be allayed. Thus Japan, hoping for American participation, wants the United States to share the economic risks. The U.S. is also needed to provide a political balance, in addition to a political justification.

Domestically, Japan is determined to move toward a greater degree of self-support. Her goal is to develop local sources to supply one-third of her crude oil needs by 1985. In 1967 the Oil Development Corporation was established, and a number of private companies entered the field. Also, foreign oil companies are concentrating on the continental shelf in the ocean adjacent to Japan. In her plans to assure a flow of sources of energy, Japan has included in her foreign assistance program a provision for developing oil reserves in countries where they exist or may exist.

While this is being done, Japan has also been moving rapidly into the area of nuclear power. License agreements have been concluded for the induction of light-water reactors.[8] Several commercial reactors of this type had been introduced and used in Japan by mid-1973.

It is hoped that by the late 1970s, the cost of nuclear power will be competitive and thus attainable. Environmental safety and the establishment of nuclear fuel cycles are two problems that must be solved before nuclear power can be used extensively. A series of agreements have been concluded with the United States for the purchase of uranium concentrate and enriched uranium.

What the Japanese view as long-term plans for the Siberian project involves securing roughly 8 percent of their fuel needs from the Soviet Union by the end of the 1970s. This figure is a compromise between what the Russians are ready to offer (175 million barrels a year) and what Japan wants (280 million barrels). But even this compromise figure is large enough to worry some Japanese—politically, not economically.

While negotiating for oil, the Japanese stumbled on another Soviet proposition—the developing of large Yakutsk coal fields. The Soviet Union needs an additional 5 million tons of coking coal annually for making steel. Should the Japanese be interested in an investment of a mere $350 million in the form of loans, the Russians would probably look with favor on Japan's entry into other sources of Soviet energy.

There was a large silence on the Japanese side for a long time after the proposal was made, but another reaction has been noted regarding petroleum. World population growth for the next decade or so is being projected at a rate of 2 percent, while world economic growth is expected to be about 5.1 percent. The demand for energy per unit of GNP is expected to increase by 11.7 percent. In order to meet this demand, it will be necessary to discover additional reserves of 20 to 35 billion tons.

The huge capital investment required, the Japanese concluded, plus the risks involved, transcend the possibilities of a single business corporation or even a single nation. Multinationalism is the answer. When looking at the potential in Siberia—and the problems—the Japanese also see multinational involvement as the answer. This is why the Siberian oil and gas deposits may have to wait awhile before being tapped.

Types of Agreements

The United States and Europe have voiced similar misgivings, but they have gone ahead and signed a few documents. A letter of intent was exchanged in 1973 between the Soviet Foreign Trade Ministry and El Paso Natural Gas Company and Occidental Petroleum Corporation. It was a grandiose document. If implemented, it would involve the outlay of about $10 billion, permitting the importation of Siberian natural gas to the American west coast. Other American companies were also involved but were unwilling to go even as far as a letter of intent. There is a considerable difference of opinion among Western observers as to the degree of risk that El Paso and Occidental were taking. Some even consider the move as an excellent psychological breakthrough for potential deals in the future, deals with a more realistic base than that of Siberian gas.

There have been other instances of Western willingness to move. A West German company has agreed to provide the U.S.S.R. with large-diameter transmission pipe. A line of credit was extended, amounting to 1.2 billion DM, repayable in 10 years at 6 percent interest. The final provision stipulates that payments be made through Soviet deliveries of natural gas to West Germany. This was the element of risk that the West Germans were willing to take. Repayment was thus conditional on the successful development of gas fields and on the assumption that proven gas reserves exist.[9] The Germans have concluded a barter agreement.

A different type of cooperation was stipulated by the North Star project, in which three large American companies are involved—Texas Eastern Transmission, Brown & Root, and Tenneco. While El Paso and Occidental plan to move about 2 billion cubic feet of Soviet natural gas daily through a pipeline to the port of Vladivostok and then to the United States, the other three companies are concentrating on the Tuymen gas fields. Their goal is even more ambitious: 3 billion cubic feet daily to Murmansk and then to the U.S. east coast.

If realized, the North Star project will provide for extraction, liquefaction, and export of gas. The proposal of an agreement could have wide repercussions transcending economic significance. On-site inspection will have to be allowed, not only in order to make an intelligent estimate of the actual reserves, but also to calculate the cost of extraction.

The investment called for is substantial. The American companies are suggesting credits of $3 billion, with a $700-million cash fund provided by the Soviet Union, to be used for the purchase of American-made transmission equipment. This will consist, among other things, of compressors and 1,500 miles of 48-inch steel pipe capable of operating in temperatures of −60 degrees Fahrenheit. A liquefying plant is to be erected at Murmansk to facilitate shipment by tanker. Twenty such special tankers are to be built by the American partners in the venture, for an estimated price tag of $2.6 billion.

Funds for making credits available are to be obtained from the Export-Import Bank. The amount the bank is expected to provide is $1.5 billion, repayable at 6 percent interest. The rest of the money is to be obtained from commercial American banks, insurance companies, and future suppliers.

These moves indicate both competitiveness and a convergence of American and Japanese interests in the Siberian development project. For the time being, there is more convergence than competition, due to the size of the investments needed and the understandable reluctance of both countries to undertake alone an enterprise of such dimensions in a not entirely friendly environment.

There is also another type of convergence, one of economic interests and sociopolitical changes. The injection of large Western credits into the Siberian oil and gas explorations will require not only on-site inspection, but also proper technical and living facilities for technicians from the U.S. and the other countries involved. Would the Russians agree to this? Would they let engineers, builders, drillers, and machine operators enter, and would they assure them the freedom of movement they are accustomed to? Henry Kearns, chairman of the Export-Import Bank, the key institution for securing large credits, has given part of the answer. The Soviet authorities, he said in response to a congressional inquiry, do not provide as much information as is normally needed to grant very large credits. He also warned about undue optimism regarding the Siberian project.[10]

In any liquefied natural gas exploration project, the bank requires careful study of reserves and the possibility of delivering the fuel at a price the market will bear. The bank has considerable expertise in this type of financing, due to its negotiations in the past with a variety of countries. Altogether, 14 such projects went through the bank's negotiating process; one with Algeria took 10 years to bring to fruition. These agreements, Kearns observed, are usually very complex. Some of the data which must be obtained in each case concerns currency and gold reserves. The Soviet Union considers such information highly sensitive.

The conclusion springs to mind with blinding force: a revolution must occur. The Soviet Union needs credits in order to develop her natural resources, a development which may prove essential to her economic growth, strengthen her political options in Asia, and earn her additional currencies. It could also help her to continue as the chief supplier of oil and lubricants to eastern Europe.

In order to secure such credits, the Soviet Union may be forced to play the game the way her creditors want her to play it. If she does, it will be a revolution in itself, with social and political implications that will be difficult to predict.

If the Soviet Union does not, her resources will remain idle, aside from what she alone will be able to do in terms of investment and exploration. The pace will be slow; results will lag behind need. The east Europeans may look for other sources of supply. The Japanese may start paying closer attention to the Chinese potential. Another kind of revolution would then start.

Once again, the outcome is linked closely to political psychology. Fear of losing the status quo may once again stop natural progress. Boldness in seeing long-term advantages would have the opposite effect, but the Soviet political and economic structure has much to lose should normal Western practices, as suggested by Henry Kearns, be allowed to enter Russia's closed society.

The choice is difficult. The outcome—no matter what the decision is—is of the highest importance to the Soviet Union, as well as her current or would-be partners.

CHAPTER 10

The Interaction of Trade, Détente, and Change

Dogma and the Exigencies of Reality

Fear of change is part of human nature. Change challenges the attitudes, habits, and prescribed methods of behavior. "Millions sleepwalk their way through their lives as if nothing has changed since the 1930s, and as if nothing ever will," wrote Alvin Toffler in *Future Shock.* The vast majority of people, he added, find the idea of change so threatening that they attempt to deny its existence. Therefore, the opposition to change became part of the social scene and of human behavior.

In the ever-moving, ever-evolving pattern of international politics, opposition to change usually produces autarchic economies and authoritarian political systems. In the juxtaposition of the two basically different and inimical systems, change is often interpreted as a sign of weakness rather than a movement indicating progress. It signals flexibility, which is considered a sin within the dogma of prescribed faith. That faith often indulges in predictions and commandments. Looking at each other across ideological barriers, capitalism and socialism indulge in all of these luxuries.

In *Das Kapital,* Marx predicted the fall and disintegration of capitalism. "Along with the constantly diminishing number of magnates of capital . . . grows the revolt of the working class, a class always increasing in numbers, and disciplines, united, organized by the very mechanism of the process of capitalist production itself. . . . The productive forces of society come into contradiction with the existing productive relationship. . . . The knell of capitalist private property sounds. The expropriators are expropriated."

After communism became a reality in the Soviet Union, its fall became part of capitalist dogma, triggering the ill-fated military intervention after the October Revolution. It brought about a vacuum in the relations between the principal capitalist states and the new Russian government. The brief unity of purpose in World War II was followed by the cold war, in which the two sides, each wedded to its theories of mutual exclusion, wished each other's political death.

Both theories proved wrong. Both dogmas created mutual fear and distrust. Both sides went through a period of calcified convictions, which on more than one occasion brought the world to the verge of a major conflict. The incredible destructive power of modern weapons has reduced the globe to peripheral dangers. Instead of Danzig or Sarajevo, the world has seen Vietnam, Korea, and the Middle East. Capitalism and socialism regard each other across limited battlefields manned by small nations.

While the superpowers fought limited skirmishes, they began to throw side glances at the possibility of convergence of outlook. What, according to political and economic dogma, was considered heretical, was reduced by practical necessity to simple sin. Mutual interests emerged in spite of such heresies. They were superimposed by the human genius of creativity. Science and technology did more to bring Russians and Americans to the conference table than any other factor. Science and technology have built weapons of such destructiveness that nothing but a death wish could justify their use. So there have been negotiations. Science and technology created the new, unexplored areas for the betterment of human life. So again, there were negotiations.

With creativity has come change. The two human characteristics fought each other the way a disease encounters inner resistance in the human body. Fear of change and adherence to the known—the safe and the accepted—has gradually been pushed back by the desire for change, the urge for change, the encouragement for change in the noncontroversial field of scientific endeavors. In looking at the future of the two systems, Robert L. Heilbroner sees social fatalism being replaced by social purpose. "The long period of acquiescence before the gods, whether manifest in the forces of nature or masquerading as priests and rulers, is coming to an end. For better or worse, the passivity of the general run of men is waning. Where there was resignation, there is now impatience. Where there was acceptance, there is now the demand for control."[1]

Heilbroner also sees in the future a better adaptability of economic institutions of socialism to the exigencies of survival than those of capitalism, in spite of socialism's failure to develop incentives and to eliminate the cumbersomeness of a planning mechanism. He expressed hope that political institutions of liberal capitalism will show themselves to be more functional than those of authoritarian socialism. Approaching what Adolph Lowe calls "the end of social fatalism,"[2] the world must pay more attention, pay more heed, play a more active role in the potential of convergence of the two systems.

This is where trade and economics come in, but it is also where the fear of change is greatest. Political stability has been accomplished in the socialist camp by eliminating freedom of choice. Fear that such freedom can be indirectly restored through change persists. On the capitalist side, a different fear is opposed to change, a fear that change or no change, freedom isn't going to be restored. Underneath this seemingly impossible impasse, forces of human creativity have begun to bore a tunnel of convergence.

Warnings and Reflections

Andrei D. Sakharov, the leading Soviet physicist, issued his own warning. For the first time in postwar history, for the first time since the divergence of Western and Eastern views emerged, a voice came from the Soviet Union pleading for human freedom. It is also a voice for change. He probably never expected that within a few years dissent would move too fast for the system to digest. Forcible expulsion of Alexander Solzhenitsyn, followed by others, illustrated the point. Sakharov, representing the apex of Soviet intellectual creativity, called for reform of the system. While his call went unheard, he turned to the West, warning against assisting the closed, repressive Soviet society. What he asked for was a trade-off approach, an approach that would permit the use of imported technology for the new approach to social and human values. What he warned against was the tendency of Soviet leaders to plow acquired knowledge into the existing system. Accumulation of military strength for outside use and a police force for domestic use are the two main goals of the regime. Western powers who enter into a closer relationship with the Soviet Union must keep this in mind. Their leverage is greater than they know or suspect, and it should be used.

A different kind of warning came from another Communist dissenter—Milovan Djilas. Not meant as a warning, but rather as a statement of fact related to the change as he has been observing it, it was noted and anxiously analyzed by the socialist countries. "The most significant change in eastern Europe is the dissolution of totalitarianism," Djilas wrote, "that is, the development of social differentiation and the gradual transition to the market economy. Democracy is not on the horizon, but neither can the withering away of totalitarianism be halted. Eastern European countries are wading deeper and deeper into the consumer society, even though in the West such a society is in bad repute with idealists."[3]

The two voices, one Russian and one Yugoslav, touched on the gamut of built-in problems with the East-West framework. While Sakharov called for the reintroduction of moral principles into economic dealings, he also told his Western friends not to underestimate their own bargaining power. Djilas's message had a different significance. He saw the process of convergence as much more advanced than the average man could recognize. He also served notice on his former ideological comrades that what they feared was already there: the emergence of a consumer society. It was emerging, not only in economic, but also in sociological and political terms. It has been observed by watching human attitudes. It has been moving into the forefront of young people's thinking, the post-World War II generation, for whom Communist governments were a part of their growing-up period, a fixture of modern life, an established power base.

Djilas's warning was not taken lightly in the socialist camp. It is one of the truisms, often repeated, that even purely economic contact with the West can have ideological implications. Consumerism, a word and concept frowned on by socialist leaders, is imported together with technology. Furthermore, economic contacts can lead to a strengthening of belief in the gradual convergence of the two socioeconomic systems—the way Djilas sees it—an idea which is viewed by Eastern ideologists as one of the most misleading and incorrect concepts. In fact, the theory goes, the concept has been created by Westerners in order to secure better acceptance of their trade with the East back home.

There is widespread reflection in the socialist bloc on the issue of Western contact with the East. The dangers are underscored, but the strengths have also been mentioned. Not unlike the West, the period of détente is viewed with mixed feelings. In the West, fear of détente centers on the possibility of the fragmentation of Western solidarity. In the East, fear is focused on the new necessity to reinstill the principles of socialist humanism in the people. After more than a generation of controlled socialist schooling, the young people have left their school benches with more doubts than their elders. The reasons advanced by the leaders include, first, the harmful influence of Western ideology. The external, and sometimes attractive, aspects of capitalism must be fully explained before they will be permitted to confront young minds.

A classic piece of writing on the subject appeared in Poland in mid-1972, rather early in the latest détente. It tackled the problem of limiting the adverse effects of outside contacts.[4] These contacts, unless they are carefully watched, can be harmful. They can affect socialist ideological stability. On the other hand, these contacts cannot be stopped altogether. Socialism simply has to be strengthened and made more immune to Western goods, ideas, and technology.

An improved standard of living and a drift toward consumerism cannot, in themselves, be the goal of a socialist society. Young people are more susceptible, since they never experienced the oppressive capitalist systems that existed in some east European countries before World War II. But aside from protecting them and warning them of the dangers of contacts with the West, it is true, Eastern ideologists apparently are saying that the purpose of détente is to avoid war. This does not at all imply that the socialist camp sanctions the capitalist social system or even that it implies that it has a right to exist. "The Communist party of the Soviet Union has proceeded and still proceeds," stated Chairman Brezhnev, "from the premise that the class struggle of the two systems in the sphere of economics, politics, and of course, ideology will continue. It cannot be otherwise, because the world outlook and class objectives of socialism and capitalism are opposite and irreconcilable."[5]

As a result of expanded Western contacts, principally in the field of economics, east Europeans plan to increase their ideological vigilance. The long-term goal is to develop the young people's socialist personalities, to immunize them against foreign influences, and to teach them how to insure the victory of socialism. There is nothing more convincing, telling, or persuasive, when reading about these measures, than the warning Sakharov issued.

The process of convergence has begun. Fences are being hurriedly built to make it a mechanical, rather than substantive, change. Neither Sakharov nor Djilas believes that this is possible. But looking at the socialist spectrum, one is more inclined to see effective fences in Russia than elsewhere. The role of American traders, bankers, and legislators grows more significant there. Djilas's concern with the change in eastern Europe is different; that is why a different defense is apparently being erected. Poland, Hungary, and the other socialist republics have demonstrated their willingness to accept economic change. Their new ideological offensive, which was dormant for a long time, might very well be a self-preserving mechanism. A genuine entry of a market economy into these countries can be viewed as a dangerous phenomenon by the Russians, but the Poles and others have done enough to reassure them that the problem has been noted and that the socialist countries in eastern Europe will not go too far.

Western Attitudes

The difference between the Western and Eastern attitudes toward mutual contacts illustrates the problem, one that is visible at every turn of events, every moment of change. There is no doubt (or shouldn't be) that a decision to reopen the economic channels was made with American interests in mind. The forging of closer trade links, it was assumed, was the best method for securing a détente—and détente, in Western terms, means a lot, but very little in socialist terms.

Economic and trade relations would permit arms negotiations, could lessen armament pressures, and bring about some kind of accommodation within SALT, MBFR, and the European Security Conference negotiations. These relations could conceivably permit individual socialist countries to count more on their own and on Western-imported resources than on those from the Soviet Union. Polycentrism within the bloc could be gratifying to the Western powers.

Moderation at home might evolve. This is what those like Sakharov want and what those like Djilas have predicted. Economic reforms could not have been made in a Stalinist atmosphere. They were now possible, and it was a change for the better.

The difference in approach, therefore, lay in the ideological thrust of the East as well as the strategic actions of the West. Both are politically motivated, but they are different in their objectives. The Soviet Union appears to be playing for time to catch up economically with the West. The political contest is in the form of preserving the bloc's cohesiveness. Without it, the entire game would be played quite differently.

The West seems to be concentrating on a global strategy of international security. Along with trade exchanges, this strategy is a prime objective. The side benefits of détente would be a stand-off attitude on the part of the big powers in peripheral conflicts. It would also add to mutual dependency, thus reducing the chances of big power involvement.

A successful conclusion of the SALT talks is viewed not only as a way to ease the problem of defense budgets in the West, but also as a useful domestic tool in the East. It is possible that the Soviet Union, once SALT is concluded, will be willing to reorder her priorities and pay more attention to her own economic needs, which, in turn, may easily lead to a significant change in Soviet international trade.

On the domestic fronts of the socialist countries, the influx of Western trade and the growing reformist mood among the economists could conceivably lead to more liberal, relaxed internal systems. It may also lead to greater independence from the Soviet Union of the smaller bloc countries. But this would run counter to what the Soviet leaders desire. A plan for a drastic change in the economic and social structure brought Soviet armies into Czechoslovakia. Hungary's successful economic experiment is a tightrope walk between economic progress and political acceptability. Sakharov's warning was a signal that the Soviet Union continues to maintain her internal grip despite her opening to the West. Sakharov felt that it could be loosened by a tougher Western stand, but it is possible that internal manifestations of totalitarian controls are maintained partly in order to emphasize the durability of the Soviet system. The recurring theme in the Soviet press is not that Soviet-Western economic openings will cause the two systems to converge. On the contrary, such openings are bound to change capitalist society; they are bound to strengthen the socialist nations.

The complexities of the newly begun relationship were simplified somewhat by Henry Kissinger during one of his numerous appearances at congressional hearings. "Some factors," he said, "such as the fear of nuclear war, the emerging consumer economy, and the increased pressures of technological, administrative society, have encouraged the Soviet leaders to seek a more stable relationship with the United States. Other factors such as ideology, bureaucratic inertia, and the catalytic effect of turmoil in peripheral areas have prompted pressures for tactical gains."[6] Then Kissinger added: "But now both we and the Soviet Union have begun to find that each increment of power does not necessarily represent an increment of usable political strength."

Also, on the Western side (including the American), there is a fair amount of healthy skepticism about how much trade can be an element in the détente policy and how much it is a factor in Soviet political thinking.

There seems to be a limited ratio of interaction to the growth of trade and the descent of political détente. Aside from the 1972 wheat sale, the growth of Soviet-American trade has been relatively limited. Memories persisted of the earlier periods when Soviet trade was viewed as an undiscovered gold mine and when it was proved to have been no mine of any kind. In a way, official statistics prove the point, despite demonstrated growth. American exports to the whole socialist bloc amounted to $872 million in 1972 and are projected in terms of $2.5 to $4.7 billion by 1978. Imports in 1972 were worth $354 million and are projected by the U.S. Department of Commerce at the level of $1.2 to $1.7 billion by 1978.

By themselves, these figures look fairly good, but there are two aspects of them which should be discussed. One is that, even if predictions come true, the entire trade volume with the East would barely comprise 2 percent of the U.S. foreign trade total. In 1930, before the Soviet Union was recognized by the United States, 3 percent of American exports went to the Soviet Union. American trade with the Russians will never be more than a small fraction of American trade with, say, Canada. It will not be a factor in the American economic situation despite the fact that it would help ease the American balance-of-payments situation. The balance of payments brings up another aspect: the Soviet Union's balance of payments and balance of trade, if the forecast is accurate.

U.S. imports have trailed behind exports from the socialist bloc. A relatively small positive balance of trade in 1972 in the Americans' favor ($574 million) would grow to a substantial figure of between $1.2 to $3 billion by 1978. Is this a situation that the Soviet leaders would tolerate, permit to develop consciously, counting on either another moratorium or a dramatic change in the Soviet export commodity structure, which would permit more Soviet exports to the West?

Another kind of Western skepticism has also been heard, which is more political than economic. An expanded trade consisting of Western capital and technology is bound to be used to strengthen an ideological enemy. Giving credit to a potential enemy is risky. Suppose that when the Soviet energy sources are developed with the assistance of Western investments, to be repaid with raw materials, political dependency ensues. A look at the Arab countries playing oil politics should be enough to sober those who dream of replacing some of the Middle East supplies with those of Siberia.

These voices are, however, rare and somewhat subdued. Western attitudes, in spite of warnings from both sides, lean toward doing business with the Russians. The signs of change on various socialist horizons encourage these attitudes. Security, détente, and the need for expanded markets are all pushing in the direction of closer economic relationships.

Soviet Attitudes

Different misgivings appeared in the East. The ideology was not at the center; economic and technological considerations were.

The détente has been hailed as one of the principal aims of Soviet foreign policy as the best way to deal with the other superpower, the way to coexist. Yet not for a moment were differences glossed over. Not for a moment was the Soviet reader permitted to forget the basic weakness of the capitalist system. Détente meant a ceasefire, a respite, a way to avoid nuclear war, a way to strengthen the socialist system. The notion that trade, commerce, and the importation of technology were badly needed was repeatedly rejected.

The Soviet Union could easily continue to exist without much importing from the developed world. What led to the détente has been the change within that world. These changes were forced by the dynamics of socialism. "The growing might of socialism," Brezhnev said at the International Conference of Communist and Workers' Parties in Moscow, "the liquidation of the colonial regimes, and the force of the workers' movement are having an ever-increasing influence on the internal processes and policies of imperialism. Many important features of present-day imperialism are explained by the fact that it is being forced to adjust to new conditions, to the conditions of the struggle between two systems."[7]

Thus the struggle goes on. It will continue to be a major factor in Soviet-American relations in the years to come. That struggle will also continue to be characterized differently by the two systems. For the Russians, it will be a class struggle. For the Americans, it will be a competitive struggle for better markets, better services, more abundant production.

The Soviet Union sees the trade issue as part of the struggle. There may be nothing wrong with this approach, an approach born out of ideological beliefs, but rather, one translated into pragmatic terms of deals and agreements. The only remaining issue for the Americans to understand is the nature of the deals and their motivations. In the totality of the socioeconomic system of the defensive socialist bloc, trade is not a way to earn a better living; rather, it is a tool in the arsenal of socialist weapons, to be used whenever it is needed. That use can be commercial, economic, or political. In the past, it has been a combination of all three, with its political underpinning coming directly to the surface.

The Soviet attitude is also colored by the actual needs of the Soviets, which are numerous and diverse. They range from basic consumer goods to grain and technology. They include long-term credits, an essential element in the future Soviet development patterns.

The most promising way to promote the development of Soviet-American trade was seen in the special cooperation agreements. American capital, for instance, would enter the Soviet Union to develop such natural resources as petroleum, natural gas, ores, nonferrous metals, lumber, and pulp. The investors would be repaid in products rather than cash. Development of joint patenting and sales of licenses would be another way. Joint participation in constructing industrial facilities in Third World countries is still another way.

The Soviet economists and political leaders who advocated this line of action have also suggested a reciprocal possibility. In the United States, enterprises can be created in those sectors in which Soviet technology appears to be superior.[8] Metallurgy, coke, blast furnace and converter production, hydroelectric and thermal power stations, the construction of high-voltage transmissions were mentioned. The interesting part of this proposal has been its target. The story was published in the Soviet Union but was not circulated abroad. While Soviet technology is being sought by several American companies, this type of cooperation in the United States would be quite a departure. Its feasibility has yet to be tested.

Appeals for Western credits remain the crux of the Soviet approach. Examples of existing cooperation agreements with several west European countries were cited as the ideal concept: credits extended, paid off with gas and oil delivered from the Soviet Union. Or, as in the case of France, Italy, and Austria, from whom the Soviet Union imports machinery, equipment, pipe, and various industrial materials, paying in oil and gas. Prospects for this type of international trade are waved in front of many dazed American businessmen. When Occidental Petroleum signed its preliminary agreement early in 1973, it was hailed as exactly the kind of deal which should be encouraged and repeated. Long-term credits will be used by the Russians to purchase equipment to permit production of large amounts of ammonia and urea. Once the complex is constructed, the Soviet Union will purchase annually one million tons of superphosphoric fertilizer from the United States. Payments will be made in the form of other commodities, such as Soviet-produced ammonia, urea, and potassium chloride.

The value of the total operations has been estimated by the Russians at $6 billion. There has been some doubt among Americans as to the feasibility of such a large transaction ever being consummated.

In the private discussions which many of the Soviet representatives held with their American counterparts, there were indications that genuine need exists and that the Soviets' attitudes are influenced by those needs. In several cases, the negotiating technocrats are ready to forgo the ideological jargon, which pleases their counterparts no end. The fact that the technocrats are only doing their job often escapes the uninitiated eye of an American negotiator.

What the current Soviet technological requirements amount to can best be summarized in five major points.[9] Large-scale petroleum and natural gas extraction, transmission, and distribution—including solution to problems of permafrost and oil recovery—is just one of the major areas of need. There have been efforts to secure outside assistance in the form of credits and equipment. Japan and the United States figure prominently in Soviet plans as potential suppliers.

The other area is transportation. Mass production of cars and trucks is envisioned. The Togliatti plant in which Fiat is involved, and Kama, where substantial American credits have been pledged, are the biggest efforts to date.

Management control systems using computer facilities, animal husbandry, and the development of tourist networks, including the building of hotels, transport, and the development of package tours, are the remaining areas of potential growth. For all of them, Western capital and technology have been requested.

The degree to which individual industries are dependent on imports is not clear. An extreme example illustrates this. All of the equipment in a large electric station is produced domestically in the Soviet Union. The only exception is a high-voltage switch, which has to be imported. Without the switch, which costs a fraction of that of the plant, the efficiency of the power plant cannot be achieved.[11] The relationship between local production and imported technology cannot be measured adequately. Should the switch be considered the key to the production of the power plant or as merely an adjunct? Should it be viewed as dependency (efficiency) or as marginal import?

Soviet attitudes are as difficult to define as is this type of semidependency on Western imports.

Multinationals—The New Soviet Allies

The change, the détente, and Soviet needs have produced one of those topsy-turvy situations which delight sociologists and bring political scientists to the depths of despair. The Soviet Union, the first socialist country in the world, the arch-enemy of cartels, monopolies, and the like, began glancing in the direction of multinational companies. The courting began in a moment when the giant companies needed friends more than ever. Under considerable scrutiny within their own family environments in the capitalist world, the multinationals are delighted.

It was Jermen Gvishiani, deputy chairman of the Soviet Union's Council of Ministers for Science and Technology, who signaled the new approach. Considered one of the chief spokesmen of the Soviet liberals who want to explore and exploit all possible avenues of economic growth, Gvishiani has been commuting to the United States for some time. His message is always clear: the Soviet Union is ready to cooperate and do business. In his multinational approach, he even went one step further. He talked about international economic cooperation as a platform for social improvements. He also denounced the theory of the limits of growth. This, he said, would be harmful rather than beneficial to the resolution of social problems.

The Soviet official chose an appropriate platform for floating his new peace offer to the multinationals. The occasion was the International Industrial Conference in San Francisco in 1973. It attracted a large number of industrialists from as many as 75 countries. But the location and participation heavily favored the multinationals, who were represented by some of their top officers who, in turn, listened with surprise and probably pleasure to the Soviet speaker. "We have particularly urged cooperation from American international companies," he asserted. "We are undertaking feasibility studies now and I would not exclude that in the not too distant future, we will come to some very interesting agreements."[12] The road is long and difficult, he added. Soviet-American economic cooperation has been neither smooth nor of lasting quality. But it is now ready to take off, realizing that economic growth ought to be the principal goal for both capitalist and socialist countries alike. Gvishiani talked about poverty and starvation. "The problem is not to stop or limit considerably the economic growth, but to insure it in the most effective way. Only economic growth creates the real conditions for the improvement of the quality of life," he added.

These points raised a number of interesting issues. There has been an extra dimension lately to the activities of the multinational corporations, thanks to a new shift in American foreign policy. The

Sino-Soviet split and the opening of China to the U.S. offer new potential. Major deals are contemplated, and in some cases, were made by the multinationals with Peking. Boeing, RCA, and others have been active there at the same time that Gvishiani visited San Francisco and signed a contract with the Stanford Research Institute. Some observers felt that his capitalist-oriented approach might have been due more to Russia's concern over American trade with China than his actual faith in the probability of large and profitable deals with American multinationals.

The other issue raised was the solidarity of the Western nations. In the past, most American trade policy initiatives have been motivated by concern over avoiding economic cleavages in the alliance system. Such splits have led inevitably to a weakened position vis-à-vis the Communist countries. This has not been true of the years of détente. Instead, the opposite was true. The American inclination in the periodic confrontations with her allies over basic monetary and economic issues is an example. The multinationals, split between their allegiance to their home base and the economic well-being of their European outlets, did not always agree or follow the new policy. The issue of the limit of growth, opposed vigorously by capitalist centers, has also been one of the bones of contention between the multinationals and some Western governments.

The issue of the quality of life opened up the entire subject of potential. It is unlikely that it was meant as a signal that the Soviet Union will be willing to apply imported technology to change her way of life. It is unlikely that she will suddenly be ready to recognize that the nature of technological change presupposes social and economic change. But by introducing the theme into his presentation, the Soviet spokesman released part of the tension. He declared publicly his country's understanding of the problem. He did not speak out of context. The ninth Five-Year Plan projected significant improvement in the Soviet quality of life. The projection, however, has been solely in material terms. It has not been accompanied, as it was in Hungary, by the possibility of a more liberal, more relaxed sociopolitical system.

The entire approach probably did not signal a major departure from the traditional Soviet stand. It might have been a signal of new tactics and a new, more liberal approach to former ideological foes. The approach has also been read—and properly so—as evidence of

Soviet needs, which are vast enough to call for the multinationals to step in.

Contradictions and Needs

Some of the multinationals did come in. International Harvester and Caterpillar Tractor entered Soviet markets with millions of dollars' worth of pipe-laying equipment; industrial electronic gear was brought in by Hewlett-Packard, and the Swindell-Dressler Company, a Pittsburgh division of Pullman, imported foundry equipment for the Kama River truck factory.

These were just a few of the most spectacular and best-known examples. They whetted the Soviet appetite for more. The need for restructuring, planning, and management concepts came to the surface when technological progress started to be felt. How could the march forward be combined with the requirements which threatened the traditional political structure? How could the Soviets relax without relaxing? How could they make it possible for foreign technology to enter without increasing contacts with the foreigners? Instead of bringing forward movement, these contradictions merely brought fast-moving circles.

In the West, especially the United States, different forces were acting as a brake. In the Congress there was stiff resistance to granting trade and credit concessions as long as the Soviet Union placed restrictions on the rights of her citizens to emigrate. Human rights were linked to international trade.

These brakes are important. American industry can, theoretically, deliver a vast amount of equipment and advanced technology to the Soviet Union. The only condition is a favorable political climate. Détente is needed to secure credits, but would détente suffice to solve the domestic problems of the Soviet Union?

This is where the new dependency on the capitalist states has to be explained. This is where traditionalists have to be appeased, so that even the appearance of convergence of the two systems is not suspected. This is where new planning techniques have to be designed, to permit the inclusion of foreign financing and foreign technology. To do so, foreign partners must be willing to commit themselves for longer periods of time, which, in turn, makes it difficult for

Westerners whose interests are economic but whose successes or failures are rooted in the durability of political structures.

Much psychological reorientation will be required in the Soviet Union before significant growth can be expected in Western technological imports. Russian national pride and the newly acquired socialist pride have to be taken into consideration. There has always been a reluctance on the part of the Russians to admit either dependence on or even acquisition of foreign industrial help. In moments of crisis or of greatness, this was possible. Lenin was willing to admit that without capitalist industrial assistance, the newly created Soviet state would not have been able to progress. Stalin acknowledged American help during World War II. But such moments were both rare and embarrassing; as soon as they occurred, the forces of Russian obscurantism rushed to the forefront to erase the impression given and to work on an opposite proposition. National pride could not support the notion of an effective contribution from outside.

In the city of Togliatti, foreign newsmen seldom meet Italian technicians. The impression visitors should take home is that this is a purely Soviet undertaking. Foreign-made machinery and equipment are not easily visible in Soviet plants and factories. Domestic as well as foreign themes have stressed self-sufficiency. This has been seen during prewar days, lend-lease interpretations, and the current Soviet rhetoric. Yet the Soviet economy alone is not able to cope with the complex growing demands. Reportedly, she has some of the world's best passenger planes, but the servicing and air traffic facilities are inadequate. She has started to build passenger cars and will soon be producing a huge volume of trucks, but the highway system is poor and service stations are few and far between.

The traditional simplicity of the Soviet economy is gradually fading away. The underdeveloped economy is being pushed back by technological progress. The Soviet government is trying to introduce reforms by creating a network of government corporations. They will have a voice in research and development and in the promotion of export products. Individual plant managers will operate on a performance basis, which means more direct responsibility and less bureaucratic dependency.

Whether the change will make a difference is unknown. Every day the Soviet economy faces contradictory politics and ideology, which is one of the reasons why Western businessmen are baffled.

The mood of international détente has to be coupled with an internal détente. In a way, the smaller socialist countries, which are not burdened with global responsibilities, can achieve this more easily. For the Soviet Union—nationalistic, dogmatic, inflexible—the dilemma of a modern, flexible economy in which interaction is one of the life-giving sources, is a lot to cope with.

The Impact of Détente: U.S.–U.S.S.R. Relations

There is little doubt that the period of détente has produced results. Some ice has been broken, some suspicions eliminated. On both sides, serious consideration has been given to the possibility of doing business with each other, regardless of the many barriers, the biggest of which will continue to be a psychological one. Deeply felt fears of Soviet expansionism and political subversion persist in the West; deeply felt fears of Western intentions to undermine socialism persist in the East.

Both fears are not entirely irrational, yet progress has been made. A series of agreements were signed between the United States and the Soviet Union. Basic principles between the two countries were outlined. One of these deals exclusively with trade. "The USA and the USSR," it read, "regard commercial and economic ties as an important and necessary element in the strengthening of their bilateral relations." Aside from the Lend-Lease Settlement, the Trade Agreement, the Maritime Agreement, and an agreement establishing a joint U.S.-U.S.S.R. commercial commission were all concluded during 1972. The last one was to be the pivotal agreement, around which everything else revolved.

In a weekly compilation of presidential documents published on June 5, 1972, the role of the commission was defined. It was to negotiate a trade agreement, including reciprocal most-favored-nation treatment; it was to negotiate the reciprocal availability of government credits, setting up an arbitration mechanism and the reciprocal establishment of business facilities to promote trade. It is a formidable task, one which puts the commission somewhat in limbo. The underlying assumption of favorable political relations remains. Nowhere, however, is there a reference to the role of the commission as an arbitration body, if politics took over and threatened trade.

The commission, composed of technicians and lower-level negotiators, could, in theory, continue its function even should outside events of a noneconomic nature damage trade relations. It was given authority to monitor all U.S.-U.S.S.R. commercial and economic relations. In a certain part of the agreement, three of the terms of reference and rules and procedures of the joint commission provide some leeway. After stating the monitoring aspect of the commission, it is stated: "when possible, resolving issues that may be of interest to both parties."

The trade agreement has been of major importance. Signed in October 1972, it contemplates that total American-Soviet trade in the 1972–75 period will triple the volume of the 1969–71 period, to at least $1.5 billion. Substantial orders were pledged by the Soviet government, to be placed in the United States. They were to include machinery, equipment, agricultural products, and industrial and consumer goods. A telling example is that, at the time of the signing, the Russians indicated a desire to purchase several million dollars' worth of U.S. equipment to manufacture tableware.

Various American firms applied for export licenses for equipment valued at over $1 billion, in anticipation of bidding successfully on the Kama River truck plant contracts. A beginning had been made; both sides looked cheerfully to the future, anticipating that MFN status would be approved by the congress and that détente would continue. Within the Department of Commerce, a new bureau was created to deal with East-West trade. According to its first director, this role was to be to "help to equalize the odds."[13] The independence and creativity of the American businessman was considered by the bureau to be the main factor in the success of trade with the East. The government should in no way get in his way. The attitude of laissez faire was to prevail in spite of well-recognized problems, spelled out in the first official handout of the department, announcing the establishment of the bureau. These problems quite correctly listed major differences between the economic systems, differences in the legal framework affecting trade, obstacles related to national security and export control, pricing problems, and political influences.

The Commerce Department created a natural and potentially useful instrument, but it rendered it toothless from the start. A platitude related to businessmen's creativity and independence can be viewed in a number of ways. Hopefully, it was not put in to divorce the government from that highly political trading area in order to shift the responsibility to business. No amount of banking or industrial creativity could force Congress to grant MFN status to the Soviet Union. No amount of creativity could have avoided the Middle East conflict. Both issues weigh heavily on the success or failure of American-Soviet relations.

Less than a year later, another series of agreements surfaced in the glare of summit publicity: cooperation in agriculture (research and development, the exchange of scientific and technological data), in studies of the oceans, in transportation, on contacts, exchanges, and cooperation, on matters of taxation, and on scientific cooperation in peaceful uses of atomic energy. They were accompanied by a sea of rhetoric, some of which indicated recognition of the problems and misgivings. Acknowledging the self-sufficiency of the two contracting parties, Brezhnev, speaking over nationwide television in the United States said "That was how things were in our relations. However, we, as well as many Americans, realize only too well that renunciation of cooperation in the economic, scientific, technological, and cultural fields is tantamount to both sides turning down substantial extra benefits. . . . It is alleged at times that the development of such cooperation is one-sided and only benefits the Soviet Union. But those who say so are either completely ignorant of the real state of affairs or deliberately turn a blind eye to the truth."[14]

Brezhnev did not leave the matter of trade without making it clear that both sides viewed the development of long-term economic cooperation as an element contributing to a better political climate. Without political détente, no meaningful trade is possible. But trade, in itself—the transfer of technology and exchange of data and personnel—is conducive to more meaningful political relations. Brezhnev's recognition of this, even if only for the benefit of the American audience, was an important point in his speech.

Among the many agreements, some of which have been significant, there was one which, in a way, is unique. It deals with the exchanging information and conducting joint Soviet-American research on the problems of the environment. It was significant, because its implementation may mean much more mutual access to the sources of information than the Soviets have been willing to provide in the past. It may also mean that one of the topics—the role of domestic law and the regulations in environmental protection—

could lead to serious examination of the forces within both societies. If the exchange of information is frank and candid, it will show where the power resides and how it is exercised, how the policy is made and carried out, and how the bureaucracy functions or fails to function.

The significance of this point is underlined by the fact that it was introduced by the Soviets. It was incorporated in the agreement and forms one of its articles (Art. XI).

The other item of the agreement, largely overlooked by most observers, is Article IX, on earthquake prediction.[15] If implemented, it may be revolutionary. The article permits the installation of jointly operated earthquake measurement instruments and detection equipment, which should allow the United States to detect nuclear explosions, as well.

Does this mean that the Soviet Union, under the guise of environmental agreements, signaled a policy shift? Does it mean that relations have entered a more concrete phase than simply an intangible shift in mood? In analyzing the provisions of Article IX, some experts see in it the beginning of a dialogue between technicians and bureaucrats talking about common problems, which could lead to developments of vested interests in keeping channels of communications open. This, in turn, might have a favorable impact on policy-makers.

Thus détente keeps producing results. The stakes are still high, while the risk of retrenchment remains equally high. The Eastern market, regardless of the obstacles—political, psychological, and economic—has great potential. At the end of 1972, the East had a population of over 370 million and accounted for a gross national product of about $750 billion. These numbers were not reflected in the role the market has played. It was small and in a way more relevant for the East than for the West: 4 percent of the total value of Western trade was a tiny fraction of the possibilities. Of that, 4 percent, the American share was even smaller—3 percent. It is true that the 1972 period produced a big jump in Soviet-American trade and American trade with the entire Eastern bloc. The jump in definite value numbers reached $1,293,000, an increase of almost 50 percent over the previous year. Exports remained high, imports modestly so—$817.5 million worth of American products were shipped eastward, against $475.5 million worth of commodities coming into the opposite direction.

No amount of statistics can portray the dimensions of East-West relationships. They oscillate, depending on time, place, and conditions. They reflect a matter of the highest importance to both protagonists, that of political and institutional survival. Economics is a function of the others, the underpinning of more important elements. Nowhere has the well-worn slogan of men not living by bread alone been proved more forcefully than in East-West economic relations. They should flourish, if logic alone be used; they should boom, if material needs are important. The Soviet Union's empty lands ought to be studded with Western seismographs, drilling and pumping equipment, highway planning, and a mushrooming network of tourist facilities. Instead, they stand empty, waiting for a compromise, a thin flicker of Western capital permitting the purchase of Western equipment.

Both sides continue to give priority to defense. Both fear the other's political motives. Both remember only too well the not too distant past: Lenin's buying Western products through concessions which permitted capitalists to own a part of Soviet productive machinery, a part of the Soviet means of production. They are reminded of the pains and tribulations of the lend-lease agreements, of strategic embargoes and their impact on the world at large. Both countries are wary and anxious—wary about the new period of another marriage of convenience, yet eager to make it work. Both need each other. But political survival overshadows everything. So trade, commerce, and "trans-ideological cooperation" are all swept under the rug and labeled national interest.

The best hope today lies in the rapid development of human creativity, not businessmen's nor political leaders', but rather, scientific and technological. It pushes humanity beyond the limits of its political growth, toward a goal difficult to define. Discovery of new elements, isolating particles of science, inching toward greater and more intelligent control over nature, makes it necessery—imperative—for adjustment and change. That change has been observed. It is slow and painful; it is forward-moving and retrogressing on occasions. But the two systems—capitalism and socialism in its Communist interpretation—do gradually converge. They adopt, sometimes unwillingly and grudgingly, sometimes unconsciously, each other's tools. The reform movement in the East reflects a sobering process. The new efforts on the part of the West to cross the Eastern psychological barriers are an innovative process. The two giants face each other in a mood of better understanding, not because they wish to understand, but because their own creative genius makes it a political must. The issue of political survival has been linked, thanks to science, with the issue of interdependency. The old notion of war-type competitiveness is fading from the world scene, not out of the goodness of human nature, but out of the divine wisdom of granting man the gift of limited creation.

It is change that matters. It is that type of an evolution that brings about the idea that psychology rather than numbers will play a major role in the troublesome relations between the two superpowers in the last quarter of the twentieth century. The mutual needs exist, as statistics, commodities, and credit listings indicate. The mutual will to meet these needs is what is ultimately required.

Heraclitus of Ephesus once said: "Only in change is there permanence. No man ever steps into the same river twice." There are hopeful signs that this type of changing permanence within the framework of our global political relations is in the making.

Notes

Chapter 1

[1] Alec Nove, *An Economic History of the USSR*, p. 18.

[2] Serge N. Prokopovicz, *Histoire économique de l'URSS*, p. 112.

[3] Nove, *op. cit.*, p. 18.

[4] Robert E. Ebel, *Communist Trade in Oil and Gas*, New York, 1970, p. 6.

[5] Budish & Shipman, Amtorg Trading Corporation, "Soviet Oil Industry," p. 28.

[6] *Economic Review of the Soviet Union*, Moscow, July 1929.

[7] Samuel N. Harper, ed., *The Soviet Union and World Problems*, p. 26.

[8] Article 14, USSR Constitution of 1936.

[9] Ian M. Drummond, "Empire Trade and Russian Trade: Economic Diplomacy in the Nineteen-Thirties," *Canadian Journal of Economics*, February 1972.

[10] Australia had other worries earlier. The Russians, eager to improve their breeding techniques of livestock and to secure the transfer of what could be called "agricultural technology," purchased a large number of pedigreed breeding sheep from Australia. Australian public opinion rose in unison, and the Australian parliament embargoed the export of sheep for breeding purposes. The embargo, aimed at preserving the purity of Australian sheep, remained in effect long after the danger of Soviet "contamination" passed.

Chapter 2

[1] Robert Huhn Jones, *The Roads to Russia*, p. 33.

[2] Raymond H. Dawson, *The Decision to Aid Russia, 1941*, p. 77.

[3]U.S. Department of State Bulletin (V), 1941, pp. 109–10.

[4]Jones, *op cit.*, p. 84.

[5]*Foreign Relations, 1942* Vol. III, pp. 723–24; *Soviet Supply Protocols* 16, pp. 35–36.

[6]Antony C. Sutton, *Western Technology and Soviet Development*, vol. 2, p. 206.

[7]"Report on War Aid Furnished by the US to the USSR," Office of Foreign Liquidation, U.S. Department of State, 1945, p. 16.

[8]Robert E. Ebel, *Communist Trade in Oil and Gas*, p. 27.

[9]"Vneshnyaya torgovlya SSSR, statisticheskyi sbornik, 1918–1966," (Foreign Trade of the USSR: Statistical Digest), 1966.

[10]Hans Heymann, *We Can Do Business with Russia*, p. viii.

[11]Nikolai A. Voznesensky, *The Economy of the USSR During World* War II (tr. by the American Council of Learned Societies), 1947.

[12]*Ibid.*, p. 16.

[13]John R. Deane, *The Strange Alliance*, p. 96.

[14]Jones, *op cit.*, p. 129.

[15]"Soviet Economic Performance 1966–1967," Joint Economic Committee, Subcommittee on Foreign Economic Policy, 90th Congress pp. 255–57.

[16]"State Five-Year Plan for the Development of the USSR National Economy for the Period 1971–1975," Joint Publications Research Service, September 7, 1972, Part I, pp. 53–54.

Chapter 3

[1]"Economic Survey of Europe in 1948," United Nations (ECE), pp. 244–78.

[2]It has been estimated that in the early 1960s the Soviet Union drew only 3 percent of her national income from foreign trade, two-thirds of which resulted from inner-bloc trade.

[3]William Diebold, Jr., "East-West Trade and the Marshall Plan," *Foreign Affairs*, July 1948, p. 709.

[4]*Ibid.*, p. 719.

[5]"The Battle Act Report 1963," U.S. Department of State, April 1965, p. 6.

[6]Gunnar Myrdal, foreword in Gunnar Adler-Karlsson, *Western Economic Warfare, 1947–1967*, p. xii.

[7]Bernard Hutton, "The Traitor Trade," *The Economist*, October 18, 1952, p. 58.

[8]Stanislaw Wasowski, ed., *East-West Trade and the Technology Gap— A Political and Economic Appraisal*, p. 165.

[9]Richard V. Burks, "Technological Innovations and Political Change in Communist Eastern Europe," Rand Corporation, 1969, p. 12

Chapter 4

[1] *The New York Times*, September 18, 1955.

[2] U.S. Senate Committee on Foreign Relations, *East-West Hearings*, Washington, D.C.: U.S. Government Printing Office, 1964, p. 18.

[3] V.I. Lenin, *Selected Works*, vol. 9, p. 17.

[4] N. Koval and B. Miroschnichenko, *Fundamentals of Soviet Economic Planning* (Moscow: Novosti Press Agency Publishing House, 1972), p. 5.

[5] Alec Nove and D.J.I. Matko, "How the Trade Tide Swelled for Russia," *London Times*, September 17, 1968.

[6] "East-West Trade: A Common Policy for the West," Committee for Economic Development, May 1965, p. 14.

[7] "East-West Trade," *Planning*, Vol. XXXI, No. 488, May 1965.

[8] "Secretary of State Rusk Transmits Proposed East-West Trade Relations Act of 1966 to the Congress," U.S. Department of State, No. 107, May 11, 1966.

[9] "East-West Trade," Joint Economic Committee, U.S. Congress, 1965.

[10] Koval and Miroschnichenko, *ibid.*

[11] Consultative Assembly, Council of Europe, January 22, 1970, Doc. 2691.

[12] Wirtschaftsberichte (Economic Reports), 1970, no. 6 from *Soviet and Eastern European Foreign Trade*, a journal of translations, vol. 7, nos. 3–4, 1972, p. 314.

[13] *Fortune*, July 1967.

[14] Jan Stanokovsky, *Economic Reports*, Credit Institution–Bank Union, Vienna, 1972, No. 1, pp.

[15] John P. Hardt and George D. Holliday, *U.S.-Soviet Commercial Relations*, June 1973.

[16] Michael Boretsky, *Comparative Progress in Technology, Productivity and Economic Efficiency in USSR and US*, p. 150–1, 1963.

[17] "Soviet Economic Prospects for the Seventies" A Compendium of Papers, Joint Economic Committee, U.S. Congress, June 27, 1973.

Chapter 5

[1] Lange, Oscar, *Pisma Wybrane*. Warsaw: 1963, p. 138.

[2] G. Varga, "The Reform of the Management of the National Economy," cited in J. Wilczynski, *Socialist Economic Developments*, p. 62.

[3] *The New York Times*, September 22, 1973.

[4] David Morse and Samuel V. Goekjian, "Joint Investment Opportunities with the Socialist Republic of Rumania," August 1973.

[5] Zbigniew Kamecki, "Possibilities of Increasing East-West Trade and Industrial Cooperation," Warsaw: June 1971, East-West Trade Conference, Management Europe.

Chapter 6

[1]Otto Gado, ed., *Reform of the Economic Mechanism in Hungary—Development 1968–1971* (Budapest: Akademiai Kiado, 1972),

[2]*Ibid.*, p. 20.

[3]*Ibid.*, p. 110.

[4]"East-West Trade and U.S. Economic Reform and Potential Investments in Hungary," *The New Hungarian Quarterly*, Winter 1971.

[5]*Experiences in the Economic Reforms in Hungary* (Budapest: Pannonia Press, 1970), p. 15.

[6]*Nepszabadsag* (Budapest), September 22, 1968.

[7]*Statisztikai Havi Kozlemenyek* (Statistical Monthly Publication), Budapest, 1972/1–10.

[8]"Overseas Business Report," U.S. Department of Commerce, July 1973, Obr. 73–33, pp. 11–12.

[9]*Statistical Pocket Book of Hungary*, 1973. Hungarian Central Statistical Office, Budapest.

Chapter 7

[1]Radoslav Selucky, *Economic Reforms in Eastern Europe*, Political Background and Economic Significance, p. 165.

[2]K. Cipek, "Economic Management Reforms in European Socialist Countries," as cited by Selucky, p. 167.

[3]Documentary material for the Eighth CC Plenum of the Polish United Workers Party, Part II, special issue, "Nowe Drogi," Warsaw, pp. 51–52.

[4]H. Flakierski, "The Polish Economic Reform of 1970," *Canadian Journal of Economics*, April 17, 1973, p. 5.

[5]*Ibid.*

[6]E. Harrasim, "The British Market for Agricultural Produce and the Problems of Polish Exports to This Market," in *Zagadnienia Edkonomiki Rolnej*, Warsaw, No. 6/71, pp. 51–52.

[7]*The Economist*, July 15, 1972, p. 41.

[8]"Polityka—Eksport—Import," No. 1, Warsaw, April 1972.

[9]By the end of 1973, Polish estimates were closer to 35 percent.

[10]Robert L. Miller, "Hotel Requirements in Eastern Europe—United Companies Should Act Now," Senior Seminar in Foreign Policy, Department of State, 1972–73.

[11]Witold Trzeciakowski, "Polish Foreign Trade: A Retrospective View," in *Canadian Slavonic Papers*, vol. 15, nos. 1 and 2, Canadian Association of Slavists, Ottawa, 1973, p. 81.

[12]Selucky, *Economic Reforms in Eastern Europe*, p. 117.

Chapter 8

[1]George Garvy, *Money, Banking and Credit in Eastern Europe.* Most of the first part of this section is based on Garvy's study.

[2]*Gesetzblatt der DDR* (Law Digest of the German Democratic Republic), 1/9, 1968, p. 223

[3]Jozef Wilczynski, *Socialist Economic Development and Reforms*, p. 156.

[4]Robert S. Kretschmar, Jr. and Robin Foor, *The Potential for Joint Ventures in Eastern Europe*, p. 3.

[5]*Ibid.*, p. 89.

[6]Hardt and Holliday, *U.S.-Soviet Commercial Relations*, p. 693.

[7]The banking house is located in New York and does a fair amount of business with the East.

[8]*"Multilateral Policies for East-West Trade and Payments,"* PEP, September 1972.

[9]A.H. Herman, *"East-West Finance,"* The Banker, August 1971,

Chapter 9

[1]UPI, Moscow, June 13, 1973, item no. 0257/73.

[2]"Soviets, US Near Gas Deal," *Washington Post*, November 3, 1973.

[3]Robert E. Ebel, *Communist Trade in Oil and Gas*, New York, 1970, pp. 101–102.

[4]*Ibid.*, p. 108.

[5]*Ibid.*, p. 111.

[6]Japan-Soviet Economic Committee, "Report on the Oil Committee's Mission of Specialists to the Soviet Union," Tokyo, July 1972, p. 5.

[7]"Nihon Keizai Shimbun," (Japanese Economic Journal) November 27, 1972, cited by Kenzo Kinga in *Russo-Japanese Economic Cooperation and Its International Environment*, Pacific Community, April 1973.

[8]In ordinary (or light) water, one molecule of water in every 6,000 molecules is constituted from heavy hydrogen atoms (or deuterium, heavy isotope of hydrogen) with oxygen atoms. To produce "heavy water," all molecules with heavy hydrogen are concentrated, and light hydrogen is discarded. So, heavy water is only constituted from heavy hydrogen (or deuterium) plus oxygen.

[9]John P. Hardt, "Siberian Oil and Gas," *Problems of Communism*, May-June 1973, p. 32.

[10]Leo Gruliow, *Christian Science Monitor*, April 9, 1973.

Chapter 10

[1] Robert L. Heilbroner, *"Has Capitalism a Future?"* New School of Social Research, 1972.

[2] Adolph Lowe, "Is Present-Day Higher Learning Relevant?" *Social Research*, Autumn 1971, Vol. 38, pp. 563–580.

[3] *The New York Times*, August 24, 1973.

[4] J. Sokol, "Peaceful Coexistence and Ideological Subversion," *Wojsko Ludowe* (People's Army), Warsaw, May 1972.

[5] *Novoye Vremya* (New Times) (Moscow), May 4, 1973.

[6] *Congressional Record*, June 19, 1972, p. S9600.

[7] *Kommunist*, No. 3, February 1973, pp. 101–113.

[8] *Izvestia*, May 8, 1973, p. 4.

[9] Hardt and Holliday, *U.S.-Soviet Commercial Relations*, p. 31.

[10] *Ibid.*

[11] "Dependence of the Soviet Investment Programme on Imported Machinery and Equipment," East-West Research and Advisory, Brussels. Special Report No. 2/73, April 1973.

[12] *The New York Times*, September 22, 1973.

[13] *Commerce Today*, U.S. Department of Commerce, January 8, 1973.

[14] Recorded at San Clemente, California on June 23, 1973 and broadcast June 24, 1973. Text provided by the White House Press Office.

[15] *World*, January 16, 1973 (World Environment Newsletter by Philip Quigg).

Bibliography

Books

Adler-Karlsson, Gunnar. *Western Economic Warfare, 1947–1967: A Case Study in Foreign Economic Policy.* Stockholm: Almqvist & Wiksells Boktryckeri A.B., 1968.

Burks, Richard V. *Technological Innovation and Political Change in Communist Eastern Europe.* Santa Monica, Calif.: The Rand Corporation, 1969.

Carr, Edward H. *A History of Soviet Russia. Vol. I. The Bolshevik Revolution, 1917–1923.* New York: The Macmillan Company, 1951.

Counts, George S., and Lodge, Nucia. *The Country of the Blind: The Soviet System of Mind Control.* Boston: Houghton Mifflin, 1949.

Dawson, Raymond H. *The Decision to Aid Russia, 1941: Foreign Policy and Domestic Politics.* Chapel Hill: The University of North Carolina Press, 1959.

Deane, John R. *The Strange Alliance: The Story of Our Efforts at Wartime Cooperation with Russia.* New York: The Viking Press, 1947.

Ebel, Robert E. *Communist Trade in Oil and Gas: An Evaluation of the Future Export Capability of the Soviet Bloc.* New York: Praeger Publishers, 1970.

Florinsky, Michael T. *Russia: A History and an Interpretation.* New York: The Macmillan Company, 1953.

Fontaine, André. *History of the Cold War. Vol I. From the October Revolution to the Korean War, 1917–1950.* New York: Random House, 1968.

Garvy, George. *Money, Banking and Credit in Eastern Europe.* New York: Federal Reserve Bank of New York, 1966.

Giffen, James Henry. *The Legal and Practical Aspects of Trade with the Soviet Union.* New York: Praeger Publishers, 1971.

Heymann, Hans. *We Can Do Business with Russia.* Chicago: Ziff-Davis, 1945.

Hill, Christopher. *Lenin and the Russian Revolution.* London: Hodder & Stoughton for the English Universities Press, 1947.

Jones, Robert Huhn. *The Roads to Russia—United States Lend-Lease to the Soviet Union.* Norman, Okla.: University of Oklahoma Press, 1969.

218

Keller, Werner. *East Minus West = Zero: Russia's Debt to the Western World.* New York: G.P. Putnam's Sons, 1961.

Kimball, Warren F. *The Most Unsordid Act: Lend-Lease 1939–1941.* Baltimore: The Johns Hopkins Press, 1969.

Kretschmar, Robert S., Jr., and Foor, Robin. *The Potential for Joint Ventures in Eastern Europe.* New York: Praeger Publishers, 1972.

Lange, Oscar. *Pisma Wybrane.* Warsaw: 1963.

Lenin, V.I. *Selected Works.* London: Lawrence & Wishart, 1936–39.

Lukaszewski, Jerzy, ed. *The People's Democracies after Prague: Soviet Hegemony, Nationalism, Regional Integration?* Bruges, Belgium: College of Europe, Postgraduate Institute of European Studies, 1970.

Malish, Anton F., Jr. *United States East European Trade: Considerations Involved in Granting Most-Favored-Nation Treatment to the Countries of Eastern Europe.* Washington, D.C.: United States Tariff Commission, 1972.

Nove, Alec. *An Economic History of the USSR.* Middlesex, England: Penguin Books, 1969.

Owen, Henry, ed. *The Next Phase in Foreign Policy.* Washington, D.C.: The Brookings Instution, 1973.

Pisar, Samuel. *Coexistence and Commerce: Guidelines for Transactions Between East and West.* New York: McGraw-Hill, 1970.

Prokopovicz, Serge N. *Histoire économique de l'URSS.* La Portulan, France, 1952.

Selucky, Radoslav. *Economic Reforms in Eastern Europe: Political Background and Economic Significance.* New York: Praeger Publishers, 1972.

Sherwood, Robert E. *Roosevelt and Hopkins: An Intimate History.* New York: Harper & Brothers, 1941.

Stalin, J. *Problems of Leninism.* Moscow: Foreign Languages Publishing House, 1945.

Sukijasovic, Miodrag. *Foreign Investment in Yugoslavia.* The Institute of International Politics and Economics. Belgrade and Oceana Publications, New York, 1970.

Sutton, Antony C. *Western Technology and Soviet Economic Development. Vol. I. 1917–1930.* Stanford, Calif.: Hoover Institution Press, 1968.

_____. *Western Technology and Soviet Economic Development. Vol. II. 1930–1945.* Stanford, Calif.: Hoover Institution Press, 1971.

Thomson, Gladys S. *Catherine the Great and the Expansion of Russia.* London: Hodder & Stoughton, 1947.

Voznesensky, Nikolai A. (Deputy Premier of the USSR and Chief of the State Planning Commission) *The Economy of the USSR During World War II.* Washington, D.C.: Public Affairs Press, 1948.

Wasowski, Stanislaw, ed. *East-West Trade and the Technology Gap: A Political and Economic Appraisal.* New York: Praeger Publishers, 1970.

Wilczynski, Jozef. *The Economics and Politics of East-West Trade.* New York: Praeger Publishers, 1969.

_____. *Socialist Economic Development and Reforms.* New York: Praeger Publishers, 1972.

Wolfe, Bertram D. *Three Who Made a Revolution: A Biographical History.* New York: The Dial Press, 1948.

Pamphlets and Special Publications

Boretsky, Michael. *Comparative Progress in Technology, Productivity and Economic Efficiency in the USSR and US.* Washington, D.C.: Government Printing Office, Department of Commerce, 1963.

Budish, J. M., and Shipman, Samuel S. (Economic Division, Amtorg Trading Corporation). *Soviet Foreign Trade: Menace or Promise?* New York: Horace Liveright, Inc., 1931.

Condoide, Mikhail V. *Russian-American Trade: A Study of the Soviet Foreign-Trade Monopoly.* Columbus, Ohio: The Bureau of Business Research, College of Commerce and Administration, Ohio State University, 1946.

De Gara, John P. *Trade Relations Between the Common Market and the Eastern Bloc.* Bruges, Belgium: College of Europe, Postgraduate Institute of European Studies, 1964.

Gado, Otto, ed. *Reform of the Economic Mechanism in Hungary: Development 1968–1971.* Budapest: Akademiai Kiado, 1972.

Gayer, Arthur. *The Problem of Lend-Lease: Its Nature, Implications, and Settlement* (Series in "American Interest in the War and the Peace"). New York: Council on Foreign Relations, 1944.

Hardt, John P., and Holliday, George D. *U.S.-Soviet Commercial Relations: The Interplay of Economics, Technology Transfer and Diplomacy.* Prepared for the Subcommittee on National Security, Policy and Scientific Developments, of the Committee on Foreign Affairs. Washington, D.C.: Government Printing Office, U.S. House of Representatives, 1973.

Harper, Samuel N., ed. *The Soviet Union and World Problems.* (Lectures of the Harris Foundation, 1935). Chicago: The University of Chicago Press, 1935.

Koval, N., Miroshnichenko, B. *Fundamentals of Soviet Economic Planning.* Moscow: Novosti Press Agency Publishing House, 1972.

McQuade, Lawrence C. *U.S. Trade with Eastern Europe: Its Prospects and Parameters,* Law and Policy in International Business, Vol. 3, No. 1, Winter 1971.

Simai, N. *Economic Growth and the Development Level.* Budapest: Hungarian Scientific Council for World Economy, No. 7, 1972.

Thornton, Richard C. *The Bear and the Dragon.* Sino-Soviet Relations and the Political Evolution of the Chinese People's Republic, 1949–1971. American-Asian Educational Exchange, Inc., 1972.

Tuthill, John W. *The Decisive Years Ahead.* Paris: Saxon House, for The Atlantic Institute for International Affairs, January 1973.

A Background Study on East-West Trade. Prepared for the Committee on Foreign Relations, United States Senate. Washington, D.C.: Library of Congress Legislative Reference Service, 1965.

A New Trade Policy toward Communist Countries. New York: Committee for Economic Development, (CED) September 1972.

Department of State Bulletins. Washington, D.C.: Government Printing Office, 1941, 1965, 1966, 1972, 1973.

East-West Trade, Vol. XXXI, No. 488, Planning. Political and Economic Planning, An Independent Research Organisation, London, May 1965.

East-West Trade: A Common Policy for the West. New York: Committee for Economic Development, May 1965.

East-West Trade. A compilation of views of businessmen, bankers, and academic experts. Washington, D.C.: Committee on Foreign Relations, United States Senate, 1964.

Experiences of the Economic Reform in Hungary. An interview with Rezso Nyers, Secretary of the Central Committee of the Hungarian Socialist Workers Party. Budapest: Pannonia Press, 1970.

Handbook of Hungarian Foreign Trade. Budapest: Corvina Press for the Hungarian Chamber of Commerce, 1972.

Moscow's European Satellites. Department of State Publication 5914. Washington, D.C.: Government Printing Office, November 1955.

Polityka–Eksport–Import. Warsaw: Polska Izba Handlu Zagranicznego (Polish Chamber of Foreign Trade), 1972.

Satellite Agriculture in Crisis: A Study of Land Policy in the Soviet Sphere. New York: Frederick A. Praeger, for the Research Staff of Free Europe Press, 1954.

Statistical Pocket Book of Hungary, 1973. Budapest: Hungarian Central Statistical Office, Statistical Publishing House, 1973.

Statistical Pocket Book of the German Democratic Republic 1972. Berlin: State Central Administration for Statistics, 1972.

The United States and the Developing World Agenda for Action—1973. Robert E. Hunter, Project Director. Washington, D.C.: Overseas Development Council, 1973.

U.S.-Soviet Commercial Agreements 1972. Texts, Summaries, and Supporting Papers. Washington, D.C.: U.S. Department of Commerce, Domestic and International Business Administration, Bureau of East-West Trade, January 1973.

Periodicals

Canadian Journal of Economics, University of Toronto Press, Toronto, Ontario, 1972 and 1973.

Canadian Slavonic Papers, Quarterly of the Canadian Association of Slavists. Ottawa. Vol. XV, Nos. 1 and 2, Spring and Summer 1973.

East-West Research and Advisory, Brussels, Belgium, 1973.

Foreign Affairs, Council on Foreign Relations, New York, 1948.

Fortune, July 1967.

Gospodarka Planowa (Planned Economy), No. 2, 1972, Panstwowe Wydawnictwo Ekonomiczne (State Economic Publishing House), Warsaw, February 1972.

Hungary, 1973/1, Budapest: Buda Press, December 31, 1972.

International Studies Quarterly, Vol. 16, No. 4, December 1972. Published by the International Studies Association, Sage Publications, Beverly Hills, London.

Le Courrier des Pays de l'Est. No. 133. Centre National du Commerce Exterieur. Secretariat General du Gouvernment, Direction de la Documentation. Paris, September 1970.

Pacific Community, Jiji Press, Ltd., Tokyo, 1973.

Polish Perspectives, Vol. XVI, No. 4, April 1973. Published under the auspices of the Polish Institute of International Affairs, Warsaw.

Problems of Communism. Washington, D.C.: Government Printing Office, 1973.

The Banker, The Financial Times Limited, London, 1971.

The Economist, London, 1952 and 1972.

The New Hungarian Quarterly, Vol. XII, No. 44, Winter 1971. Lapkiado Publishing House, Budapest.

Trends in World Economy, No. 8. Gy. Becsky. *The International Monetary Situation and the Global Economic Strategy of the USA.* Budapest: Hungarian Scientific Council for World Economy, 1972.

Index